Voices of Israel

SUNY Series in Modern Jewish Literature and Culture
Sarah Blacher Cohen, editor

Voices of Israel

Essays on and Interviews with

Yehuda Amichai
A.B. Yehoshua
T. Carmi
Aharon Appelfeld
and
Amos Oz

Joseph Cohen

State University of New York Press

Published by
State University of New York Press, Albany

© 1990   State University of New York

For information, address State University of New York
Press, State University Plaza, Albany, N.Y., 12246

Library of Congress Cataloging-in-Publication Data

Cohen, Joseph, 1926–
    Voices of Israel : essays on and interviews with Yehuda Amichai,
  A.B. Yehoshua, T. Carmi, Aharon Appelfeld, and Amos Oz / Joseph Cohen.
      p. cm.–(SUNY series in modern Jewish literature and culture)
    Bibliography: p. 213.
    Includes index.
    ISBN 0-7914-0243-6.–ISBN 0-7914-0244-4 (pbk.)
    1. Authors, Israeli–Interviews.   2. Israeli literature–History
  and criticism.   I. Amichai, Yehuda.   II. Title.   III. Series.
  PI5014.C64 1990
  892.4'09006–dc20   89-11512
                                                                            CIP

10 9 8 7 6 5 4 3 2 1

For Ruth

Contents

Acknowledgments ix

Preface xiii

Introduction 1

Chapter 1: Yehuda Amichai 9

Chapter 2: A. B. Yehoshua 45

Chapter 3: T. Carmi 81

Chapter 4: Aharon Appelfeld 107

Chapter 5: Amos Oz 141

Conclusion 193

Notes 197

Selected Bibliography 213

Index 219

Acknowledgments

I am happy to acknowledge my indebtedness to those who helped to bring this book into existence. Foremost among them are the five Israeli writers, Yehuda Amichai, A.B. Yehoshua, T. Carmi, Aharon Appelfeld and Amos Oz who not only willingly consented to being interviewed when the Jewish Studies Program of Tulane University brought them to New Orleans but who subsequently responded to my requests for further information, reviewed texts, and offered suggestions and encouragement all the way. For her help in arranging the visits to Tulane, I wish to thank Ruth Wheat of the B'nai B'rith Lecture Bureau in New York.

After the final interview was taped in 1986, the task of transcribing all of them fell to Margaret L. (Maggie) Wittke, the Jewish Studies Program secretary. They were not easy tapes to work with, given soft-spoken accented voices amidst varying background noises, to say nothing of the widely ranging and often changing and challenging subject matter, but Maggie worked her way through them, putting successive drafts into the office computer. Hers was a Herculean effort, superbly accomplished, and I am pleased to acknowledge my enormous indebtedness to her. When the first version, consisting of the interviews and brief introductions was complete, it was read by several other Jewish Studies colleagues (and cherished friends), David Goldstein and his wife, Shoshanah. Their encouragement was an imperative to proceed. And in the final stages of the work, Alan Avery-Peck, who succeeded me as director of the Jewish Studies Program, has shared his biblical expertise and knowledge of Israel and has been helpful in other supportive ways for which I am grateful. I appreciate the support of the Jewish Studies Program in underwriting costs incurred on the way to production.

For other secretarial and word-processing help, I owe thanks to Paula B. Rault and Sandra Haro, with the assistance of Mildred M. Gillespie and Rosemary K. Eddins of the Tulane English Department.

Additional encouragement came from Sarah Blacher Cohen, the editor of the SUNY Series in Modern Jewish Literature and Culture, and to her and her colleagues at the State University of New York Press, particularly editors Carola Sautter and Diane Ganeles, I express my deep appreciation for their professionalism, sophistication, courtesy, and interest in guiding this work into print. I am grateful also to their several anonymous expert readers whose gentle but firm prodding convinced me to extend the scope of the book to include full-scale analytical essays about the Israeli writers and their *oeuvre*. One of them gave me a B+ for the early version; now, I hope to get an A.

It was the poet Dannie Abse who taught me much about the art of interviewing. I am glad to have the opportunity here to thank him, particularly for teaching me the cardinal rule of never out talking the interviewee.

The one who has shared this experience with me closely from the first word to the last one is my wife, Ruth. My most stringent but lovingly sympathetic critic, she is the best informed and most sensitive expert grammarian/wordsmith it has ever been my good fortune to encounter. In her sustained and perceptive love of literature, nurtured through careers in anthropology and the law, she insists that standards in the language are never to be compromised. Whatever respectability my prose has achieved, I owe to her.

The interview "A Conversation With Aharon Appelfeld" is reprinted by permission from the late Trude Weiss-Rosmarin, Editor and Publisher, *The Jewish Spectator*. The interview "A Conversation With Amos Oz" is reprinted by permission from Ernest L. Weiss, Editor and Publisher, *Judaica Book News*.

Acknowledgment is made to the following individuals and publishers for permission to reprint materials in this book:

Yehuda Amichai. Excerpts from *Selected Poetry of Yehuda Amichai*, by Yehuda Amichai, ed. and trans. by Chana Bloch and Stephen Mitchell, copyright 1986, English translation copyright 1986 by Harper & Row, Publishers, Inc., reprinted by permission of Yehuda Amichai, Stephen Mitchell, Chana Bloch and the publisher. Excerpts from *Not of This Time, Not of This Place*, by Yehuda Amichai, copyright 1963 by Schocken Publishing Ltd., English translation copyright 1968 by Harper & Row Publishers, Inc., reprinted by permission of Yehuda Amichai and the publisher. Excerpts from "Yehuda Amichai: An Interview By David Montenegro," *The American Poetry Review*, copyright 1987, reprinted by permission of David Montenegro.

Aharon Appelfeld. Excerpts from *Badenheim 1939*, by Aharon Appelfeld, copyright 1980, English translation copyright 1980 by David R. Godine, Publisher, reprinted by permission of the publisher. Excerpts from *The Age of Wonders*, by Aharon Appelfeld, copyright 1981, English translation copyright 1981 by David R. Godine, Publisher and Wallace Literary Agency, Inc., reprinted by permission of the publisher and agent. Excerpts from *Tzili The Story of a Life*, by Aharon Appelfeld, copyright 1983, English translation copyright 1983 by E.P. Dutton and Wallace Literary Agency, Inc., reprinted by permission of the publisher and agent. Excerpts from *The Retreat*, by Aharon Appelfeld, copyright 1984, English translation copyright 1984 by E.P. Dutton and Quartet Books Ltd., reprinted by permission of the publishers and the Wallace Literary Agency, Inc. Excerpts from *The Immortal Bartfuss*, by Aharon Appelfeld, copyright 1988, English translation copyright 1988 by Weidenfeld & Nicolson and the Wallace Literary Agency, Inc., reprinted by permission of the publisher and agent. Excerpts from "A Talk With Aharon Appelfeld," by Philip Roth, *The New York Times Book Review*, copyright 1988, reprinted by permission of Philip Roth.

T. Carmi. Excerpts from *The Brass Serpent*, by T. Carmi, copyright 1964, reprinted by permission of T. Carmi. Excerpts from *At the Stone of Losses*, by T. Carmi, translated by Grace Schulman, copyright 1983, English translation copyright 1983 by Jewish Publication Society of America/The University of California Press, reprinted by permission of T. Carmi, Grace Schulman and the publishers. Excerpts from *The Penguin Book of Hebrew Verse*, ed. and trans. by T. Carmi, copyright 1981, English translation copyright 1981 by Penguin Books Ltd, reprinted by permission of the publisher. Excerpts from *Modern Hebrew Poetry A Bilingual Anthology* by Ruth Finer Mintz, copyright 1966, English translation copyright 1966 by The University of California Press, reprinted by permission of the publisher.

Excerpts from *Justine*, by Lawrence Durrell, copyright 1957, E.P. Dutton and Faber and Faber Ltd, reprinted by permission of the publishers. Excerpt from *Balthazar*, by Lawrence Durrell, copyright 1958, E.P. Dutton and Curtis Brown & John Farquharson, reprinted by permission of the publisher and agents.

Excerpts from *Birds, Beasts and Flowers*, by D.H. Lawrence, copyright 1974, Haskell House Publishers, reprinted by permission of Viking Penguin, Inc.

Excerpt from *Under the Volcano*, by Malcolm Lowry, copyright 1947 by author, renewed copyright 1975 by Margerie Lowry, Harper & Row Publishers, Inc., reprinted by permission of the publisher.

Excerpts from *The Collected Poems of Wilfred Owen*, by Wilfred Owen, ed. C. Day Lewis, copyright 1963, New Directions and Chatto and Windus, reprinted by permission of the estate of Wilfred Owen and the publishers.

Amos Oz. Excerpts from *My Michael*, copyright 1968 by Amos Oz, English translation copyright 1968 by Amos Oz, reprinted by permission of Amos Oz, Vintage and Chatto & Windus. Excerpts from *Elsewhere, Perhaps*, by Amos Oz, copyright 1966 by Sifriat Poalim, English translation copyright 1973 by Harcourt Brace Jovanovich, Inc., reprinted by permission of Harcourt Brace Jovanovich and Martin Secker & Warburg. Excerpts from *Touch the Water Touch the Wind*, copyright 1973 by Amos Oz. English translation copyright 1974 by Harcourt Brace Jovanovich, Inc., reprinted by permission of Harcourt Brace Jovanovich and Chatto & Windus. Excerpts from *Unto Death*, copyright 1971 by Amos Oz, English translation copyright 1975, 1971 by Amos Oz, reprinted by permission of Harcourt Brace Jovanovich, Inc. and

Chatto & Windus. Excerpt from *The Hill of Evil Counsel*, copyright 1976 by Amos Oz and Am Oved Publishers, Ltd. Tel Aviv, English translation copyright 1978 by Amos Oz, reprinted by permission of Harcourt Brace Jovanovich, Inc. and Chatto & Windus. Excerpts from *A Perfect Peace*, copyright 1982 by Amos Oz and Am Oved Publishers, Ltd. Tel Aviv, English translation copyright 1985 by Amos Oz, reprinted by permission of Harcourt Brace Jovanovich, Inc. and Chatto & Windus. Excerpts from *Black Box*, copyright 1987 by Amos Oz and Am Oved Publishers, Ltd. Tel Aviv, English translation copyright 1988 by Nicholas de Lange, reprinted by permission of Harcourt Brace Jovanovich, Inc. and *Chatto & Windus*. Excerpts from Nathan Alterman's Hebrew poem "Weeping," copyright by Hakibbutz Hameuhad Publishing House, Ltd. Tel Aviv, English translation copyright 1988 by Nicholas de Lange, reprinted by permission of Nicholas de Lange, Harcourt Brace Jovanovich and Chatto & Windus. Excerpt from *Israeli Mythogynies*, by Esther Fuchs, copyright 1987 by the State University of New York Press, reprinted by permission of the publisher.

Excerpt from *Poems of a Jew*, by Karl Shapiro, copyright 1953 by Random House, Inc., reprinted by permission of the publisher.

A.B. Yehoshua. Excerpts from *Three Days and A Child*, copyright 1970 by A.B. Yehoshua, English translation copyright 1970 Doubleday & Co., reprinted by permission of Doubleday & Co. and Peter Owen Ltd. Excerpt from *The Lover*, copyright 1977 by A.B. Yehoshua, English translation copyright 1978 by Doubleday & Co., reprinted by permission of Doubleday & Co. and William Heinemann Ltd. Excerpts from *Five Seasons*, copyright 1987 by A.B. Yehoshua and Hakibbutz Hameuchad Publishing House, Ltd. Tel Aviv, English translation copyright 1989 by Doubleday & Co., and William Collins Sons & Co. Ltd., reprinted by permission of the publishers.

Preface

In the short space of the decade of the 1980s, a number of Israeli writers have become widely known to American readers, Jewish and non-Jewish alike. Though few Americans may acquire and read the works of these writers in Hebrew, translations of their volumes of poetry and novels occur with increasing frequency, so that they have become widely accessible not only in the United States but also throughout the Western world; in some cases, even behind the Iron Curtain. When the translations of the recent novels of Amos Oz, Aharon Appelfeld and A. B. Yehoshua were published in the United States, each of them was given the lead review in *The New York Times Book Review*. That prominent attention in itself is evidence of the stature these writers have acquired in a relatively brief span of time.

These Israeli writers, increasingly, are invited by colleges and universities all over the United States to spend a semester or an academic year in residence, enriching the cultural milieu not only of the campuses that become their temporary homes but also the far distant schools and communities where they appear on overnight visits for poetry readings and lectures. Or they may make whirlwind trips, commuting as it were, from Tel Aviv to Terre Haute, Jerusalem to Palo Alto, and Haifa to New Orleans. Their availability and their accessibility, combined with the popularity of their books, the critical acclaim they have received, and no small amount of personal charm, have made them welcome to our podiums, and given them a place in our heads and in our hearts. Even when they are openly and outspokenly critical of the American-Jewish community—as when they chide us for not making *Aliyah* en masse. Perhaps we find them endearing because they are outspoken.

The Jewish Studies Program of Tulane University, which was instituted in 1981, recognized from the outset that the availability and accessibility of these highly mobile Israelis could, through their visits, enhance the cultural life of both the university community and the larger community in New Orleans. The Jewish Studies Program has in the short period of its existence sponsored (and in some instances, cosponsored with other university departments and local Jewish organizations), the appearances of Yehuda Amichai, A. B. Yehoshua, T. Carmi, Aharon Appelfeld, and Amos Oz. Other distinguished Israelis whose appearances have been sponsored and cosponsored by Jewish studies include Yehuda Bauer, Aliza Shinhar, David Hartman, Emmanuel Sivan, Aaron Klieman, Josef Olmert, Haggai Erlich, Jacob Rosen, Naomi Chazen, Yoram Peri, Abba Eban, and Yehuda Blum.

As the director of the Jewish Studies Program from its inception through 1987, it was my responsibility to oversee the arrangements for the visits of these distinguished Israelis. But in my other academic capacity, that of professor of English literature, I was particularly interested in getting to know Yehuda Amichai, A. B. Yehoshua, T. Carmi, Aharon Appelfeld, and Amos Oz. It was an imperative for me, even though at the time of their visits I had only a limited familiarity with their translated works. Some of these works receive more attention in the interviews than others, because it was these titles that were uppermost in my thoughts when their authors were in New Orleans.

While I would have liked to have been in a position during the interviews to range more widely over the whole of their writing, I was at the time principally interested in obtaining accounts of their lives and experiences. I was also interested in identifying their connections with modern Western literature since my own field is twentieth century American and British poetry and fiction, Jewish and non-Jewish. The latter emphasis determined the approach the analytical chapters would subsequently take: the consideration and documentation of the extent to which these Israeli writers could be placed in the Western tradition.

Each of the writers graciously consented to an interview, in the course of which, in every instance, I found a new friend and kindred spirit. What each of them had to say was so significant that I have felt an obligation to share their thoughts with that larger public that has come to know and admire their works, which have been translated into English. Although the taped conversations were informal, the interviews did follow a format of sorts. Generally, our dialogues established the writer in his time and place in terms of family and background, education and military service, with some emphasis on the role Jewishness has played in his life and work. From this foundation, we went on to discuss the development of modern Hebrew literature, the difficulties of writing in an ancient language rapidly undergoing transformation into a modern tongue, the ties to the past, the continuing impact of the Hebrew Bible, and the influence of the early twentieth century literary giants in Palestine, principally M. J. Berdycewski, Y. H. Brenner, and S. Y. Agnon.

Beyond these subjects, I asked for assessments of the current literary scene in Israel, which led to some illuminating observations by several of the writers about one another's work. Equally interesting were the attitudes these authors displayed about the Holocaust and its impact on their lives and writing. Not unexpectedly, we also talked about American Jewish literature, with frequent mention of Saul Bellow, Bernard Malamud, Philip Roth, and Cynthia Ozick; this, in turn initiated discussions of European influences, both British and Continental. Other topics included the use of Jewish Mysticism, the pervasiveness of the desert in their writing, temporal and spatial experimentation, and problems of translation from Hebrew into English and, in Carmi's case, translation from English into Hebrew.

In the hour or so to which the interviews were limited, we covered a lot of ground. Yet I have no doubt that readers of these conversations will experience the same frustration I felt when each conversation came to an almost abrupt conclusion; we were usually still immersed in conversation when we realized we had to drive immediately to the airport in order to avoid missing the writer's plane. To alleviate my own frustration and perhaps the reader's as well, I set myself the task of writing amplifying introductions to each of the interviews. These were brief in the beginning, with the exception of an essay on most of Appelfeld's Holocaust novels, which was originally written for presentation in a Mellon Foundation sponsored series of lectures at Tulane. To redress the imbalance, and at the suggestion of my editor, I undertook to write uniformly detailed critical analyses of all the translated works.

While the preparation of the critical analyses satisfied my own need to know more about these writers and Israeli literature, it further increased my regret that many of the works were not mentioned in the individual interviews. The extended analyses here will, I hope, prove useful to those readers already seeking greater insight into a marvelously varied and versatile body of literary work, one which has not yet been treated in the United States and Great Britain to the critical investigation it deserves. Of course, individual novels and volumes of poetry have been reviewed and some highly illuminating critiques written by American and British specialists in Hebrew literature, and I am indebted to them for their insight. I have listed their reviews and articles in my notes, and I recommend them to those readers who want to pursue these discussions further. Since I am not a Hebrew scholar and do not read Hebrew, and since my expertise in literature, such as it may be, is in American and British poetry and fiction, I make only the most modest of claims for the critiques in this book. I would be the first to admit that whatever those claims may be, they are inversely proportional to the degree of *chutzpah* I displayed in undertaking to write authoritatively about a body of literature I could not read in the original and with which I had only the most tenuous previous connections. It became an irresistible challenge. In my efforts to rise to that challenge, I immersed myself in the subject matter, thereby treating myself to one of the richest literary experiences I have ever had in a professional career that is now in its thirty-fourth year.

But my enthusiasm for and fascination with the works of these writers was tempered by the limitations of relying entirely on translations. I am keenly aware of the pitfalls of basing scholarly analysis on translated works. Long interested in bibliography, I have repeatedly lectured to graduate students over the years on the absolute necessity of basing critical analysis only on authenticated texts. In this instance, the only truly authenticated texts were all in Hebrew. I was also aware that in the case of several novels, most notably Amichai's *Not Of This Time, Not Of This Place* and Oz's *Elsewhere, Perhaps,* the translations were very different versions from their originals. However the danger of misinterpretation has been somewhat ameliorated by the fact that several of the Israeli writers, knowing English well, have collaborated with their translaters on most of their works or have been fortunate enough to have sensitive and perceptive translators whose translations they, the writers, have approved. Whatever their shortcomings, I hope the critiques will nonetheless prove to be helpful, particularly to those scholars, students and readers who, like myself, have been precluded from reading these authors in Hebrew.

It remains to place each of these writers into the context in which the interviews occurred. Of Amichai, it would take a book longer than this one to do justice to his poetry and his presence. Modest and soft spoken, he came to New Orleans on April 8-9, 1984, filled with the wonder of being in a new place of enchantment. He made of his two days here an adventure. It was one for me, too. From the moment his plane set down, we found ourselves in a continuing dialogue, our remarks overlapping one another's, colliding, running ahead, anticipating what was to be said and heard next as though we were kin reunited after a separation of many years. All this torrent of talk went on while we viewed Greek Revival houses in the Garden District, visited cemeteries with their aboveground tombs, walked along the levee of the Mississippi River, strolled the narrow passageways of the French Quarter, and ate our way through some well-known restaurants. I told him everything I could think of about Jewish life in this fabled city whose Mediterranean flavor he soon found compatible; he shared with me stories of his long sojourn in his own fabled city, Jerusalem.

A. B. Yehoshua's visit to Tulane on March 5-6, 1985, followed Amichai's visit by almost a year. Unlike the relaxed, leisurely pace with which Amichai imbibed the sights, sounds, and smells of New Orleans, Yehoshua was moving fast. He was on a one week non-stop talking marathon that began in Boston, moved to New York, and then in succession to Lawrence, Kansas, Houston and Austin, Texas, thence to New Orleans and back again to New York. If his trip seemed exhausting, one would never have known it by listening to him or watching him, for he was all animation and lively intelligence. His hands and arms were in constant motion, perfectly synchronized with his conversation to the extent that it was impossible for a listener not to become entranced, caught up in a lovely near-stereophonic symphony of sound and action.

T. Carmi came to New Orleans on March 10-11, 1986, a year after Yehoshua had been here. His demeanor was totally different from that of either Amichai or Yehoshua. Where the former was relaxed and easygoing, and the latter in motion all the time, Carmi reminded me of a machine-gun, temporarily at rest and then suddenly coming to life, sending its messages in short bursts, full of power, waiting in the quiet moments to zero in on the target of a new idea or image. Smoking incessantly, Carmi displayed an intellectual and nervous energy that seemed to be in high gear all the time.

Appelfeld's visit on September 25-26, 1986, followed Carmi's appearance by only a few months. It coincided with the American publication of his novel *To The Land Of The Cattails* and it was a busy and exciting time for him. It had been preceded by the rapid publication in the United States of four novels in six years. Because of his astonishing track record I prepared myself, as his plane landed, to welcome a prodigious force. Prodigious as his work is, he himself turned out to be smallish, round, with twinkling eyes, cherubic and at the same time almost impish. He was a melody of grace, courtesy and gravity, soft-spoken, warm, endearing, and dignified but possessed with an unusual degree of humility. He will be the last one to be taken in by his own success.

Amos Oz came to New Orleans November 19-21, 1986, eight weeks after Appelfeld was here. His reputation in the United States was already extensive, fueled through his highly publicized participation in the Peace Now movement in Israel and by the popularity of his book of reportage *In The Land Of Israel*, translated by Maurie Goldberg-Batura and published in 1983. Like that of his close friend, Yehoshua, Oz's schedule was tightly structured. As soft-spoken as Appelfeld and equally gentle and easygoing, Oz has an astonishing appeal. At once both exuberant and reflective, serious and lighthearted, he revealed underneath his boyish charm an enormous talent and intellectual strength, to say nothing of his fierce political commitment to his principles and ideals.

Vitality and versatility mark Oz's work as, indeed, they do those books of his several countrymen represented in these pages. They are, of course, not the only fine writers Israel has produced. One thinks immediately of Natan Zach, Chaim Gouri, Meir Wieseltier, Amalia Kahana-Carmon, S. Yizhar, and Aharon Megged among others. A companion volume to this one could well come into being in a few more years. For the time being, however, the opportunity to share the insights and the views of Amichai, Yehoshua, Carmi, Appelfeld, and Oz in the interviews assembled in this single compilation is special and, perhaps, even unique.

In conclusion, I want to express my deep appreciation to each of the five distinguished Israelis included here for his willingness to be interviewed. Willingness apart, each author gave of himself unstintingly, with gusto and great warmth. I am indebted to them further for granting permission for the publication of the interviews and for their subsequent responses to my inquiries for bibliographical and other information. Most of all, I am grateful for the new dimensions of enrichment they have brought to my life and for their friendships, which are the best of treasures.

Introduction

The five Israeli writers who are the subject of this book stand today at the forefront of contemporary Israeli literature. Their achievement is attested to by the literary prizes and awards they have garnered, by the popularity and the controversy surrounding their works, and by the seriousness with which scholars and students in Israel and increasingly—throughout the Western world—study their books. While there are other significant writers in Israel who unfortunately could not be included in the present work, these writers are representative of their age; they are the literary voices of Israel.

The age they inhabit in the particular setting of their small country is a peculiarly fortuitous one for serious writers. In the Amos Oz interview, he likens the literary situation in Israel today to "a volcano in action," not unlike the cultural ferment that was "bubbling and simmering" in Elizabethan England, producing the greatest drama in its history, an inspired drama that functioned at extraordinarily impressive metaphorical, metaphysical, and psychological levels in order to reflect precisely and accurately all the nuances of the complex social and political conditions of life at that time and in that place. Just as the Elizabethan playwrights responded to the demands of their time, so these Israeli poets and novelists have responded to the bubbling and simmering ferment of contemporary Israel, and they, too, have functioned (and are functioning) at the same extraordinarily impressive levels.

These writers are part of a movement now referred to as the New Wave. "New" because they are the most recent writers with a distinct point of view and methodology for expressing it, and a "Wave" because they have rejected and supplanted the major group that preceded them, the Palmah or Generation of 1948 writers who were nurtured in the years before the War of Independence on Zionist idealism, kibbutz socialism, and Russian "pioneering" literature. The New Wave writers came to their maturity after the War of Independence, and in a sense, grew up with the nation. Two of them are Sabras, A. B. Yehoshua and Amos Oz; the remaining three came to Palestine before the War of Independence, Yehuda Amichai from Germany in 1936,

1

Aharon Appelfeld from Bukovina and T. Carmi from the United States by way of France, both in 1947. There could have been few places in the world more auspicious for molding a career as a poet or novelist.

No other sovereign state in modern times has continuously been a powder keg with an often-lit short fuse. Nowhere else has an ancient tongue been created anew overnight, a whole technological vocabulary added to it, a language adapted to the vicissitudes of modern life in a world vastly more complex than that of the Judea and Samaria of old. The Israel of the past and the Israel of the present sit at the point where three great continents converge, and from the various lands of those continents diverse peoples have come to Israel to form one of the most cosmopolitan communities in the world. The cross-cultural influences are enormous: they include the British of the Mandate period, the French of the Levantine, the Palestinian Arab, North African Yemenite and Ethiopian, the Mediterranean, the Russian, Polish, German, and more recently, the American influence. Sephardic and Ashkenazic traditions, dialects, and points of view meet, sometimes clashing, sometimes blending. Death camp survivors locked into the tragedies of their past rub shoulders with young Sabras in uniform facing an uncertain future.

Moreover, in Israel intense rivalries in religion and politics are as commonplace as breakfast cereal, and everywhere there are seemingly irreconcilable differences and problems. Israel is a country that has lost its early vision and its giant statesmen. Zionism, however innocent this visionary movement may be of the charges lodged against it by its enemies, both internal and external, may no longer be relevant to the nation's survival and development. Israel's cities are growing faster than their services can be expanded to meet the needs of the people; the kibbutz movement is heavily in debt and may not survive; Israelis are leaving for America in droves; the Russian dissidents do not want to settle in the ancient homeland; the PLO, despite its long history of terrorism, has won worldwide sympathy and support; and behind everything else there still stands the implacable hatred of the hardcore Arabs, led by Syria and Libya, determined to push the Israelis into the sea.

The Israelis have had no choice but to respond to this continuously threatened annihilation with military ardor, and consequently there is a siege mentality[1] that permeates Israeli life; and an ever increasing emphasis upon military diplomacy gives rise to fears that unless a peaceful solution can be found to the Palestinian question, Israel will become an embattled police state, eventually more fascist than democratic, an outcast among nations. There is an ever increasing need to escape from this pressure cooker environment on the part of the Israeli middle class, saddled with taxes, high inflation, and bureaucratic intransigence. There is a touch of madness and frenzy in the daily lives of these Israelis and, if the New Wave writers are to be taken seriously, the lives of the people who make up the middle class are under so much strain that family life is being disrupted at an alarming rate with marriages breaking up and families torn asunder. In such a climate, the ethical and humanitarian values traditionally emphasized in Jewish life get short shrift.

The drama of contemporary Israeli life, then, is more than a bubbling and simmering cauldron, more even than a powder keg. It is a complete microcosm of a people attempting to cope with a war that has never ended, of terrorism that unveils itself in a variety of lethal forms: border clashes, unrest in the occupied territories, bomb explosions in the markets and assaults on land, sea and in the air, inside Israel and elsewhere throughout the world. It is in short a microcosm of the human condition under siege, with so much action occurring that no writer could remain aloof from it.

Aloofness is not now and never has been the style of the New Wave writers. On the contrary, they sought *engagement* from the outset. Apart from the fact that all of them have fought in Israel's wars, there was no intention on their part to distance themselves as writers from all that was happening around them in order to recollect the turmoil in tranquility. According to Nurith Gertz, their writing anticipated the troubled conditions of Israeli life well before the Yom Kippur War in 1973 "shocked the Israeli consciousness out of its sense of inviolability."[2] For the six years before that conflict, when, she says, Israeli "morale was at its peak, Israeli literature constantly dwelt on terror and destruction."[3] She observes that "this theme was either kept below the surface, treated metaphorically, or relegated to sub-plots. When it did appear undisguised, it was not recognized by critics or readers."[4] They saw this emerging body of literature as one in which the "stories were seen to be not political but psychological studies in political settings."[5] When they discerned the writers' true intent, they faulted them for a lack of aesthetic distancing between fiction and reality. The reality and the fiction, however, went hand in hand:

> ... it is precisely when Israel was strongest that its literature dealt with the fears of the persecuted Jew still without refuge, even in his homeland— either because past destruction and disaster must inevitably be repeated— (Aaron Apelfeld), *sic*, or because in Israel past and future belong not to the Jew but to the Arab (A. B. Yehoshua), or because "this evil land" and its inhabitants, the jackals and the Arabs, are hostile to the Jews (Amos Oz), or because the threat of war is ever present.[6]

To understand how the New Wave writers arrived at their substantially grim views of Israeli life, we must know something about the literary situation in Israel when they were growing up. The survey that follows is far from exhaustive, it is merely a broad outline intended only to place in context the remarks of the writers in the interviews about their predecessors. In general, they acknowledge the influence of the early giants in the revival of Hebrew literature in modern times, H. N. Bialik, Y. H. Brenner, S. Y. Agnon, and M. J. Berdyczewski, and of those who came afterwards, particularly the poets

Nathan Alterman and Abraham Shlonsky. Mastering the works of these writers constituted their basic "homework." In growing up and attending the university, they absorbed an extraordinary amount of Western literature, the ancient Greek classics, Renaissance drama, Gustave Flaubert and Marcel Proust, the Russian masters, particularly Fëdor Dostoevsky, Leo Tolstoy and Anton Chekhov, Franz Kafka, William Butler Yeats and James Joyce, and the American writers, Edgar Allen Poe, Herman Melville, Ezra Pound, T. S. Eliot, William Faulkner and Ernest Hemingway among others.

While they were engaged in this absorptive process, The Palmah[7] generation moved into literary prominence. Their writing, by and large, had a political visionary stance. It was exhortative, explicit and by contrast with the New Wave, simplistic in its aims and techniques. The protagonist in a typical Palmah novel usually lived and worked on a kibbutz and was trained to be a fighter as occasion demanded. In the novel's enveloping action, according to Gertz, the hero confronted a problem that pitted "personal fulfillment" against the "collective good."[8] Usually, society's goal prevailed in accord with the collective will and its value system. That is to say the themes of struggle, hard work and when necessary, engaging in combat, were enveloped in an idealistic aura, a romanticism that transcended the difficult realities of everyday life in Palestine. Gertz identifies the following writers as members of the Palmah movement: Aharon Megged, Nathan Shaham, Yigal Mosinzon, and Hanoch Bartov.

Writing about the Palmah Generation, Gershon Shaked, in *The Shadows Within: Essays on Modern Jewish Writers*, has pointed out that the "images that derive from the romanticism of the pioneering movement—return to the earth and adoration of the 'noble savage' in the persons of the Arab and the sabra—carry within themselves the seeds of irony [in the] gap between the vision and its realization."[9] As nationhood came into being, the Palmah Generation faced an existential crisis: its goal of political autonomy had been achieved and its vision had reached its limits as the new state began to develop along lines other than those of Zionist commitment to the recovery of the land and the extension of socialist models in the kibbutzim. Shaked believes that the decline of the Palmah Generation was hastened by the 'seeds of irony' inherent in its romantic stance. It invited "harsh criticism" from both the "political Left and Right,"[10] opening the way for sustained journalistic satire ridiculing "the innocents and dreamers from the lost paradise."[11] This satire, since it exposed the superficiality of the transcendental romantics by holding their glimmering world view up to the harsh glare of reality, opened the way in turn for the New Wave realists.

Yehoshua, in the interview here, put it this way:

> There used to be a kind of structured Zionist, socialist center and writers wrote comfortably from within its boundaries. They were very much concerned with what we would call the national experience. It placed a lot of

responsibility on those writers who wanted to express not only their personal experience but the experience of the nation in general, relating it to the use of the Hebrew language. Hebrew contributed to the awareness of a national consciousness. This has long been a trend. From the beginning, Hebrew literature wasn't detached as are other literatures. It is analogous to the concern for national problems one finds in Tolstoy, Dostoevsky and even Chekhov who were always probing the Russian condition. In a way, this concern with the national experience gave direction to Israeli writing. Each of us placed himself at a certain angle to this central consciousness, saying "this I accept, this I reject." This center has now collapsed and we cannot act as if it still exists. In the coming years we will have to find our way in an Israel that no longer has a center.

In fact, the center was dissipated in the birth pangs of the new nation. As its problems increased in number and complexity, it did not take long for the ancient fears of the Jews—the ones in the passage from Gertz quoted above—to surface, and surface they did in the work of the New Wave writers.

It might be said that the New Wave was literally programmed for the realistic stance it took. The romantically inclined ruling literary clique had been discredited and, if it could be said that the satirists created a vacuum, the New Wave came to fill it, nurtured on the fiction of S. Yizhar, whose major work the *Days of Tiklag* is unfortunately not known in the West. An important writer born in 1916 who has escaped classification with any one coterie, Yizhar is distinctive for having produced works of realism in the late 1940s in opposition to the dominant Palmah romanticism.[12] Also germinal were the works of Flaubert, Dostoevsky, Kafka, Joyce, the French existentialists and a whole host of other Western writers who internalized reality, legitimated psychodrama, prophesied the collapse of the Western value system in the twentieth century in a never ending stream of grim fables and pessimistic poems, and altered the concepts of time and space to make simple chronology and linearity outmoded. That is to say that the basic reason the New Wave writers, poets and novelists alike, have so much appeal in the Western world is that while they are Israeli to the core, they are essentially Western writers who espouse its traditions and employ its techniques. The names of the Western models recur frequently in the interviews; the names, themes, motifs, and techniques of Western literature are everywhere to be observed in their poetry and fiction. The main burden of this study is to demonstrate the propositions that the five Israeli writers considered here are steeped in the Western tradition, are adept in its use, and are at their best when they merge Western tradition with the central elements of Israeli life.[13]

My concept of the term "Western tradition" in the context of this study embraces a number of significant approaches to modern literature: the realism of Flaubert and Dostoevsky, the nihilism of Nietzsche, the sinister, anonymous authoritarianism described by Kafka, the subjectivity of Proust, the trench mentality of the World War I English poets combined with T. S. Eliot's view of the modern world as a wasteland, the impact of Sigmund Freud's psychoanalytical theories of the unconscious and the role of dreams, combined with the interiorization of reality by Conrad, Joyce, Woolf, Lawrence and Faulkner, the primal archetypes of Carl Jung, and the positivism of Søren Kierkegaard's Christian existentialism combined with the *angst* of the atheistic existentialists, particularly Albert Camus and Jean-Paul Sartre. My analysis of the individual works of the New Wave writers will offer illustrations from their books of the extensive use of these approaches in Western tradition, both in theme and in technique. Once presented, these illustrations will be analyzed and matched with their ostensible Western sources, or compared to their Western counterparts. The thematic connections need not be catalogued here, they are many and diverse, but one modern Western technique, since it is still new and largely unfamiliar, needs to be discussed in some detail at this point.

I am referring to the adaptation of principles from Einstein's relativity theory to contemporary literature. As we shall see, these principles, simultaneity, the breakdown of causality and the indeterminacy theory of Werner Heisenberg, turn up significantly in the fiction of Amichai, Yehoshua, Appelfeld and Oz. (Carmi does not write fiction.) Perhaps more than any other single technique, the use of relativity places these writers in the mainstream of modern, serious Western fiction. Like a number of important Western writers, including Jorge Luis Borges (*Labyrinths*), Lawrence Durrell (*The Alexandria Quartet*), Malcolm Lowry (*Under the Volcano*), Thomas Pynchon (*Gravity's Rainbow*), and Cynthia Ozick (*Levitation: Five Fictions*) the Israelis have mastered the adaptation of these principles as promulgated by Einstein, Bohr and Heisenberg, employing them to achieve freedom from dependence on the objective Newtonian absolutes that heretofore have governed our attitudes and responses to space and time.[14] While the Israelis' fiction is presented to us in an aesthetic context, its understructure is metaphysical. How are these metaphysical concerns reworked for literature?

The literary usage of relativity and the Newtonian absolutes is not formalized. It consists largely of generally agreed upon subjective adaptations.[15] For that reason a restating of the basic scientific laws and formulae in both systems is not required here for an understanding of their application to fiction.

Without underestimating the complexity or the seriousness of these scientific systems, we can observe that the New Wave writers in specified narratives, Amichai's *Not of This Time, Not of This Place*, and *The World Is A Room And Other Stories*, Yehoshua's "Early In the Summer Of 1970" and *The Lover*, Appelfeld's *Badenheim 1939* and *To The Land Of The Cattails*, and Oz's *Touch The Water Touch The Wind* challenge the comfort and security we take in the Newtonian absolutes, in three-dimensional space and a separate dimension of time, and in a view of reality based on the premise that the things we see around us move at much slower velocities than the speed of light. At velocities approaching the speed of light, as we know, space and time are fused, and we detect matter for what it really is, highly concentrated energy. When John Donne wrote that "No man is an island" in his *Devotions Upon Emergent Occasions* he could not have known how right he was, for our very bodies, which at ordinary velocities we view as discrete and separate and think of as being composed of matter, are made up of intense concentrations of the same energy that fills the cosmos in the form of subatomic particles.

These billions upon billions of subatomic particles share certain properties. They possess a wavelike function, bond and break, and move about furiously with a certain randomness and indeterminacy. Whatever our traditional view of reality, the one most cogent and applicable is the one that reflects the movement of these particles. Intensity and tension are the hallmarks of the process.

The implications of the process have not been missed by a number of serious modern writers of fiction, including these Israelis, who recognize that the nature of our universe is one of interconnectedness throughout, of simultaneous occurrence, of random action and unpredictability. Cause and effect are no longer locked into an eternal marriage, and anything becomes possible. Nothing can be measured with any final degree of accuracy.

For a number of serious writers relativity has come to provide an alternate, legitimate means of dealing with space and time, freeing them from the linear rigidities of the Newtonian absolutes. Novelists and short story writers are no longer chained to a chronological occurrence of events and sequential plot devlopment. Instead they now engage the multiplicity of the universe through an emphasis upon simultaneity, expanding the range of possibilities in human interaction by freeing themselves from the principle of causality and by accepting Heisenberg's indeterminacy theory that precludes the singularly unchallengeable measurement of any object. Multiple endings or the absence of any closure have become commonplace. To view everything as relative is to give the writer of fiction a range of freedom that theoretically extends to infinity.

Simultaneity, the breakdown of causality, and indeterminacy came to be numbered among the principal techniques of Borges, Lowry and Durrell in the early middle decades of the twentieth century. Subsequently, John Fowles, John Barth, Kurt Vonnegut, Jr., Thomas Pynchon, Tom Robbins, Don Delillo, Cynthia Ozick, Philip Roth and, now, these Israeli writers have joined their ranks. As the discussions throughout of the Israeli writers' use of the technique will show, even the critics have not recognized either the extent to which relativity is used or its legitimacy as a working tool. The critics invariably refer to the simultaneity, the breakdown of causality and indeterminacy as a writer's "game" or "tricks" or "magic," when of course it is none of these at all.

The frequency with which Lawrence Durrell's *The Alexandria Quartet* is referred to or discussed in the interviews and the analyses calls for a brief comment here. Not only is his novel seminal in the development and use of relativity in modern literature, it is a major work by a sympathetic British writer intimately familiar with the eastern Mediterranean area, its peoples, its modern history, its politics, and its emotional ferment. The points of contact between it and the fiction of the Israelis are many, and it is a useful artifact by which to measure their mastery of Western tradition.

The interviews provided me with the unusual opportunity to raise some intriguing questions about the role of the writer in Israel, his social and political commitment, the relationship between literature and politics, the essential similarities and differences between contemporary Israeli and Western literature. The essays pursue these matters further in an effort to elucidate a singularly remarkable body of literature. Such overviews as may be pertinent will be brought together in my concluding remarks.

Chapter 1

Yehuda Amichai

Yehuda Amichai is Israel's best known poet. A transplanted German Jew, Amichai came to Palestine in 1936 with his parents when he was twelve years old. Since he was taught Hebrew as a child, his adjustment to the language in Palestine posed no unusual problems. After completing high school Amichai went to Hebrew University where he prepared himself for a secondary school career teaching Hebrew literature and the Bible. Before long, however, his avocation as writer overtook his vocation as a teacher, and he now has an estimable international reputation not only as a poet but also as a a novelist, short story writer and dramatist. He began composing poetry in 1949, and he published his first volume of poems, *Akhsahav u-ve-yamin Aherim* (Now and in Other Days) in 1955. A steady succession of volumes of poems has followed. From these volumes, eight collections have thus far appeared in English,[1] along with translations of his novel, *Lo Me-Akhshav, Lo Mi-Kan* (Not Of This Time, Not Of This Place) and his volume of short stories *Ba-ruah ha-nora'ah ha-zot* (The World Is A Room And Other Stories).

While a number of the volumes of translated poetry are in print, the quotations of poems in the discussion that follows are all from the *Selected Poetry of Yehuda Amichai*, edited and translated by Chana Bloch and Stephen Mitchell, published by Harper & Row in 1986. That compendium contains translations of work from ten volumes of Amichai's poetry, moving from his earliest published verses to his most recent ones, and it is, therefore, the most representative selection as well as the most currently accessible one for American readers.

Since several fundamental subjects in Amichai's poetry, particularly his evocation of the impact of war and of love on himself and on humanity are addressed in the interview, they require only incidental comment. The poems of war and of love, so important in Amichai's canon, are, in a sense, prologues and epilogues to his great ongoing dialogue with God. They are always in the forefront and afterthought of that dialogue which, more precisely, takes the form of a debate over God's presence and His absence, His caring and not caring, His actions and inactions. The parameters of this argument form a backdrop to much that is articulated throughout Amichai's poetry. Since the dialogue is cumulative, it is natural to think of Amichai's successive volumes of poetry as comprising one monumental argument with the Almighty. The observations about Amichai's poetry in this book are mainly, but not exclusively, concerned with that dialogue, its expression, and its implications.

A secular but positive Jew who turns frequently to the Hebrew Bible for his themes and images as complements to his views of the contemporary world, Amichai, like the prophets of old, continually confronts God, demanding explanations for humankind's never ending calamities and catastrophes. In her introduction to the *Selected Poetry of Yehuda Amichai*, Chana Bloch maintains rightly that it is "Amichai's sardonic quarrel with God" that "stamps [his] poetry as so unmistakably Jewish."[2]

This quarrel is central to the Jewish experience. It has perhaps been summed up best by Karl Shapiro in the introduction to his *Poems Of A Jew*. In that remarkable volume of poetry published in 1958, Shapiro, after having seriously considered converting to Catholicism, reaffirmed his Jewishness. Attempting to define the meaning of Jewishness, he said:

> No one has been able to define *Jew*, and in essence this defiance of definition is the central meaning of Jewish consciousness. For to be a Jew is to be in a certain state of consciousness which is inescapable. As everyone knows, a Jew who becomes an atheist remains a Jew. A Jew who becomes a Catholic remains a Jew. Being a Jew is the consciousness of being a Jew, and the Jewish identity, with or without religion, with or without history, is the significant fact. The Jew is unique among mankind, once he accepts this identity, and the word *Jew* retains its eternal shock, a shock that has nothing to do with Christ or the Crucifixion. The shock has to do with the Covenant, the intimacy of Jew and God. This intimacy is not sentimental; on the contrary, it is unfriendly. And it is the kind of intimacy that precludes religion itself . . . and, secondarily, art itself.[3]

Amichai, like Shapiro, keeps his intimate, unfriendly Covenant with God, preclusive of religion and art, by constantly challenging Him.

The Amichaian challenge, while not friendly, is for the most part positive. It confirms God's presence in human affairs, and it bespeaks a bond that is reconstituted endlessly by the awareness in those affairs of both joy and sorrow, of the pleasures of love however ephemeral, and of the pains of war however permanent. At its core is an ambivalence that is on the one hand potentially loving, but on the other hand predominately angry, frustrated, and oppositional. This disdain for God is frequently articulated in the poems.

In a very early war poem, "God Has Pity on Kindergarten Children," one that is widely known, Amichai makes distinctions based on age, between those whom God will protect and those whom He will leave exposed:

> God has pity on kindergarten children.
> He has less pity on school children.
> And on grownups he has no pity at all,
> he leaves them alone,
> and sometimes they must crawl on all fours
> in the burning sand
> to reach the first-aid station
> covered with blood. (1)

Only the youngest of helpless innocents are the objects of God's concern, not those who are older and more vulnerable. Adult soldiers in combat are ordinarily far more exposed to destruction than are small children, but for them God provides no watchfulness. The image of the bloodied, wounded soldiers is reminiscent of Wilfred Owen's soldiers who crawl like caterpillers in his poem "The Show," and whose limbs are "knife-skewed/ Rolling and rolling there/Where God seems not to care" in his poem "Greater Love."[4] Caring or pity, however, is one thing, protection against danger is something else. In Amichai's poem, pity carries with it no omnipotent obligation, no guarantee of protection. Ultimately, living beings are responsible for themselves, Amichai suggests, except for small children and several other categories of people whose innocence and vulnerability may or may not entitle them to God's attention. These include true lovers, and an "old man/ sleeping on a public bench" (1).

There are other associations in Amichai's poem to Wilfred Owen: the emphasis on pity itself—"My subject," Owen said in his famous preface, unpublished at the time of his death in combat, "is War, and the pity of War"[5]— and an Owenesque wistfulness in Amichai's closing stanza that establishes the efficacy of human compassion as a substitute for or an addition to the non-protective uncertain concern of God:

> Perhaps we too will give them
> the last rare coins of compassion
> that Mother handed down to us,
> so that their happiness will protect us
> now and in other days. (1)

As Edward Hirsch has pointed out, this poem and others published with it also show an indebtedness to W. H. Auden. Amichai is, Hirsch asserts, "a tender ironist ... (especially in his conjunction of the private and political spheres)."[6] There is, of course, a direct line of literary descent for the combination of tenderness with irony, from Owen through Auden to Amichai; to make this connection is simply to acknowledge how thoroughly modern and Western Amichai's poetry is.

In another early poem, "Ibn Gabirol," Amichai comments on the frequency of pain in life and expresses the need to escape. The most powerful image of the poem is one of God's "peer[ing] into the universe" through "the wound in [the poet's] chest" (6). Elsewhere, in "God's Hand in the World," God's hand is seen as mechanical; Amichai compares its actions to the perfunctory removal of a fowl's entrails:

> God's hand is in the world
> like my mother's hand in the guts of the slaughtered
>   chicken
> on Sabbath eve.
> What does God see through the window
> while his hands reach into the world?
> What does my mother see? (10)

The answer is that God sees pain but, unlike a mother nurturing her family, He does nothing to alleviate the pain; perhaps, the inference is He is the cause of it. In a critique of this poem, one of Amichai's translators, Glenda Abramson, observes that "The expression 'the hand of God' is frequently used throughout the Bible to denote God's power; his hand in the world destroys, generally for the good of his people, and it moves in the universe against evil. At the same time the image connotes a terrifying and implacable force which devastates while it is doing good."[7] The difference between biblical usage and Amichai's position is that he finds little evidence of God's hand "doing good."

In "And That Is Your Glory," the words that form the poem's title and refrain, based upon a key passage from the liturgy of the Days of Awe, the *Vehi tehillatekha*, change the praise of God in the original to a condemnation. Amichai complains that "God is hiding," and that "Underneath the world, God lies stretched on his back,/always repairing, always things get out of whack" (11). All the speaker of the poem can see are the soles of the shoes of this careless mechanic. Called into question are God's need to hide from His people and his creation of a faulty universe. The conclusion drawn is that what should be God's glory is now His shame.

Coupled to God's absence is His insensitivity. In "Look: Thoughts and Dreams," Amichai presents us with a God who is neither capable of comprehending people's wishes nor even aware that the natural growth patterns of life have been reversed:

> Look: thoughts and dreams are weaving over us
> their warp and woof, their wide camouflage-net,
> and the reconnaissance planes and God
> will never know
> what we really want
> and where we are going.

Only the voice that rises at the end of a question
still rises above the world and hangs there,
even if it was made by
mortar shells, like a ripped flag,
like a mutilated cloud.

Look, we too are going
in the reverse-flower-way:
to begin with a calyx exulting toward the light,
to descend with the stem growing more and more solemn,
to arrive at the closed earth and to wait there for a
 while,
and to end as a root, in the darkness, in the deep womb. (7)

It is futile to ask why the natural expectations of life have been reversed, why
the exultation "toward the light" turns into the solemnity of darkness. The
voice asking the question about the direction in which humankind is headed
just hangs unanswered in the heavens. In its war imagery "Look: Thoughts
and Dreams" is also reminiscent of another of Owen's poems, "Futility":

Move him into the sun—
Gently its touch awoke him once,
At home, whispering of fields unsown.
Always it woke him, even in France.
Until this morning and this snow.
If anything might rouse him now
The kind old sun will know.

Think how it wakes the seeds,—
Woke, once, the clays of a cold star.
Are limbs, so dear-achieved, are sides,
Full-nerved—still warm—too hard to stir?
Was it for this the clay grew tall?
—O what made fatuous sunbeams toil
To break earth's sleep at all?[8]

Amichai's technique is similar to Owen's in contrasting the destructiveness of
war with the normalcy of natural processes and in asking why this unnatural
inversion of life has superseded generational growth and survival.

In other poems, the linking of God to an inverse value system, mainly
connected to war, is continued. In lines from that magnificently sustained,
long autobiographical poem, "Travels of the Last Benjamin of Tudela," Amichai
links God to a modern technology geared toward violence, destruction, and
militarism: "Tanks from America, fighter planes from France, Russian/ jet-
doves, armored chariots from England" (81). Images of peacetime, mainly
religious objects, are transposed into the weaponry of war:

                                        Multiple automatic
prayer beads and also in single shots. Muezzins armed with
three-stage missiles, paper-rips and battle-cries
of holy wars in all seven kinds,
shtreimls like mines in the road and in the air, deep philosophical
depth-charges, a heart lit up with a green light inside
the engine of a red-hot bomber, Elijah's ejection-seat
     leaping up
at a time of danger, hurling circumcision knives,
     thundering
dynamite fuses from heart to heart, a Byzantine tank
with a decorated window in which an icon appears
lit up in purity and softness, mezuzahs filled with
explosives .... (81)

"The Joint Chiefs of Staff" are Job and "his friends, Satan and God." The modern world is a reenactment of Job's travail at the hands of a God who is a stiff-necked militarist willing to be manipulated by the devil. The transposed imagery continues with additional Jewish religious objects drawn into the arsenal of combat: "eight empty bullet-shells for a Hanukkah menorah," "a submachine gun carried in phylactery straps," "hand-grenades in the shape of a spice box" (82). Amichai concludes this "manual of arms" with a listing of acronyms that link militarism to technology, big business, institutional religion, violence and government. The final link is to God:

               M.I.R.V., S.W.A.T., I.C.B.M., I.B.M.,
               P.O.W., R.I.P., A.W.O.L.,
               S.N.A.F.U., I.N.R.I., J.D.L., L.B.J.,
               E.S.P., I.R.S., D.N.A., G.O.D. (82)

God has become a merchant of death. In the "Songs of Zion the Beautiful," He is no longer a successful salesman of religious objects, which is to say, a purveyor of religion:

               Every evening God takes his glittery merchandise
               out of the shop window:
               chariot works, tablets of law, fancy beads,
               crosses and gleaming bells,
               and puts them back into dark boxes
               inside, and closes the shutter: "Another day,
               and still not one prophet has come to buy." (114)

     In "A Great Tranquillity: Questions and Answers," the title poem of the volume in which it appears, Amichai ponders the question whether God is a delusion for religious enthusiasts, from whom he must escape:

> The people in the painfully bright auditorium
> spoke about religion
> in the life of contemporary man
> and about God's place in it.
>
> People spoke in excited voices
> as they do at airports.
> I walked away from them:
> I opened an iron door marked "Emergency"
> and entered into
> a great tranquillity: Questions and Answers. (142)

The people in the bright auditorium have answers, but they are answers the speaker of the poem finds incomplete. They possess only half a world, a world of answers to which no questions are attached. From this half world, the speaker of the poem must escape into his whole world of both "Questions and Answers," for only there is the world complete and tranquility possible. One question that might be asked has to do with the worth of a God who appeals to superficial zealots. If God is to be found at all, He is more likely to be in the questions than in the answers.

Does God exist at all? With wry irony, Amichai answers the question negatively in another section of "Songs of Zion the Beautiful" by linking God's existence to two disproven theories of the cosmos, the three assertions placed ironically into an insistently affirmative refrain:

> And because of the war
> I repeat, for the sake of a last, simple sweetness:
> The sun goes around the earth, yes.
> The earth is flat as a lost drifting plank, yes.
> There's a God in heaven. Yes. (106-107)

The delusion notwithstanding, Amichai acknowledges God's presence in the universe in several instances by expressing his anger. God is there, but He will never answer to His presence. Recalling his childhood in "Travels of the Last Benjamin of Tudela" Amichai tells us that he learned very early not to expect an answer:

> ... And on holy days *Kohanim* [priests] blessed me
> from inside the white caves of their prayer-shawls, with
> fingers
> twisted like epileptics. I looked at them
> and God didn't thunder: and since then his thunder has
> grown
> more and more remote and become a huge
> silence. (62)

The silence only provokes the greater need to know why God has withdrawn from converse with his people. Still thinking of his childhood and describing himself as one who has "become a collector of pains in the tradition of [Israel]," Amichai asks the crucial question but must provide his own answer: "'My God, my God, why?' Hast Thou forsaken me. My God, my God. Even then/ he had to be called twice. The second call/ was already like a question, out of a first doubt: my God?" (63) If God is so obstinately silent, the poet must wonder if such a deity should continue to be worshipped. The identity with a God who is so provocative is frustrating and suffocating.

The poet's frustration mounts because the Covenant is too one-sided. This voiceless deity expects too much: "Not just one finger of God but all ten of them/Strangle me" (67). This again is the hand of God working in the universe. Here He again appears to be malevolent. It is, at least, a sign, albeit a negative one. Is He also benevolent, positive? Amichai's answer is that He is both good and evil, a conclusion that does not reduce the poet's discomfort in the unpredictability or harshness of God's actions. God, Amichai argues in these lines from a different section of "Travels of the Last Benjamin of Tudela," is not to be trusted because He is capable of anything. One can wager on His unpredictability and on His harshness:

> I want to make a bet with Job,
> about how God and Satan will behave.
> Who will be the first to curse man.
> Like the red of sunset in Job's mouth,
> they beat him and his last word
> sets in redness into his last face.
> That's how I left him in the noisy station
> in the noise, among the loudspeaker's voices.
> "Go to hell, Job. Cursed be the day
> when you were created in my image. Go fuck your mother, Job."
> God cursed, God blessed. Job won. And I
> have to kill myself with the toy pistol
> of my small son. (72)

By contrast, Satan behaves better than God because he is not the first one to curse man. He is not the one to threaten Job, and by inference, he is no threat to contemporary humankind. God is the threat, partly because He is unpredictable. One never knows whether God will bless or curse. He is as likely to do one as the other—or both. Here He does both. In spite of His harsh curses Job is blessed, and the poet loses the wager. But the loss of the bet is incidental to the lesson learned about God's behavior: He is inconsistent and He plays games with human beings. In angry mockery the poet offers a rebuke to God by engaging vicariously in the same kind of sport: he will pretend to kill himself with his son's toy gun. There is a kind of grim whimsicality here on both God's part and the poet's part. Amichai's stance is not unlike Pursewarden's sardonic belief, expressed in Lawrence Durrell's *The Alexandria Quartet*, that "God is a humorist."[9]

Yet if there is anger, mockery, and contention in Amichai's attitude toward God, there is also some tenderness. God may be a ruthless, relentless killer in war after war, but He is conscious of human loss and He mourns the dead. For all his strictures against God in "Travels of the Last Benjamin of Tudela," it is also in that poem that Amichai credits God with grieving over the deceased: "This valley is the rip," he says, that "God made in his clothes, in the ritual mourning for the dead," (78) an image that acknowledges God's power as the Creator of the earth and of everything in it. The context is neither ironical nor negative but benevolent. Other images of a benevolent God occur elsewhere. In "Poems for a Woman" lovers find rest "on God's quiet slope" (17). And in a passage from "Songs of Zion the Beautiful," Amichai writes of four entrenched synagogues whose presences and interiors constitute gifts from God:

> In the first, Holy Arks with candles hidden away,
> and sweet preserves of God's Word from a blessed season,
> all in beautiful jars, for children
> to stand on tiptoe and lick with a golden finger.
> Also ovens with *cholent* and oatmeal running over.
>
> In the second four strong pillars for an everlasting
> wedding canopy. The result
> of love.
> The third, an old Turkish bathhouse with small, high
>   windows
> and Torah scrolls, naked
> or taking off their robes. *Answer, answer us*
> in clouds of vapor and white steam,
> *Answer, answer* till the senses swoon.
>
> The fourth:
> part of God's bequest. (112)

The plea for answers, for a response from God in this instance is not the cry of the forsaken that we observed earlier. It is a cry, an utterance that is more in the nature of a prayer of thanksgiving.

If Amichai's struggle with God is softened somewhat by these passages, it does not alter the balance. God remains distant and demanding; His actions are beyond the comprehension of mortal men. In Amichai's "The Real Hero," his version of the *Akedah*, the story of the near-sacrifice of Isaac by Abraham to prove his faith in God, the honors go not to Abraham for his faith or to God for providing a sacrificial substitute at the last minute for Isaac. They go instead to the offering, the ram. In "The Real Hero," Amichai stubbornly insists on parity between man and God and an end to God's destructive irresponsibility. Because it is a recent poem (1983) that confirms again Amichai's stance, consistent over the decades, of refusal to accept omnipotent malevolence, it bears quoting in full:

> The real hero of the Isaac story was the ram,
> who didn't know about the conspiracy between the others.
> As if he had volunteered to die instead of Isaac.
> I want to sing a song in his memory—
> about his curly wool and his human eyes,
> about the horns that were so silent on his living head,
> and how they made these horns into shofars when he was
>   slaughtered
> to sound their battle cries
> or to blare out their obscene joy.
>
> I want to remember the last frame
> like a photo in an elegant fashion magazine:
> the young man tanned and manicured in his jazzy suit
> and beside him the angel, dressed for a party
> in a long silk gown,
> both of them empty-eyed, looking
> at two empty places,
>
> and behind them, like a colored backdrop, the ram,
> caught in the thicket before the slaughter.
> The thicket was his last friend.
>
> The angel went home.
> Isaac went home.
> Abraham and God had gone long before.
>
> But the real hero of the Isaac story
> Was the ram. (151)

In the twentieth century, the theme of the *Akedah* has been used by many writers, by novelists as diverse as Robert Penn Warren in *The Cave* and Bernard Malamud in *God's Grace*, and by poets, most notably, in addition to Amichai, Wilfred Owen in "The Parable Of The Old Men And The Young," and Amir Gilboa in "Isaac." (The renderings by Owen and Gilboa are quoted and discussed in the interview with T. Carmi.) All these modernized versions have in common a closure that differs from the original biblical version. Usually Isaac, or his modern counterpart, is sacrificed. His death is seen as the result of criminal irresponsibility, either on the part of the father or of the son. Amichai's treatment of the *Akedah* is closest to that of Malamud in assigning the criminal irresponsibility primarily to God, the initiator of the "conspiracy" that ended in the death of the ram.

Amichai's ongoing quarrel with God is, to be sure, a direct result of the poet's ambivalence and guilt over his rejection in adolescence of orthodox Judaism and the disappointment and suffering that act caused his father to whom he was always close. It has assumed the form of an unresolved conflict that demands a continuing dialogue (taking place in Amichai's mind, since his father died years ago) as if a resolution were a viable option. Downplaying the conflict Amichai, in an interview with David Montenegro, stressed both the idea of the continuing dialogue and his specific identification of his father with God. Their exchange follows:

> DM: ... you mentioned that you're not religious anymore. Does that still bring up conflicts in you?

> YA: No, no, no, no, no. Actually, I'm going on with the discussion I had with my father [laughs]. We loved each other very much, but we had this problem—big problem—so we go on, I go on discussing it with him. The liturgy has one famous phrase: "*Al venu malkanu,*" which means, "Our Father, Our King." It is a bit metaphoric, because if you say our father, our king in a prayer to God, it also means: our father, our God,—god-father. If God is a father then father is God. The metaphors are equal. So my father is actually my private god.
>
> When I was a child, like every child, I thought my father was really a god, and when I rebelled against him, he still was God. But then I found out, of course, that he was a human being. I think it's the same with God.[10]

While Amichai chooses to remove the onerous conditions of rejection and sustained conflict from his relationship to his father and thus to God by euphemizing the conflict as "dialogue," the continuing tension he experiences in this situation has, through its expression in poetry, given the world a score of beautiful poems. This tension is somewhat akin to the tension in Stanley Kunitz's poetry over that poet's lifelong need to resolve a reverse problem of rejection: his father's suicide a few months before Kunitz was born. It has produced, among other verses, Kunitz's famous poem "Father and Son" in which the "rebellion" by the father against the son has precluded the possibility of attaining a Jewish identity. Kunitz pleads with his father to return to instruct him in "the Gemara of your gentleness."[11]

In her essay "Amichai's God," mentioned above, Glenda Abramson discusses at length Amichai's identification of his father with God. She first makes a useful distinction between the images of the Almighty in the poet's earlier work, maintaining that his first complaints were articulated against a "primitive, anthropomorphic deity who walked on earth among men," and the images in his later poetry, moving away from a "concretized" God to a representation of "the God of the Talmud who no longer dabbles capriciously in human affairs" and is "no longer a personal adversary or a manipulator of man's destiny . . . ." "The blending," she writes, "of the images of the father (*av* or *avi*) and God in the later poetry provides the abstract, ethical image of the deity."[12] She assigns the coalescence of the two images of God and father to the period of Amichai's first novel, *Not of This Time, Not of this Place*, first published in Hebrew in Israel in 1963.[13] After the novel was written, she suggests, Amichai's poetry demonstrates "an almost obsessive consistency" of "the domination by God and the father."[14] Because of his rebellion against the combined authority figures, Amichai had come to feel more and more guilty. Guilt over his trespasses occupies a large domain in his poetry. The "Travels of the Last Benjamin of Tudela," Abramson says, "is a long *mea culpa* for diverting what should have been piety and religious fidelity into the paths of love and other, secular, concerns," adding that "there is, consequently, an imputation of reproach in the image of the father as he appears in the poetry, particularly in his unbroken silence, his elusiveness and unapproachability."[15]

Ultimately, Amichai's battle is not so much with an externalized deity as it is with an internalized mixture of that deity with his father. Because it is internalized, it must continue to find an outlet in Amichai's poetry for the rest of his life. Perhaps an interesting fictional parallel to Amichai's relationship with his deceased father is that of Saul Bellow's Herzog in the novel of that name. Herzog, too, had disappointed his father who told him he would never amount to anything, and Herzog's near disintegration becomes a self-willed enactment of the father's prophecy. Only by coming to terms with himself and by learning to care for others does Herzog begin to turn his life around and to embark on the slow, hard process of moving toward an idealized *Menschlichkeit*. Amichai, it hardly needs saying, is a man of compassion and caring, already a *Mensch*, but his ongoing "dialogue" with his father will not be concluded so easily as was Herzog's. As long as it is not concluded, the prospects remain for more poems on the same filial/theological themes.

Apart from Amichai's themes, the special qualities that mark Amichai's verse are a capacity to make profound ideas appear simple without reducing their profundity; an ear and voice that pick up and articulate nuances and meanings, however complex, in informal, affectionately warm colloquial speech patterns; and an ability to juxtapose seemingly disparate images that when considered together, reveal an underlying affinity and create a solidly cohering unity. Because he is an emotional poet, Amichai's poems achieve their beauty and movement in the expression of his feelings which, however strong or intense, are always under control. Pain and pleasure are balanced, sadness, melancholy and loss are compensated for by the anticipation and fulfillment of love, and world-weariness is mitigated by fresh optimism. Ancient biblical themes and history are juxtaposed to the conditions of life in contemporary Israel and each informs the other by the interchanged perspectives. The imagery is vital, clear, and filled with Jewish compassion and wisdom.

Amichai's main poetic genius is his versatility in the creation of meta-phors. Few poets are his peers in the ability to link and join seemingly unrelated objects, events, ideas, and symbols to provide his readers with fresh ways of seeing reality and experience. Everywhere one turns in his poetry, the metaphors and the similes stand out, delighting and informing the reader simultaneously of some new hitherto unimagined way of looking at his sub-ject matter.[16] Amichai's poem, "The Visit of the Queen of Sheba" [to Solomon] is not only one of the most memorable love poems[17] in modern literature, but it also is a magnificently sustained example of the poet's metaphorical virtu-osity. In metaphor and simile Sheba is presented to us first as she prepares for the journey, arranging gifts of peacocks and ivory boxes. As she wants to know everything about Solomon in advance of her visit, we are told

> her curiosity
> blossomed like leprosy,
> the disheveled sisters of her corpuscles
> screamed through their loudspeaker into all her muscles,
> the sky undid
> its buttons, she made herself up and slid
> into a vast commotion,
> felt her head
> spin, all the brothels of her emotions
> were lit up in red.
> In the factory
> of her blood, they worked frantically
> till night came: a dark night, like an old table,
> a night as eternal
> as a jungle. (22-23)

In this one short passage alone, there are eight dissimilar comparisons, as follows: curiosity-leprosy, sisters-corpuscles, screaming-loudspeaker, sky-dis-robing, brothels-emotions, factory-blood, night-table, and night-jungle. Each pair of objects is brought together and all are linked to give us a portrait of Sheba's erotic anticipation of Solomon.

The third section of the poem, "Setting Sail," continues this cascading of metaphorical figures:

> She called her thighs to return to each other,
> knee-cheek to knee-cheek, and her soul
> was already a zebra of moods, good and bad.
> In the oven of her body, her heart
> rotated on a spit. The morning screamed,
> a tropical rain fell.
> The forecasters, chained to the spot, forecasted,

> the engineers of her sleep went out on weary camels,
> all the little fish of her laughter fled
> before the shark of her awakening rage. In her armpits
> faint-hearted corals hid,
> night-lizards left their footprints on her belly. (23-24)

Here thighs are independently animated to hear Sheba's voice, her soul is animated to display its moods as a zebra does its temperament, her body heat is reflected in images of fire and roasting food, the morning is personified in the voice of one screaming, the catalysts of sleep move as though they were part of a camel caravan, laughter and rage become prey and predatory fish, and corals are personified in their capacity to hide.

The poem becomes more and more explicitly erotic, and the metaphorical imagery matches the heightening desire:

>   Captains
>   plotted their course by the map
>   of her longing. Her nipples preceded her like scouts,
>   her hairs whispered to one another
>   like conspirators. In the dark corners between sea and ship
>   the counting started, quietly.
>   A solitary bird sang
>   in the permanent trill of her blood. (24)

When Sheba reaches Solomon's palace, he must summon his wisdom to counter her beauty. Solomon's desire, like Sheba's, is expressed in a series of comparable metaphors and similes that begin in the ice of rejection and end in the heat of acceptance:

>   In the bedroom of his heart he pulled down the shades,
>
>   he covered his blood with sackcloth, tried
>   to think of icebergs, of putrefied
>
>   camel flesh. And his face changed seasons
>   like a speeded-up landscape. He followed his visions
>
>   to the end of them, growing wiser and warm,
>   and he knew that her soul's form was like the form
>
>   of her supple body, which he soon would embrace—
>   as a violin's form is the form of its case. (25-26)

Their attempts to master each other are first compared to a ping-pong game. All their strategies are then played forth in a battery of complementary images:

> He made black waves with his beard
> so that her words would drown in it.
> She made a jungle
> of her hair, for him to be lost in.
> Words were plunked down with a click
> like chessmen.
> Thoughts with high masts
> sailed past one another.
> Empty crossword puzzles filled up
> as the sky fills with stars. (26)

The word-play, composed of a series of minor metaphors in this climactic section of the poem, becomes overall a major metaphor for the sexual union of Sheba and Solomon. Both have used all their wiles in their sexual power-struggle; they are cunning linguists as, indeed, is Amichai. The final section of the poem "The Empty Throne Room," is a kind of postcoital epilogue: the wordplay and love-play are over, the throne room is empty both literally and symbolically. All that remains are the linings of the containers that held their wiles:

> All the word games
> lay scattered out of their boxes.
> Boxes were left gaping
> after the game.
>
> Sawdust of questions,
> shells of cracked parables,
> woolly packing materials from
> crates of fragile riddles.
>
> Heavy wrapping paper
> of love and strategies.
> Used solutions rustled
> in the trash of thinking. (26-27)

In the closing stanzas Sheba leaves, and up until the very end Amichai maintains the unity of his sexual metaphor. The poem ends on a note of postcoital sadness:

> Later, in ponderous parade, the King's soldiers arrived.
> She fled, sad
> as black snakes
> in the dry grass.
>
> A moon of atonement spun around the towers
> as on Yom Kippur eve.
> Caravans with no camels, no people
> no sound, departed and departed and departed. (27)

The combination of a steady, successive battery of metaphors and similes all culminating in the one large metaphor for the sexual encounter between Sheba and Solomon is the work of a master.

In the interview with David Montenegro mentioned above, Amichai discussed the importance of metaphor and simile to his poetry. His statement is a seminal one. When Montenegro asked Amichai, "Metaphor and simile; what work do they do, what do they satisfy?"[18] Amichai replied:

> Well, I think first of all they're a way out of loneliness. If you use even a very worn-out metaphor or simile—for instance, you are beautiful like a rose—you are not alone. The rose becomes an equal, and it's like stretching a hand out. . . . So I think metaphor is a reaching out. We are groping for words. We say, "Ah, I'm looking for words. I can't express myself." So we need something, again something *real*. I might say, "His heart is stone," which is also an over-used expression, but you are groping for words. You want to keep your head above water, so words become a kind of, I would say, *solid* thing, which you can hold on to in order to make yourself understood. I personally believe that the invention, so to speak, of the metaphor is the greatest human invention, greater than the wheel or the computer.[19]

This observation speaks for itself, and it explains why, in many respects, Amichai is regarded as a poet's poet. Yet as important as this observation is in indicating the value Amichai places on metaphor, none the less significant is his opening observation on poetry's use as a means of escaping loneliness and as an instrument for reaching out. Perhaps good poets have always known this, but I suspect that most readers, even the most perceptive ones, do not share that knowledge. Amichai is right to emphasize that it is this function that makes it possible for good poetry to provide the richest of cultural experiences in its communicative function. The connection goes beyond that of the metaphorical function of comparing object and object or object and symbol; it further establishes the crucial link between poet and reader in the *sharing* of the comparison which, when first made, enlarges the world for the poet and, subsequently, when read, does the same for the reader.

It will not be surprising, then, to find that Amichai relies on metaphor and simile as much in his prose as he does in his poetry. His novels and short stories, to which I will now turn, are substantially dependent on these figures of speech in their time-honored function of comparison. In this respect, reading Amichai's prose is a parallel experience to reading his poetry. Indeed, the same metaphors and similes that appear in his poetry frequently turn up in the prose. While some critics have complained that this repetition becomes excessive, detracting from the normal rhythm and pace of fiction,[20] it should be noted that one form of metaphorical usage has provided Amichai with a structural design for his prose that is uniquely modern. That technique is personification, also time-honored, in which the inanimate objects of the world take on the traits and activities of the living. That is, in the new metaphorical functions borrowed from poetry and assigned to them in fiction, they are given human capacities to do and to think. I am suggesting here that personification, pushed far enough, moves directly into relativity, for even the most inert objects in our universe, in the scope of relativity theory, are composed not of matter but of energy, and this energy activates everything that exists.

Any number of good examples of personification culminating in relativity may be found in Amichai's first novel, *Not of This Time, Not of This Place*, translated by Shlomo Katz and published in the United States by Harper & Row in 1968. (A British edition, published by Vallentine, Mitchell, appeared in London in 1973.) On a summer night in Jerusalem, Joel, the protagonist, married but moving away from his marriage to Ruth, makes love to Patricia, an American doctor, non-Jewish, also married but separated from her husband. Afterward, when they are falling asleep, we are told that Joel thinks with his mind and Patricia with her body. Thinking, at least in the degree of sophistication it has achieved, is an exclusively human function, one that distinguishes *homo sapiens* from everything else in the universe. This exclusivity Amichai explodes instantaneously, for at the same time that Joel and Patricia are thinking, he tells us

> The various objects in the room think—the dresser with its door open a crack, the big black trunk which Patricia covered with a colorful cloth and put a small plant on it. Everything thinks, the gay dress and the somber one, the skirt made of sailcloth and Joel's unlaced black shoes near the bed.... The stone on the window sill thinks, as does the leaf petrified inside it.[21]

Everything in the universe always has been animated, the petrified leaf out of the past and the stone that encompasses it in the present. The basic unit of existence is the energized subatomic particle, forever bonding and breaking and moving randomly.

In addition to the relativity achieved by extending the function of personification, Amichai's novel relies heavily on relativity in other ways. Modern fiction is obsessed with the dimensions of time and space, and this obsession is reflected in the title of Amichai's book. The negative "nots" of the title constitute a rejection of traditional linearity, for the message of the novel is that the Holocaust has produced in those Jews who experienced it or memorialize it a displacement in both time and space. Jewish life has been wrenched from its linearity, its sense of chronological progression, and though the seasons continue in their annual round, the sense of continuity in the memory of the Jews has suffered a massive interference, a breakdown in the normal processes of causality, accompanied by an incapacity to gauge or determine accurately the meaning and the implications of the monumental tragedy. The need to go back and relive the experience of a lost childhood—in large part the subject of Amichai's book—while one's life is either stalled or moving forward elsewhere, results in a context of simultaneity.

Thus it is that the theories of Einstein, Bohr and Heisenberg with relativity's emphasis upon the pervasiveness of energy in the universe, random movement, the breakdown of causality, indeterminacy and simultaneity, have come to be peculiarly appropriate to the condition of post-Holocaust Jewry, especially in the consciousness of the Israelis whose nation came into existence as a consequence of the Holocaust. It is remarkable that Amichai perceived all this so early in his career. If my supposition is correct, it was his understanding of the ultimate uses to which personification and metaphor could be put that brought him to an awareness of the literary applications of relativity, and to the realization that relativity was the natural medium for his story. It is no coincidence that at one point in the novel a bust of Einstein adorns Joel's living quarters in a monastery on Mt. Scopus where he is working on an archeological project. In Joel's first letter, "written without a salutation; without addressing it to a single person," he begins by saying, "It seems to me that I have been here in this weird monastery a long time. I share a room with Einstein. His wise head may be having an influence on me" (330). Whether Einstein did get a firm grip on him we never know, for Joel is killed shortly afterward when he carelessly steps on an undiscovered mine, presumably left from the 1948 war; but we can be certain that Einstein had a strong influence on Amichai.

In referring to the "peculiar structure of the novel," Robert Alter describes it to be "a brilliant but not fully worked out invention of Amichai's," and the unidentified reviewer of the book in *The Times Literary Supplement* notes that "the shifting from one present to another is, of course, a game—a writer's game—and the unsettling rightness and profundity of the novel comes from its density of exploration and from the author's delight in making it work."[22] Alter sees the structure as "a kind of diagrammatic illustration of the difficulties Israeli writers have in trying to imagine this ultimate catastrophe [the Holocaust] and how one can live with the knowledge of it."[23] While I would agree with both critics that the novel is "brilliant" and profound, it is debatable whether it is "not fully worked out," as Alter contends, or that it is "a writer's game," as the *TLS* reviewer maintains. On the contrary, the novel gives every evidence that Amichai thought through the application of relativity to the structure of his book and that far from playing games, he was totally serious about its use. My judgment is that he was consistent and successful in the entire undertaking. Nothing will undermine a reader's confidence in a novelist more rapidly than his failure to impose a disciplined temporal and spatial structure on his narrative and, given the demands that relativity makes on the reader, the writer had better have his temporal and spatial arrangements under firm control if he is to keep the reader's interest and respect. Amichai demonstrated this control throughout his story. He was as positive and as assured in his use of these techniques in the early 1960s, when he was writing the novel, as Philip Roth is in his novel *The Counterlife*, published in 1987.

As a matter of fact, Amichai's book and Roth's have much in common. Each could appropriately have used the other's title, for their narratives concern their protagonists' counter lives, which are not of this time, not of this place. At the outset of *Not of This Time, Not of This Place*, Joel is attending a party for Mina, a Virginia Woolf-like Israeli, prone to nervous breakdowns of increasing intensity. She is on the verge of such a breakdown and later that night will be committed to a mental hospital, the arrangements for her internment having already been made. Joel, who was brought to Palestine by his parents when he was twelve years old, as was Amichai, is now watching his life as a successful archaeologist and good husband in its initial stages of disintegration—a different kind of breakdown from Mina's—a disintegration whose causes are buried in his need to return to his childhood and his home in Germany to make his peace with the catastrophic disruptions of his past. Their discussion of Joel's situation sets the whole action of the novel into motion:

> "Well, Joel? Have you found what you were looking for?"
>
> Instead of answering her, he told her of the dream he had some days before the party, and of his longing for the town of Weinburg, in southern Germany, where he wanted to be with his little dead Ruth.
>
> "So you're lucky. Now you have a program in the summer," she said. "Return to childhood. Get involved with things that don't exist anymore."
>
> "But you suggested that I stay in Jerusalem and get involved in a love affair. Have you forgotten already?"
>
> "I have not forgotten. You will do both."
>
> "And what should I do first?"
>
> "You can do both at the same time."
>
> "You are drunk or mad."
>
> "Both drunk and mad. So you will go yet stay. Then you will decide which is better and drop all the rest." (9)

In a context of simultaneity, legitimated by relativity theory, Amichai presents Joel, soon after his conversation with Mina, embarking on his counter lives. In one of those lives, he leaves for Weinburg in order to come to terms with his past, to seek out any survivors of the Holocaust who knew him as a child or knew his parents, to wreak vengeance on the Germans, and to bring into sharper focus his years of mourning for "little Ruth," the daughter of Dr. Pappenheim, Weinburg's rabbi, who has survived and come that same summer, an old man, to die in Eretz Israel. It was expected that Joel and "little Ruth" would marry when they grew up. A cripple, she was transported to the crematorium when she was nineteen. It is no accident that Joel has married a Sabra with the same name. Throughout the novel, he tells his story about his experiences in Germany in the first person. These narratives are interspersed with the story of Joel's other life, of his remaining in Jerusalem, which is told in the third person. The lives counterpoint each other, and the interspersed narratives are frequently linked by the same events, phrases, and motifs.

In Weinburg, Joel locates and visits Henrietta, a death camp survivor now in a home for the aged, who helped look after him when he was a child. He also visits the site of his former home, and other familiar sites including the synagogue he attended, which was destroyed in 1938 on Kristallnacht. The site is being excavated for a supermarket. He has promised Rabbi Pappenheim he would try to locate the lost manuscripts of the rabbi's sermons. They are discovered at the excavation site, but the wind blows the sheets away and Joel doesn't try to recover them, a symbolic indication of the distance he feels from the strict orthodoxy of his youth. He plots vengeance with an imaginary army, but the more he plans the more he comes to realize that the past cannot be recaptured, either for consolatory reasons or for punitive ones. He interviews German railway officials and others who participated in the deportations of the Jews from Weinburg, only to discover that the Germans, unable to deal cathartically with the world's rebuke or to expiate their guilt in the mass murders, have either invented a monstrously hypocritical mask of innocence or have gone to the opposite extreme of self-inculpation as a defense against outside condemnation.

Simultaneously, an American movie company is on location in Weinburg, filming the wartime destruction of the city. According to Vernon Young in his review of Amichai's volume of poems entitled *Time*, Wurzburg, Amichai's native city and the model for Weinburg, "was on March 16, 1945 'eighty-five percent' demolished by Allied bombers in ... thirty-five minutes."[24] Joel becomes friendly with the film's producer, Melvin, who as an American artillery officer—Amichai changes the aerial attack to one that is ground based—was responsible for carrying out the bombardment that leveled Weinburg. Melvin is also the estranged husband of the very same Patricia who is carrying on a torrid love affair with the Jerusalem-Joel. While the Jerusalem-Joel is hearing about Melvin in Israel, the Weinburg-Joel is hearing about Patricia in Germany, and in ever-encircling complexities, the Jerusalem-Joel crosses paths once with Melvin in Israel, while the Weinburg-Joel meets Patricia in Germany. Other simultaneities occur. When Henrietta dies in Weinburg in the middle of the night, Rabbi Pappenheim dies in Jerusalem in midmorning. Their deaths, because of the difference in time zones, occur simultaneously. In the end, the Weinburg-Joel leaves to return to Israel still as vague and as discomfited as he was when he arrived, without having satisfied any of his longings. Amichai's message is that the return to the past as a resolution to the problems of the present, particularly in terms of the Holocaust experience, is futile.

While the Weinburg-Joel is drifting in Germany, the Jerusalem-Joel falls in love with his Patricia, and their nights of passion are related with an eroticism as explicit as that found in "The Visit of the Queen of Sheba" and other love poems by Amichai. Patricia is described as the Queen of Sheba in her voluptuousness and sexual ardor. While Joel permits himself this indulgence, he never escapes from his guilt over abandoning his wife or his departure from the strict ethical code taught to him by Dr. Pappenheim. The unresolved guilt, of course, is thematically linked to Amichai's ongoing dialogue with his God/father authority figures. The conflict and torment the Jerusalem-Joel suffers in the midst of his wild, uncontrollable sexual pleasure are all presentiments of his approaching sudden end. Like the Weinburg-Joel, the Jerusalem-Joel is seeking an escape from unresolved difficulties, the former over what the Holocaust has done to his life, the latter over his abandonment of God and wife. But there is no escape for either one of them.

According to Robert Alter, *Not of This Time, Not of This Place* was "the first important novel by an Israeli dealing with the Holocaust."[25] Its importance, in my view, is threefold: (1) its relativistic structure; (2) its sustained poetic imagery; and (3) its informed treatment of a transplanted German Jew's response to the Holocaust. Although it is likely that Amichai's prose will always be overshadowed by his poetry, and this early novel of the Holocaust will always be overwhelmed by the Holocaust novels of Elie Wiesel, Aharon Appelfeld and others, this novel is too significant to be forgotten. Yet, a copy is hard to find today.

Amichai's second novel, *Hotel in the Wilderness* (1971), not translated into English, deals with the ever increasing problem for Israel of the *Yordim*, the Israelis who desert Israel to seek a more comfortable life in America. The protagonist, an Israeli poet in New York, is hired to convince his countrymen to return home. He is patently unsuccessful. Moreover, his own life lacks a true focus and in its absence, he joins the *Yordim* and ends up writing advertising jingles for a manufacturer of women's underwear. This novel, like its predecessor, is marked by its figurative language and the comedy inherent in the protagonist's chosen line of work.

Amichai's most recent prose work is a collection of short stories, *The World Is A Room*, variously translated by Elinor Grumet, Hillel Halkin, Ada Hameirit-Sarell, Jules Harlow, and Yosef Schacter, and published by the Jewish Publication Society in 1984. Like Amichai's novels, these are the stories of a poet. They might have been written by a Jewish e.e. cummings, and it is in cummings's major prose work, *The Enormous Room*,[26] that I find the measuring stick for gauging Amichai's achievement in this fictional genre. Maverick in its form, *The Enormous Room*, now an offbeat but nonetheless genuine American classic, vividly describes the three months cummings spent in La Ferte-mace, a notorious French detention camp, following his imprisonment during the First World War. His incarceration resulted from a series of errors, compounded by French bureaucratic intransigency and suspicion, which occurred when the young poet attempted to transfer to the famed Lafayette Escadrille from the Norton-Harjes Ambulance Service, an American Red Cross unit into which he had enlisted.

The significance of cumming's novel was and is to be found in its singular evocation of the human spirit, its commitment not merely to survival in the face of destruction but to love and tenderness and human connectedness. Thumbing his nose at death, cummings responded to the dehumanization of war and concentration camp detention with a full-throated, defiant laugh. Not the least of the virtues of his book is its graphic description. The fine eye of the artist is at work here, seeing not merely the surfaces of things but probing into their subterranean depths as well. cumming's metaphors, like Amichai's, expand into entire realities. The microcosm of the poet's cell becomes the macrocosm of the enormous room, that is, of the whole world.

In Amichai's *The World Is A Room*, the same evocation of the human spirit and the same emphasis upon love, tenderness, and human connectedness are to be found. The use of graphic description from the artist's view is similar. The same kind of startling brilliance in the imagery is present, though here the setting is not La Ferte-mace but Israel in its first years of independence. Israel (with the exception of one story that is set in New York) is Amichai's microcosmic metaphor for the world at large, a "room" that lacks positive meaning until it is filled with love. And with love come light and sound, neighbors, children, and normalcy.

The search of the two poets is therefore identical. It is a search for love and for understanding and acceptance, in a setting of uneasy peace and the anticipated violence of war. In the absence of love, or when love turns bad or goes astray, the sense of loss is pervasive. The figurative language employed by both cummings and Amichai is resplendent, opening up whole universes of nuance, feeling, and meaning. They share, moreover, a penchant for sophisticated irony and whimsicality.

Of course, there are some fundamental differences between the two poets. As distinguished as cummings was by the time he died in 1962, Amichai's poetic talent is greater. His metaphors and similes in these stories, like those in the novels and the poetry, cluster and leapfrog one over the other, accelerating and accumulating with an astonishing barrage of the fertile and original images I have catalogued earlier, images that go far beyond the limits cummings set for himself. Where cummings invariably turned to ribald jests and defiance, Amichai relies upon compassion, empathy, and resignation, accepting what cummings sought to evade: the fact that one could face down death only so many times. cumming's romantic individualism gives way in Amichai to apprehension, wariness and a determination to reconfirm the fact of one's existence by repeated acts of love, sensual and compassionate.

Apart from the work of cummings, Amichai's short stories in *The World Is A Room* function differently from those of any other contemporary writer with whom I am familiar. Short fiction depends for its effect upon a critical conflict between two clearly defined opposing forces. This is hardly the case here. In the stories that use the War of Independence as background, the protagonists' enemies are less likely to be hostile Arabs than they are to be immobility, detachment, constraint, separation, transformation, the erosion of time, and the failure of two people—lovers, spouses, neighbors, or friends—to communicate, because of the disparity in their subjective comprehension of the same realities. That is to recognize that we are thrust again into a world of random movement, simultaneity, the breakdown of causality, and indeterminacy. Soldiers mobilize and wait interminably, lovers pledge everlasting fidelity and either sleep with or marry others, a *bar mitzvah* boy is given gifts of compasses to guide him on his newly initiated journey into the diaspora of time and space, two lovers begin their affair at its end and work their way backwards to its start, a son recognizes the accumulated deaths of his father, culminating in the final one that separates them forever. In this story, the same concern with dominance and guilt that we observed earlier in Amichai's work is seen to still be a continuing, obsessive force.

In several of the stories Amichai, always the poet, pays his respect to his muse, an earth goddess, earth-mother figure who reveals herself through a dozen different women, all of whom aggressively bestow and withdraw their sexual favors and maternal benevolence in a confusion of hope and despair that constitutes Amichai's vision of human relationships in our time.

In sum, Amichai's achievement, both in poetry and prose, is an enormous one, enriching not only Israel's modern literary landscape but that of the Western world as well. In his metaphorical pyrotechnics, particularly, he has many peers, but few equals. In his application of the literary techniques adapted from relativity theory, he was a forerunner, along with Jorge Luis Borges, Malcolm Lowry and Lawrence Durrell, of the narrative strategies that understructure the best of the serious novels now being published. He also anticipated the direction in which the Israeli novel of the Holocaust would go, and I will argue elsewhere in this study that he was likely an influence on Amos Oz in his treatment of the Jew's relationship to post-Holocaust Germany. Of final importance is the fact that he has given to the world an exceptional number of memorable poems that exquisitely mirror both its frustrations and defeats, and its satisfactions and triumphs.

Interview 1　Yehuda Amichai

April 10, 1984

JC: Tell me first about your family.

YA: I've been married twice. I have three children, a son who is now twenty-three from the first marriage, and I have two smaller children, eleven and six from my second marriage. They are with their mother in New York. I am a guest lecturer at New York University this academic year.

JC: When did you go to Palestine?

YA: I came with my parents. We settled in Petah-Tikvah, which was a small agricultural colony for one year, and then we moved to Jerusalem. I have lived there ever since.

JC: What about your education?

YA: I have a German-Jewish orthodox background. I was born in Wurzburg, a city in the south of Germany which had a Jewish teachers seminary and a Jewish hospital—it was a kind of Jewish center—and I started school in a Jewish kindergarten where we studied both Hebrew and German. It was a public school, a Jewish public school. I learned to read and write Hebrew in the first grade. I went to high school in Jerusalem. In 1942 I volunteered for the Jewish-Palestinian unit of the British Army, and I served for four years in World War II, all of it in the Middle East. In August 1942 we were deployed very quickly, with hardly any training, along the seashore to stop the Germans. Rommel was advancing rapidly through the desert, and everyone thought it was the end of everything. We just stood our ground along the length of the seashore. We got some training while we waited for the German breakthrough. But it didn't come because Rommel was stopped at El Alamein. So I didn't see much action in World War II. We were lucky that the Germans never invaded Palestine. After the Second World War, I spent one year in a number of Arab countries as a member of the Haganah underground, illegally smuggling arms and munitions. From the beginning of 1948 to the end of 1949, I was again in the Palmah as a commander of a unit of the Haganah. I spent two years fighting in the south of Palestine, mainly against the Egyptians. Later I again fought the Egyptians in the Sinai Campaign. Luckily, I was wounded only once. After serving with the Palmah, I taught for fifteen years in the public schools, and then I taught in the Chaim Greenberg College for overseas students.

JC: Then you fought in all of Israel's wars?

YA: Yes. All of them except the Lebanon Campaign. By then I was too old.

JC: In the past I have done a good deal of writing about war poets, especially Wilfred Owen and Isaac Rosenberg. Your poetry, like their poetry, is filled with, indeed haunted by the images and the impact of war. I think of the eleventh section from the "Songs of Zion the Beautiful" as typical:

> The city where I was born was destroyed by gunfire.
> The ship that brought me here was later sunk, in the war.
> The barn in Hamidiya where I made love was burnt down,
> the kiosk in Ein Gedi was blown up by the enemy,

> the bridge in Ismailiya that I crossed
> back and forth on the eve of all my loves
> was torn to tatters.[1]

War has become paramount in our thinking; we are never free from fears of it. When it became a totality in the First World War literature designated the poets of protest as "War Poets." That term is set now in granite, so to speak. Yet the anti-war poets of the Second World War, poets like Karl Shapiro, who came to prominence with his volume of poems entitled *V-Letter And Other Poems,* shunned the term. In a recording that you made recently you said that you do not think of yourself primarily as a "war poet," but simply as a poet who has experienced much of life.

YA: I did that recording at the Kennedy Memorial Center in Washington. Critics tend too often to label poets: this one is a Holocaust poet, that one is a love poet, this one a Jerusalem poet, that one a New York poet. A poet who uses his whole life as material for his poetry is not just a poet of one subject. I've had an interesting life and all of it is my subject.

JC: What do you consider to be the central experiences of your life?

YA: War and love are the only two things that are central, love and hate and how to deal with them. Even a complete pacifist has sometimes to face combat in order to survive. The alternative, extreme pacifism, amounts only to sitting back and getting yourself slaughtered. No one can sit back. Even a limited pacifism abridges one's commitment to life, and that's not enough for me. I am as fully involved in life as it is possible for one to be. I can't sit back; no one can sit back. I live in reality. Poets must live in reality. They cannot live like politicians, with ideas and conceptions; poets must live in the concrete world.

JC: That emphasis upon concretion I find frequently in your poetry. I am reminded of your lines:

> When I banged my head on the door, I screamed,
> "My head, my head," and I screamed, "Door,door"
> and I didn't scream, "Mama" and I didn't scream "God."
> And I didn't prophesy a world at the End of Days
> where there will be no more heads and doors. (118)

Given the Western world's dual mindset, do you see love and war as opposites?

YA: They are opposite but they are also separate, as Ecclesiastes suggests, there is a time for war and a time for peace, a time for weeping and a time for loving. In a way, I accept war as a fact of life as much as I try to keep it

out of my life, politically and otherwise. Of course, I know that mankind
has tried for the past few thousand years to eradicate war, but as new
religions have come in, or new political leaders appear, they say that they
are for eternal peace but that they need one little war to make it happen,
to get their platforms established. Because of those tiny little wars that
are made in the name of eternal peace, there is never any peace.

JC: Whether they are opposite and separate, love and war, the terms, that is,
are confused, especially in modern literature. The terms for love and
making love have come to be substituted for the terms of war. A foot
soldier *loves* his rifle and sleeps with it. Is that reversed terminology in
use in Israel?

YA: No, but there are counterparts. For example, religion confuses love with
war. The two are confused elsewhere. One notices how much war is going
on in love, or how much love goes on in war. Ecclesiastes apart, in Israel
we have to do everything at once, to laugh and to weep at the same time.
You can't just say to someone, " I can't make love to you now because
there is a war going on," or, on the other hand, "we are in love, I can't go
to the war." We have to do things as they come. I am reminded of those
lines from Rilke in the *Duino Elegies* where he says, "What is this life?
We put things into order, and then things fall apart. Until, again, we put
them into order," and so on, "until we ourselves fall apart." Living is to
put order into chaos. We are part of that process.

JC: Do you view your composition of poetry in that context?

YA: Yes. Poetry is for me the only way to put some order into the experience
of the world.

JC: In your creative writing classes, say the ones you are teaching at New
York University this year, what principles of creative writing do you advise
your students to follow?

YA: First of all, as you know, you can't learn to be a poet. The idea that you
can comes from the American belief that everything is teachable. That
isn't so. Creative writing classes should be encounter groups where students read their own work and discuss it. The main thing I tell students
is to forget that they are poets, or aspiring poets, because the moment
you become a poet, you lose contact with conventional reality. The important thing is to live openly, not to shrink from fear from anything because
one is a poet. I tell them to read a lot of good poetry. That is about the
most that can be done. I have had discussions occasionally with some
American poets who think you have to write a poem, whether good or
bad, every day to stay in form, like jogging. I don't believe in that. One
should write only when the poetry comes. Of course, a poet should do

what he can to encourage it. You can't arrange it in advance. It is a kind of game between the inside and the outside. Things from the outside help: history, politics come from the outside. Other things are on the inside. If they come together there's no problem, the poet is engaged with his material. Everyone should write as if he were engaged.

JC: You were described in an article that was widely reprinted in the American Jewish Press about a year ago as one of those who when you started out "established [him]self as one of the leaders of a group of new poets who rejected their predecessors' formality, and, with it, the automatic idealization of the land and the Jewish people. Questioning and introspection took their place, questions about history, about human relationships, about God, and most of all, about identity as a person and as a Jew."[2] Were you, in fact, a leader of a group that began to reexamine everything back in those years?

YA: No. A poet with this kind of inclination doesn't get involved with a group. There was a group. It was loosely made up. I was really not part of it. It was more conservative, more politically conservative. Actually, what T. S. Eliot, maybe Ezra Pound, did in English poetry was somewhat comparable. The group's poetry in the 1950s tended to the chaotic; it moved away from the classical forms, it used everyday speech, taking the holy down, heightening the profane. Unlike most of my contemporaries who grew up in Israel in totally nonreligious homes, I was lucky enough to be reared in a very Jewish home. My father was devoutly orthodox, and his Judaism was a treasure he passed on to me. Though I am not religious, it is a marvelous treasure, and I use it. In the same respect, you can't mention James Joyce without bringing in his Catholic Dublin background. Catholicism was always a presence for him, so, for me, our classical literature, the Bible, the rabbinic writings, the prayers, are always a presence for me. Like Joyce I did my own thing, but I used my religious background as he used his religious background.

JC: And like Joyce, your poetry, and a good deal of modern Israeli poetry, it seems to me, has more of an earthy flavor to it, a flavor that constitutes a departure from classical reverence.

YA: Yes, because life in Israel is so absorbed in reality it comes in naturally.

JC: Ever since the end of the Second World War when the somewhat obscure, highly esoteric poetry that had been advocated by Pound and Eliot was rejected, American poetry has become more and more radicalized. Allen Ginsberg's work is a good example. In this respect the most recent American poems I've read tend to be pessimistic, defeatist, confessional and sometimes so introspective it is hard for a reader to see much besides hopelessness. While the vicissitudes of life in America and Israel are dissimilar I wonder if contemporary Israeli poetry has undergone any parallel radicalization?

YA: Israeli poetry is highly individualistic. Israel is a small country and poetry is widely read there. You have many types of poetry. Our concerns are different: our thinking is shaped by the Jewish Question, Arab-Jewish relations, and war and peace. Certainly, our poetry is not defeatist. Some of my poems are sad, but they are not hopeless. Sadness is a good way out. It makes hopelessness into a sweet human experience that keeps you going.

JC: I have been impressed by the poems you have written about your father and about fatherhood, including "My Father," "I Am A Live Man," "My Father in a White Space Suit," and your story "The Times My Father Died." I suppose that one way of looking at all of Jewish history is to look at it in terms of encounters between fathers and sons. Can you comment on your own feelings about your father that made those poems so moving?

YA: As I mentioned, I grew up in a very orthodox home. My father was orthodox; I was orthodox. In my mid-teens, I broke from orthodoxy. Because my father and I loved each other very much, we tried not to talk about it. I didn't want to hurt him. He died quite young; he was only 63. My mother died last year at the age of 88. You cannot feel the same sense of loss for her because she had so many more years of life than my father had. The memory of my father is very fresh, because he died a man in his full powers. On the other hand, my mother slowly became an old woman, so I got used to her aging gradually.

JC: Your situation was different from that of many contemporary Jewish writers. For a number of Jewish poets their memories of their fathers were tragic. Take Delmore Schwartz, for example. Schwartz's father and mother awakened him in the middle of the night when he was five years old and said, "All right, choose between us, we're separating." Stanley Kunitz's father committed suicide a few months before Kunitz was born and, in a sense, his poetry has become a vehicle in the never ending search he has made for his father. For others, the Oedipal rebellion was crucial.

YA: For me, the rebellion was just that I stopped being religious, but it didn't affect my feelings for my father or his for me. I am sure it was a deep wound for him all of his life. For an orthodox Jew whose son is no longer observant it is a hard blow.

JC: And you were an only son?

YA: I have two sisters, but I was the only son.

JC: In addition to your poetry, you've written two novels and a collection of short stories. How would you describe what's happening with fiction right now in Israel?

YA: For the last ten to twenty years in Israel most of the literary action has been centered around poetry. That's still true, today. The reason is because poetry comes down to us in an unbroken tradition since the time of the Bible, through prayers. Modern Hebrew poetry started at the beginning of this century. After the War of Independence ended in 1948, Jewish poetry just took up from where it had left off in the Middle Ages, as though it were unbroken. But prose had no such tradition. The whole prose situation, in this sense, is still unsettled. I think it will take a few generations of people living in Israel for an Israeli prose to emerge. The only exception is Agnon, but he brought the Old World with him to Palestine. What we have is largely experimental. We don't have a Henry James or a Faulkner yet. We will have to wait a few generations.

JC: Are you saying that a good deal of contemporary Israeli prose is derivative? Yehoshua's *A Late Divorce* was recently translated and published in the United States. It has a strong Faulknerian cast to it. Is that derivative or is Yehoshua's authentic voice imbedded in that work?

YA: No. Even before *A Late Divorce*, Yehoshua had written a lot of interesting stories, but they all have been experimental and one can make various inferences about it. As a spoken language, Hebrew is just two or three generations old, so prose writers have a hard time. One finds everything: slang, classical Hebrew, correct Hebrew, a Yiddish-oriented Hebrew, an Arabic-oriented Hebrew.

JC: Where would you place Aharon Appelfeld?

YA: In Israel he is not yet too much appreciated. The critics and the professors like his work more than the people, probably because his work is so esoteric.

JC: In America, he has a growing reputation.

YA: Yes, I know, I know. But it is not the Israeli experience he writes about; it's the standard European Jewish experience.

JC: The Holocaust.

YA: Yes. That's another thing. In Israel, we don't read too much about the Holocaust.

JC: But doesn't Yad Vashem play a strong role in the life of the country?

YA: Not as much as one would think, either for Jews or non-Jews in Israel. It's a strange role because, actually, Israel is the answer to the Holocaust, the way out of it, the end of the Holocaust. Attitudes about the Holocaust in Israel are different from those in America. It is normal for memories of the Holocaust to be kept alive not only as long as people of that generation are still around, but as a never to be forgotten tragedy. But I am afraid that the activity of American Jews surrounding the Holocaust is basically negative in the sense that the Jew who takes up the Holocaust or Holocaust studies as the main part of Jewish learning argues that it is the great Jewish experience of the twentieth century. It's not.

JC: The founding of the State of Israel was the great Jewish experience of this century?

YA: Yes, and even that may change. It probably will change, but that is what I see right now.

JC: I'm willing to acknowledge the central importance of the Holocaust, but I would agree that it should not obscure several thousand years of Jewish history however horrible the event was. New Holocaust centers seem to be opening in America every year. I suspect that in addition to the need to remember what happened, the emphasis on Jewish losses in the Holocaust makes it easier to raise money for Israel.

YA: Another reason for that emphasis is the fear that people have that a tragedy of that magnitude could happen in America. If you keep talking about it that is one way of keeping it from happening.

JC: To my knowledge, there is only one American-Jewish writer who from time to time reminds us that there is a possibility that things will change in America and that eventually the comfortable status of the Jews here will mirror the situation in Weimar Germany that will be followed eventually by a swing to the fascist right ...

YA: Or the fascist left ...

JC: Or the fascist left and the Jews will be in trouble again in this country. That writer is Cynthia Ozick.

YA: In one of her most recent books she used a stanza from one of my poems as a motto. About the politics, I think she is exaggerating. She is outspoken about what goes on in Israel; her position is right wing, which I don't accept.

JC: How do you feel about the position she has taken that English is an alien Christian language in terms of the translations of your poems into English, into a language that is not Jewish?

YA: The important thing for me is that Jews again become people like other people, like, for example, the Italians. I'm not concerned at all about the Jewishness, the Israeliness, the Hebrewness of my poetry because it is my life that I write about and, in that sense, I don't have to be so concerned about being Jewish or being this or that.

JC: It is the universal experience that one has in common with the rest of humankind that counts.

YA: Yes, it's much more open. We don't have to concern ourselves constantly with how Jewish we are, or how Jewish my writing is. Israel is the only country where you don't have to think, that is, keep in mind, that you are Jewish. It's automatic.

JC: In your newly translated collection of short stories *The World Is A Room*, I was delighted to discover that your sense of time throughout those stories is freed from a linear, predetermined context. That's very modern, perhaps, "postmodern" might be the more accurate term, in that the spirit of Einstein is wonderfully invoked: everything is relative, nothing is certain, all things are possible, causality breaks down. Separation is the only certainty. Transformation is the only constant. The centrality of ordinary conflict is replaced by the random and therefore unpredictable movement of people as though they were particles and waves moving through the great magnetic field of the world as a room. Your Einsteinian use of time and space, too, gives to your writings an extra dimension of insight, a currency that will keep it contemporary for a long time to come.

YA: Do you know my poem "Relativity?"

JC: Yes. I like particularly the middle section with the lines:

> A four-year-old dog corresponds to a man of
>   thirty-five
> and a one-day fly, at twilight, to a ripe old man
> full of memories. Three hours of thought equal
> two minutes of laughter.
> In a game, a crying child gives away his
>   hiding-place
> but a silent child will be forgotten.
> It's a long time since black stopped being the color
>   of mourning:
> a young girl defiantly squeezes herself
> into a black bikini. (141)

Curiously, the American Jewish novelists, with the exception of Malamud, who was a fantasist, have not been tempted yet to get away from the use of linear time and space. Maybe they are simply bound in too much by linear events, by the history of the Jews. Do you read the American-Jewish novelists?

YA: I read Saul Bellow, Philip Roth, Bernard Malamud, and Cynthia Ozick.

JC: What do you think of them?

YA: I am impressed by how Americanized they are. They have a double consciousness. Part of it is thoroughly American, but the other part is very
Jewish. They are always aware as Jews of what they are doing. From their
Jewishness there emerges a kind of hidden nervousness in their perceptions. They are like nervous horses, constantly seeing either a mare around
or an enemy. Their books are marked by sensuality and sensitivity.

JC: Do you regard the sensuality as an advantage or a disadvantage?

YA: Well, for a writer, it is an advantage. The more sensual the writer is the
richer his writing will be in its meanings and its double meanings.

JC: Still, curious distinctions are made about the degrees of Jewishness a
writer possesses. Cynthia Ozick admits Bellow as a Jewish writer but
excludes Philip Roth.[3]

YA: I think Philip Roth is a very Jewish writer, especially in *Portnoy's
Complaint*. Though it is a caricature, it is a psychoanalytical approach to
basic American-Jewish mores.

JC: I've always regarded *Portnoy's Complaint* as an important work. It did, in
fact, reflect the lower middle-class aspect of Jewish life. It is an honest work.

YA: I agree.

JC: But, of course, the American-Jewish public was offended.

YA: And yet even Cynthia Ozick shows Jews to be lecherous. She gives us the
image of the Jew as the lecherous child of guilt. Nonetheless, it is a very
human Jew, emotional and erotic at the same time.

JC: Given the traditional influence of Jewish ethics, is there in Israeli literature a kind of corollary to the American dichotomy of a strong residual
puritanical sense of restraint always opposing the erotic and emotional
excesses of American-Jewish writers, particularly as in Roth's case?

YA: It's not the same in Israel because we don't have a similar kind of religious puritanism. What we have is a form of ethical extremism that is
found in the yeshivas. Sometimes it's fanatical, and it's crazy, with a lot of
laws; it's austere, but it is not puritan. In its own way it is terrible, and
sick, but it is not the nordic puritanism of American Protestantism. Israel
is much more middle-eastern, more Mediterranean Catholic in that sense.
It's easy going, except for the fanatics.

JC: I have noticed that in your own poetry there is much sensuous imagery,
many images of both male and female genitalia, and your terminology is

explicit. Has this explicitness generated any negative criticism either in America or Israel?

YA: Actually, it hasn't. In America, they say, "Oh, well, those foreigners can get away with it." In Israel, I don't think it matters. In the beginning there were a lot of academic critics who were angry about how outspoken I was. They were antagonized by my sexual images. On the other hand, that explicitness opened up poetry for a lot of people who had regarded it as unreachable, as an academic domain unfathomable to them.

JC: There are numerous references to the desert in your work. What influence has the desert had on your poetry?

YA: I love the desert. I spent two years of war in the Negev. I need the desert as a part of my life. It is an intrinsic part of my experience, like day and night. It is not a negative thing. I use it. It keeps me going.

JC: In what way does it keep you going?

YA: When you are in the desert there is nothing to take your attention away from its vastness. You are not distracted by trees and flowers. You become all the things you take with you from the city, for me, that is to say the lush greens of the lowerlands in Israel. In the desert the same experiences stay with you but they are translated into something larger, something more memorable. It provides a wonderful dimension of consciousness. It is no accident that three powerful religions, Judaism, in the beginning, and the Christian and Moslem ones later, came out of the desert. The prophets always went into the desert. In the exodus from Egypt to Palestine the forty years of wandering in the desert became part of the Jewish national, cultural experience.

JC: Is the impact the desert makes conducive to mystical experience?

YA: No, it is anything but a mystical experience. Everything in the desert is clear-cut. Where you have trees, streams, mist, there you have mysticism. The desert doesn't allow you anything, everything is clear-cut, the human mystical experiences of the prophets, the burning bush . . .

JC: But what about all the impressions we have of the desert being the source for mirages?

YA: Mirages are there, but they are not mystical. You see visions, but the visions are clearly seen: Everything is outside, just as it is in Greek mythology that allows no mystery because it is bathed in the clear light and color of the Mediterranean. It is an illumination that is unlike any other in the world.

JC: There is the blue of the sea and the sharp brightness of the sun . . .

YA: And the white sands of the desert. Everything is whiteness and shadows.

JC: What you are saying sort of gives the lie to Kabbalah and its influence in Israel.

YA: Kabbalah is much overrated. It is overly attractive to people who want to get deeply into mystical excitement. I tell a lot of American students who want to get into Kabbalah not to read it, but, instead to read the Bible, which is clear-cut. Kabbalah is okay, but it is the wrong way to enrich one's personal experience. Too much arithmetics. It may be fascinating and imaginative, but it is not helpful.

JC: Were you forbidden to read Kabbalah when you were young?

YA: No, it wasn't forbidden, it just didn't do anything for me. I think a lot of people who are attracted to it are seeking something exotic, they approach it the way other people come to Hari-Krishna, to Sufism, and to Zen. Some Jewish people look for a counter influence, a counter usage. Not me.

JC: Well, so much for Kabbalah. Tell me about your ongoing collaboration with the British poet, Ted Hughes?

YA: We have done two books together. He doesn't know Hebrew, but we work out a kind of poetic translation when we sit together. It has been a nice collaboration. I translate as best I can and then he refines the translation.

JC: I find your relationship unusual because he is so different from you.

YA: He's totally different. That's one reason why we admire each other. We have been very good friends for more than twenty years. But our differences are marked, in poetry as in everything else. I admire his verse, his ability to objectify his personal feeling about animals in nature, and he, in a way, edits me so that I can speak about my interests as I envision them.

JC: I remember Dannie Abse telling me about your meeting Ted Hughes some years ago when the two of them, along with several other British poets, were in Israel on a reading tour. He had a lot of anecdotal stories about that trip. In a published conversation with me Dannie said, "One afternoon I was walking with Ted Hughes ... and Yehuda Amichai, in Jerusalem not far from the mosque, the Dome of the Rock. Suddenly, without warning Ted deliberately flung himself on to the ground. He lay horizontal, all six foot of him, his arms outstretched, face down, as he stared through a grill into blackness. And he crooned softly, 'Blackness, blackness.' He was just assing around, but it seemed to me almost—for he was so intense—as if he was trying to summon blackness up through that hole. At last he rose and noticed, on his hands, the marks the iron grill had made. He held them up to us delighted—for on his hands were the signs of the stigmata."[4]

YA: Yes, I remember that day. Ted's intensity is a remarkable characteristic.

JC: Another story that Dannie told me was that one day several of you went swimming together . . .

YA: In the Sea of Galilee.

JC: Dannie said that the water was so cold that when he got out, he understood why Jesus had walked on it. Incidentally, I find some affinities between your poetry and Abse's, the same kind of *angst*, the same eroticism.

YA: I thought about those affinities a good deal last year when I was in England. We have the same kind of poetic mix.

JC: Let me ask you one final question. I notice that in your poems you tend to use images of doors and windows. Does the use of a door or window image indicate an opening nod into the universe or a closing one?

YA: It's both. Doors and windows are images that suggest both the inside and the outside of things, the light and the darkness.

JC: This sort of seems like stopping in the middle of things. But stop we must. Let me close by thanking you for talking with me.

Chapter 2

❖ ❖ ❖

A. B. Yehoshua

To enter the world of A. B. Yehoshua's fiction is to come into a realm that is intensely and peculiarly Israeli, as distinguished from Hebrew, Yiddish, and Continental Jewish writing; yet it is a fictional world that is marked by its strong connections with Western modernist non-Jewish literary tradition. In Yehoshua's stories, the thoughts, actions, weaknesses and occasional strengths, the perplexities and contradictions, the strained human relationships, the frenzy, the sense of alienation and futility of contemporary middle-class Israeli life are all laid bare in the white hot light of the desert sun, but this unrelenting emphasis upon realism is only the conscious surface underneath which Western modernist surreal and symbolic forces, dreams, unconscious destructive impulses, and temporal and spatial displacements are combined to reveal truths about the human condition that give us a universalized insight into our troubled lives whether they are pursued in the Middle East or in the West.

Influenced early by S. Y. Agnon and Kafka, Yehoshua's writing subsequently moved outward to embrace Joyce, and, principally, Faulkner. Yehoshua's greatest achievement, in my opinion, lies in his ability to incorporate modern Western ideologies, motifs and techniques in a context that both bespeaks the essence of the Israeli experience in particular, and simultaneously moves to the universal. To accomplish this transition, Yehoshua uses modernist symbolism, the existential despair of Kafka, the dreamlore and the probing into the unconscious in the works of Joyce, and the stream-of-consciousness technique in the works of Faulkner. Like Joyce and Faulkner, Yehoshua interiorizes reality, undermining temporal and spatial linearity, and like those two modern giants, he has a gift for lyricism in his prose that lifts us out of the ordinary world and propels us into a subjective one where "real" life goes on inside peoples' heads rather than in their external environment. Hence, his narratives function simultaneously on several different and frequently paradoxical levels.

From the beginning, Yehoshua's use of symbolism enabled him to function on these several levels. His first published story in 1962, *Mot ha-zaken*

(The Death of an Old Man), relates the tale of an ancient Jew whose life has become a burden to his neighbors in the apartment building they share. Led by an old lady in the building, the neighbors declare him dead and bury him alive. This bizarre episode introduces two themes and two techniques that have become staples in Yehoshua's fiction. One theme is generational conflict in which old people cannot communicate with or understand young ones, while the young ones have no patience with or tolerance of their elders. The second theme is the argument that contemporary Israelis, if they are to survive in the modern world, must shed their past. The suggestion is that the biblical heritage, and even Zionism, however important in Jewish history, are albatrosses. This theme has shocked Israelis who have articulated their displeasure with Yehoshua from time to time despite his known and, indeed, proven loyalty to his native land.

Symbolism, the first technique, emerges here: the old man symbolizes the Jewish past, a past in which, however glorious, modern Israelis can indulge only at their peril. He is the first of several elderly people who symbolically inhabit Yehoshua's works, anticipating the poet who renounces poetry and embraces silence in "A Poet's Continuing Silence,"[1] the Afforestation Department manager in "Facing the Forests,"[2] the seventy-year-old Bible teacher in "Early In The Summer Of 1970,"[3] the old commanding officer in "The Last Commander,"[4] Veducha in *The Lover*,[5] Yehuda Kaminka in *A Late Divorce*,[6] and the protagonist Molkho's mother (not named) and his mother-in-law, Frau Starkman, in *Five Seasons*.[7] All of them have ambivalent and tormented feelings about a world that is about to pass them by or has already done so with devastating consequences, complicating their last years and their relationships. They have none of the complacency of Robert Browning's "Rabbi Ben Ezra" or the confidence of Alfred, Lord Tennyson's "Ulysses"; they are closer to the rage and lamentation of W.B. Yeats's aged man who is "but a paltry thing" in "Sailing to Byzantium."

The second technique, the use of the bizarre, in the act of burying the old man alive in "The Death of an Old Man" quickly drew attention to Yehoshua, and readers of his early stories came to expect climaxes that combined the unusual and the unexpected with human destructive impulses. Yehoshua did not disappoint them, as practically all of his early stories employed the technique. However usefully exploited, it was not a device intended merely to titillate and to shock readers. Yehoshua, without formally acknowledging it, and perhaps, without a full awareness of it at first, was exploring those situations in human experience when circumstance, in order to effect change, forces the release of unconscious destructive urges. In a tiny nation surrounded by enemies and beset continually by war, this "trench mentality" has the same kind of macrocosmic intensity that evolved in the poetry of the Western Front in the First World War and emerged again in the drama of the absurd that followed the Second World War.

Another early short story in *Mot ha-zaken* (The Evening Journey of Yatir),[8] illustrates the presence of this trench mentality that is present in Israel even when the Israelis are at peace. An isolated village, occupied by people whose lives have become meaningless and where boredom prevails, conspires to wreck the one train that passes daily on its journey to Jerusalem. In carrying out the destructive act, the villagers imprint indelibly on themselves and the outside world the unacknowledged fact of their existence.

The collective violence of "Evening Journey of Yatir" and the individual violence of various characters in Yehoshua's earliest stories came, in time, to be ameliorated. A turning point occurred between 1963 and 1967 when Yehoshua lived in Paris where his wife was studying for a doctorate in clinical psychology. Already familiar with Western literature, he broadened his reading further, and, as he put it, immersed himself "deeply into European culture, falling in love with it emotionally and intellectually and greedily swallowing the history and the beauty which is on every corner."[9] Like Joyce, who recreated Dublin from afar, Yehoshua's living in France sharpened his perspective about his homeland: "But it was precisely in Paris," he says, "that I began writing about Israel coming back to reality. . . . The distance seemed to help me accept Israeli reality and realism. The stories became longer, still containing fantastic, grotesque, absurd, and surrealistic elements, but these became much milder, mixed with psychological reality."[10]

The form Yehoshua's "psychological reality" takes is literally the "interiorized reality" of Joyce and Faulkner, Virginia Woolf, and D. H. Lawrence. The subjective perception of the world, in the writer's mind, was, by the time Yehoshua got to Paris, coming to dominate modern serious fiction. The immediate result of Yehoshua's shift into subjectivity with its accompanying attenuation, though not the elimination, of the bizarre, coupled with his resurging interest in the minutiae of middle-class Israeli life was another collection of short stories *Mul ha-Ye'arot* (*Facing the Forests*) published in Israel in 1968.[11] The title story, plus three other novellas—Yehoshua, in writing novellas, was extending his craft preparatory to writing novels—and one short story, "Flood Tide," were translated from the Hebrew into English by Miriam Arad and published in 1970 as *Three Days And A Child*.

With the exception of the one short story "Flood Tide," which critics generally agree is an oddity[12] in Yehoshua's canon—it is an abstract parable about evil, having to do with the flooding of an island prison, probably an experimental offshoot from Kafka's "In the Penal Colony"—the four other novellas of *Three Days And A Child*, "A Poet's Continuing Silence," "Three Days And A Child," "Facing the Forests" and "A Long Hot Day, His Despair, His Wife And His Daughter," are all of substantial interest in tracing Yehoshua's central fictional progress. Though they are all similar in their depiction of the growing existential despair, aimlessness, conflict, and ennui of Israeli life, despite its appearance of frenzied activity, each novella is distinctive in

its own right. This discussion follows the order in which the tales appear in
the book.

Of "A Poet's Continuing Silence," it needs mainly to be observed that this
story of generational conflict is another statement of contemporary Israel's
predicament. The old idealism has died, its goals aborted, its adherents silent
and shuffling towards their deaths. The new generation, characterized by the
poet's dim-witted son, has superceded the older generation, but lacking the
zeal, the intelligence, and the discipline of its elders, it is plodding, mechanical, unpredictable, disorganized, heedless, and headed for ruin. If there is
idealism, it is misguided and distorted. The poet's son, understanding nothing of his father's accomplishments before he repudiated his craft and became
silent, and eager only for renewed attention, publishes a poem, a horrible
pastiche, a senseless corruption of his father's work, under his father's name,
bringing him humiliation and shame.[13]

As demoralizing personally as the son's act is to his father's sense of
poetic principle and human propriety in "A Poet's Continuing Silence," it is
hardly comparable to the destruction wrought by the young protagonist of
"Facing the Forests." Both stories round out the characterization of the
Yehoshuan anti-hero. But where the poet's son is dim-witted, the protagonist
of "Facing the Forests" is well educated, a prototype for a number of protagonists in other stories of Yehoshua's whose lives are centered in the university,
either as graduate students or as faculty members. Though the graduate student in "Facing the Forests" is bright, he has other shortcomings. Nearly
thirty, with defective eyesight, he suffers from a kind of intellectual paralysis,
unable to decide on a topic for his history thesis. A likable chap, he is engaged
in a desultorily pursued love affair with the wife of a friend, who encourages
him, as do other friends, to apply for a vacancy in the Afforestation Department as a forest ranger, more specifically, to act as a fire warden. With the
desert winds blowing across the arid land, constant vigilance is required to
protect the National Jewish Fund forests. The protagonist thinks forests in
his country are an anomaly, but because the six month appointment that he
gets offers almost total solitude and an escape from the city's distractions, his
friends convince him that he will be able to write his thesis. They suggest to
him that its subject be the Crusades.

Impatient with the bureaucratic pomposity of the elderly manager of the
Afforestation Department and his fanaticism in wanting the forest preserved,
the protagonist, apprehensive, lackadaisical and somnolent, is driven to the
distant forest where he is totally alone except for an old Arab caretaker and
his young daughter. Hostility and fear prevade the relationship between the
fire warden and the caretaker. Communication is impossible because of their
political differences, the hesitancy and indecision of the fire warden, and the
Arab's mutilated mouth, his tongue having been cut out in the last war. Though
the fire warden wonders which side did it, the perpetrators are indirectly

identified through the Arab's hatred of Israelis, for his burned village lies underneath the new forest of pine trees. Just as Ovid's story in his *Metamorphoses* of Philomela, Procne and Tereus who were turned into a nightingale, a swallow and a hawk (swarming flocks of birds swoop into the fire warden's open walled observation post, shedding feathers and dropping dung) is grounded in revenge, so the Arab is secretly storing kerosene against the day that he can even the score for his leveled village and his mutilation by putting a torch to the forest.

The fire warden is vigilant, but he sleeps so little that he lives in a state of perpetual somnolence, unable to read his books on the Crusades. During the summer, there are frequent visitors to the forest, campers, and American Jews on pilgrimages to plant trees. The warden has few visitors of his own, his father arrives uninvited and finds him more incomprehensible than before; and with the first winds of autumn, the mistress arrives, also uninvited, to discover he is more out of touch with reality than when he was in the city. He knows the Arab is storing kerosene and even empties a can of it in the Arab's presence, lighting the flammable liquid himself, but he takes no steps to prevent the coming conflagration. On the day he is to leave the forest, having resigned, the warden finds his telephone dead and the Arab setting fire to all the trees. Having himself toyed with the idea of seeing the entire forest in flames, he is overjoyed and awed when it becomes a reality. Yet he is unmoved by the disaster, though his books and papers are burned along with the few remaining objects of his once civilized existence. Arriving at the forest a human being, he is brought back to the city looking and acting like an animal. His former friends give him up for lost.

In one sense "Facing the Forests" is germinal in Yehoshua's fiction. By the time it appeared in 1968, his concerns for Israel had crystallized, though they are anything but static. Drawing on his earlier use of symbolism, the national forest can be regarded as the State of Israel itself on the one hand, and the Zionist Dream on the other hand. Growing trees is, as Nili Wachtel points out, the new crusade in the Holy Land,[14] a crusade that holds no meaning for the younger urbanized generation. The Afforestation Department manager represents the pioneers and the older generation in Israel who set specific goals for themselves in reclaiming the land. The graduate student, a symbol for the younger generation in Israel that has discarded and even trampled on the idealism of the older generation without replacing it with new purposes and resolves, is in generational conflict with both his surrogate father, the manager, and his natural father. His incapacity to complete his degree program is complemented by his haphazardly pursued adulterous affair, for both are *culs de sac* blocking off the possibility of a normal, productive life. His impaired eyesight confirms the absence of vision, and the somnolent state in which he moves reflects the disregard middle-class Israelis have for the dangers confronting them from within and without.

In "Facing the Forests" Yehoshua has written a parable warning Israel that its own weakness and indecision, its conflicts, and the frivolous preoccupations of the younger generation will bring about its destruction. The idealism of the past and the vigilance the military maintains against external enemies are not enough to safeguard Israel's future. The real threat is from within, where the bestial urges and the destructive impulses of the unconscious are ever struggling to be unleashed. Ultimately, the tale is a study in human self-hate and unresolved guilt in which Yehoshua poses a painful question, one which the Jews of the generation preceding his (and those of his own, too!) were shocked to hear from a coreligionist: Do the Jews have a right to be in Israel at all?

In asking such a question, Yehoshua was not presupposing an answer either one way or the other. He needed to confront the dilemma personally and he deals with it in other fictions and in his two published dramas, *A Night in May* and *Last Treatment*,[15] and gives it its fullest consideration in a nonfiction work *Between Right and Right*, translated by Arnold Schwartz and published by Doubleday in 1980. But it is not his dilemma alone, and his frequently and fully articulated hopes for the survival of Israel have made mandatory his raising the question for others.

Rarely does Yehoshua hold out any real prospect that things will turn themselves around. Once in a while there is a glimmer of hope. For example, in the title story to *Three Days And A Child*, the protagonist Dov, a Jerusalem-based graduate student in mathematics, temporarily blocked in resolving a central problem for his thesis, is asked by his former lover, the exquisitely beautiful, always barefooted Haya and her husband Ze'ev, who live on a Galilee kibbutz, to look after their three-year-old son Yahli for three days while they hastily prepare themselves for entrance examinations to the university. Though Dov has a new lover, Yael, a homely graduate student in biology, who is doing research on thistles (more explicitly thorns, a paradoxical symbol of both the barrenness of the younger urban generation and Israel's determination to wrest anything it can from an arid land), he is still desperately in love with Haya and filled with smouldering anger over her having married another man. His love has crossed that narrow borderline into hate, and Dov lusts for revenge, particularly as the child has an astonishing resemblance to his mother.

Dov agrees to keep Yahli even though it will wipe out the last three days of his summer vacation. In a wonderful mixture of tenderness and harshness, the manifestations of his love and hate for Haya, he takes the child on a vigorous daylong outing. They go first to the zoo, which in a sense is a symbolic return journey into primitive nature, and as we shall see in a story Dov later tells Yahli, into the primal unconscious, for all the characters in the narrative are caged animals. Their names are indicative: Dov stands for bear, Haya an animal, Yael, variously a doe, a gazelle or a mountain goat, Zvi, another biologist friend of Dov's, a deer, and Ze'ev, a wolf. He gives the child free rein, hoping for a fatal accident. He dozes on a park bench while Yahli climbs a distant slanting fence high off the ground. Terrorized, he is rescued by a park visitor before he can fall to his death.

Out of a surfeit of love and hate, Dov exhausts the child. He stuffs him with ice cream, takes him for a long walk through Jerusalem, offers to play hide-and-seek with him in a cemetery, takes him for a swim just as the first autumn wind whips up, and then for another long hike to visit Yael's parents where Yahli, flushed and feverish, vomits on Yael's father. His nose bleeds; he's a sick little boy. Dov thinks how easily he could abandon him in the darkening streets. Finally back in Dov's apartment, he takes the child's temperature. It is 103 degrees. Dov says to himself "Where can I hide my joy?" (95).

Hoping the child will die, he nurses him through the illness with gruff devotion. As the child recovers, he tells him a wild, invented story "embroiling all the beasts of the forest: a stocky bachelor bear, two old foxes [Yael's parents], a wolf, a long-legged deer [and how they go] prowling through the forest, eating and drinking and sleeping and waging desperate battles. The majority died all manner of horrible and fearful deaths, and those that survived did not deserve to" (124). Of course, it is Dov who is waging the most desperate battle of all, for he has come to a crucial juncture in his life where either his primal hate or his need for love will become the determining force in his life.

Without an ameliorating love, hatred will destroy him forever. As the child begins to turn to him in love, Dov responds to him, and reaches a compromise with himself. Continuing to tell Yahli the story, he says, "I make up my mind to exterminate every living creature and plant, save one little wolf cub" (125). He returns Yahli safely to his parents and goes home, his rage subsiding, to grudgingly accept his plain Jane, Yael. Though he is only partially redeemed, he is one of the few examples of a return to sanity to be found among Yehoshua's protagonists.

The story is rich in flashbacks, dreams, and malevolent and benevolent impulses, all of which are picture windows not merely into Dov's benevolent soul and malevolent unconscious but into the Israeli psyche and the human condition. It is also rich in humor. Dov's herpetologist friend Zvi, afflicted like the fire warden of *Facing the Forests* with defective eyesight, captures a small pit viper and being naturally careless and somewhat irresponsible, he brings it to Dov's apartment in a shoe-box. The snake escapes, subjecting the sick child to another hazard. Dov and Zvi hunt for it, forget about it, and are surprised when it turns up a day later still in the apartment. In attempting to capture it when he can hardly even see it, Zvi is bitten by the viper. He crushes its head. Having no automobile, Dov helps Zvi to get to the highway where he is picked up by a truck that will take him to the hospital. This story within a story is a mini-parable of Dov's malicious willingness to release his own pernicious and potentially lethal impulses upon the innocent child and its parents, and it is, at the same time, a showcase for the irresponsibility of the younger generation of urban Israelis and still another example of the dangers of allowing the human unconscious free rein.

If the elderly characters in Yehoshua's stories are in decline and the younger generation is irresponsible, those in between have their problems too. Not yet confronted with the deterioration of old age and well past the inexperience of youth, they are afflicted by a malaise that is peculiarly their own. The most common form this malaise takes is that of the marriage gone sour. The husband enters into middle-age growing weak as his wife grows strong.[16] His career flounders or turns into a refuge from the escalating domestic conflict at home. He develops insomnia, becoming a wanderer at night, grabbing his sleep in fitful handfuls during the day. His wife is never around any longer, having returned to the university to prepare for a career of her own. She meets younger, livelier men to whom she is attracted. The married couple's sex life disappears, producing impotence and suspicion in the husband, guilt and hostile distancing in the wife. Discord and rancor are their lot. The husband, consumed by unrequited desire, turns his attention incestuously to his adolescent daughter, to her schoolmates or to the first nubile child-woman who comes into range. Tensions mount until one day everything either explodes or simply slides into disaster. Distinctions between the cataclysmic and the trivial become blurred so that madness reigns.

In "A Long Hot Day, His Despair, His Wife And His Daughter," the closing novella of *Three Days And A Child*, a forty-two year old water works engineer, an unnamed insomniac living in Haifa, harassed by the heat and the glaring light of the Israeli sun, agrees to go to Africa to help in the construction of a dam in Kenya. His wife, Ruth, urges him to take the assignment, since she is preoccupied with finishing her studies at the university in Jerusalem where she spends four long days a week, commuting back and forth, maintaining the household in between her trips, collapsing on weekends. Their marriage is a tired one, slowly unraveling. They have a teenage daughter, Tamara, half a child and half a woman, an infuriating but lovable creature unable to control her emotions, doing poorly in school, and self-indulgent. The engineer is happy to escape from the confusion of his domestic habitat into a new adventure though he is closely tied to home and hearth.

After some months in Kenya, he becomes ill, is wracked by pain, loses consciousness from time to time, is dizzy, becomes weak and too exhausted to work. Following three days of examinations at the hospital in Nairobi, his doctor, a young black man who is antiwhite and harangues his patient while he is examining him, announces to him that he has a fast-growing malignant tumor and that he will operate the following morning. The engineer refuses the operation, leaves the hospital, and gets the first plane available to return to Israel. There he undergoes two weeks of inconclusive tests. The diagnosis, following a biopsy, is that he does not have cancer, but he is not convinced. He is sent home for a long convalescence.

The truth is that he does have a cancer, but it is sociological, not physical. His marriage is critically ill. Subconsciously aware of this sickness and its implications, he becomes increasingly unable to cope with his forced leave from work and the uncertainty of returning to it, his wife's and daughter's routines, the heat, his insomnia, and the approaching demise of the family's ancient car, hurried toward oblivion by Ruth's harsh treatment of the vehicle, her total disregard for its proper maintenance, and its need for delicate handling. When the engineer seeks to renew their conjugal life, Ruth puts him off, though she feels guilty about it. He begins to turn his sexual attentions to Tamara, though these remain veiled and unarticulated.

Tamara, in the meantime, is being pursued by Gaddy, a student companion, recently called up for military duty. He writes her daily, but the engineer intercepts the letters, hiding them in the toolbox of the car. The car becomes a second home to him, for there in the cool of the evening he is able to sleep. He tinkers with it, deciding at one point to dismantle it completely and to put it back together in perfect condition. He doesn't do it. The car, of course, like the suspected cancer, is a symbol of his deteriorating marriage. Both the marriage and the car are coming apart because of Ruth's insensitivity, disregard, and rough usage. He dotes over the car as he does over his marriage, but in the end, he is unable to salvage it though it continues to function, however poorly. Unexpectedly Gaddy, lovesick and determined, shows up on leave, and in Tamara's absence, the engineer, ambivalently friendly and hostile to the boy, gives him the letters, explaining that Tamara is still a child and would not understand their intent.

Tamara arrives, and the engineer retreats to his car, feeling guilty for his meddling. He knows that he has provoked a monumental family fight and that neither Tamara nor Ruth will forgive him for selfishly interfering in his daughter's life. Asleep in the car, he awakens to find the light out in Tamara's room. Gaddy has left. There is still an hour before Ruth comes home. He decides to go for a drive. The car won't start. In the dark, he takes it out of gear and rolls down the driveway to get the motor going, only to hit Gaddy who has been hiding, nursing his lovesickness. Gaddy suffers only minor injuries, and his glasses are broken (another instance of impaired vision), but most of all, he is humiliated, having injury added to insult. He runs off. In deep dejection the engineer lies down by his expiring car and his expiring marriage and awaits Ruth's return and the coming storm that will finally destroy his marriage completely.

The story, significant in its own right, is additionally important because it contains the germinal elements that went into the making of Yehoshua's first novel, *The Lover*. The family is basically the same. The unnamed engineer is metamorphosed into Adam, the mechanic *cum* successful garage owner

who becomes infatuated with an ancient car. Ruth is fashioned into his wife
Asya, already out of the house teaching and taking courses at the university
as well, enamored of a younger man, Gabriel. He is older than Gaddy, to be
sure, but like him, he is pressed into military service. Tamara is turned into
Dafi, an exact mirror-image. The disappearance of intimacy, the loss of domestic tranquility, the onset of impotence and the disintegration of the marriage
which Adam, like the engineer, seeks desperately to save, are all paralleled in
the two fictions. However, before we can turn to this novel, we must acknowledge the publication of another volume of novellas that preceded *The Lover*
into print.

   Early In The Summer Of 1970 contains the title story, translated by
Miriam Arad, and two other narratives, "Missile Base 612," also translated by
Arad, and "The Last Commander," translated by Pauline Shrier. Of the three
novellas, the title story, first published in America in *Commentary* in March,
1973 (39-52), is the most interesting work in terms of technique. Employing the
now familiar themes of generational decline and conflict and the "trench mentality" of the Israelis, the novella, rich in symbolic content, achieves its unusual degree of sophistication by its action being set totally in subjective time.
It requires some analysis whereas "Missile Base 612" and "The Last Commander" do not, since the former story merely gives us another instance of a
disintegrating marriage between a sleep-worn, nonproductive, wandering university lecturer and his frequently absent wife given to unexplained "night
journeys" (77), while the latter, an earlier work, indebted, I believe, like "Flood-
Tide" to Kafka's "In the Penal Colony," presents abstractly and in a disinter-
ested way the twin masks of God, one devoted to peace, the other to war.[17]

   "Early In The Summer Of 1970" is a story of an old high school bible
teacher's shock, anguish and grief when he is informed of his only son's death
in the never ending war of attrition along Israel's borders, this one in the
Jordan Valley. The thirty-one year old son, his career as a university professor
soaring, has recently arrived in Israel after an absence of many years, with his
young American wife and child, to do research. Transfixed by the tragedy, the
bible teacher, over the next several days, is put through the usual procedures
for identifying his son's remains. He goes alone to the Jordan Valley where
the sounds of fighting can be heard in the distance. Arriving at the army
hospital, he is taken by a slow-moving elevator to the morgue in the subterranean depths of the building to view the body. It is literally a trip of epic
proportions into the bowels of hell. On viewing the corpse, he discovers that
the dead soldier is someone else. Though he is relieved, he is appalled by the
ordeal the army has put him through, and emotionally distraught by the new
insight he has gained into the meaning of sacrifice and loss.

   Able for the first time to gauge the worth of a son who has been a puzzle
to him for years, the father comes to understand his own worth as a human
being and to acknowledge the value of love. An idealist, he is prepared to give

up his son to the nation's needs. As a member of the older generation, with its noble but now outmoded aspirations, he has allowed himself to be seduced by the old Horatian fraud: *Dulce et decorum est, pro patria mori.* The younger generation, he knows from the baffling responses he gets from his students, see things differently. Only through this harrowing experience does he come to the realization that the young people are right to reject the old dreams of national glory and historical necessity for the price they have to pay is too high. The principle that is confirmed for him is that it is sweet and proper to live for one's country, not to die for it. He comes finally to a true affirmation of life.

The story is, as Alan Mintz and Nili Wachtel[18] have pointed out, a modern version of the *Akedah*, the near-sacrifice of Isaac. We have noted Amichai's use of it already in his poem "The Real Hero," and other adaptations of it, Amir Gilboa's "Isaac" and Wilfred Owen's "The Parable Of The Old Man and the Young" are discussed in the interview with Carmi. In these modern renderings, Isaac is usually sacrificed, not saved. Yehoshua in "Early In the Summer Of 1970" both sacrifices and saves Isaac's modern counterpart. Though the bible teacher's son is saved, someone else's son—the symbolic unknown soldier—is sacrificed, so that the killing of the young on a universal scale goes on, while in this particular instance the individual with whom we are concerned is spared. However much suffering these several "Isaacs" undergo, the real pain is the father's. The binding of Isaac becomes the binding of Abraham. In one scene in the tour de force that this novella is, Yehoshua turns the father's suffering into knowledge, for he comes to realize the awful finitude of death and he rejects the internecine warfare and the military mentality that causes it.

As dazzling as Yehoshua's treatment of the subject is, the story is even more impressive in its subjective presentation. Told by the old bible teacher in the first person, the action of the several days is interiorized into one of those great moments where the past, present, and future merge—linear time is displaced—and the total meaning of the experience is gathered up and revealed in the psychological intensities swirling in the compression chamber of the old man's mind. It is all a dream, with reality and fantasy mixed together, a phantasmagoria of thoughts and actions cascading one over the other, so obsessive that the bible teacher must repeat the central events in three tellings, as though he will never get the shock of it out of his system.

It seems clear that by the time "Early In The Summer Of 1970" was completed, Yehoshua had moved far from the influence of Agnon and Kafka, retaining only the latter's existential despair, in the direction of Joyce and Faulkner. As he indicates in the interview, two new directions had emerged: the use of "more experimental language" and the "probing more into psychology and human relationships without putting it into a symbolic context." In terms of language, Yehoshua added, "All of us have treated language not as an instrument but as a goal unto itself. Still, the subject matter has commanded our attention, it has loomed larger than the aesthetic forms, larger than the language because the subject matter grips us. Despite that pull, I have to go for innovation in the aesthetic forms."

Yehoshua's innovation in aesthetic forms, it seems to me, is revealed in his experimentation with Joyce's and Faulkner's stream-of-consciousness techniques. The old bible teacher's torrent of thoughts, exclamations and impressions in their associational expression and his evocation of the irregular and repetitive temporal and spatial configurations of dreams where everything is relative—"Early In The Summer Of 1970" comes across with all the intensity of a nightmare—is consistent with the language patterns in the work of these two writers. And like Joyce and Faulkner, Yehoshua's compression and interiorization of reality demonstrates his probing into the psychology of his characters, although in doing so, he is no more likely to escape, and there is no reason why he should, a symbolic context than did Joyce or Faulkner. The extent to which Yehoshua had become engaged upon these seminal approaches in modern literature is evident in his novels to which we now turn.

The Lover, translated by Philip Simpson and published in 1977, is set in Haifa during and after the Yom Kippur War. The story centers around the search by the prosperous middle-aged garage owner, Adam, for his wife Asya's young lover, Gabriel, who had returned to Israel from Paris a few months prior to the outbreak of the war, anticipating his grandmother Veducha's death, to collect his inheritance. Veducha has been comatose for a year but she has refused to die. Appropriating her 1947 blue Morris, Gabriel asks Adam to put it into running condition. Adam, fascinated with the ancient automobile, then appropriates Gabriel to revitalize his stagnating marriage by providing Asya, who has moved into a dream world, with a sexual surrogate. Like Leopold and Molly Bloom's marriage in Joyce's *Ulysses*, the marriage of Adam and Asya has cracked under the surface following the death of their young son years before. Adam, unable to sleep with Asya, is still as much tethered to her as Bloom is to Molly. In his frustration he wanders all over Israel searching for Gabriel the way Bloom wanders through Dublin searching for his surrogate son, Stephen Dedalus.

Gabriel, a decade older but no more mature than his predecessor Gaddy in "A Long Hot Day, His Despair, His Wife And His Daughter," is pressed into combat. He is taken over by a gigantic, taciturn major who treats him like a deserter, and, indeed, he is one, having deserted Israel ten years earlier, returning now to claim an inheritance that he will spend elsewhere. In Gabriel, Yehoshua returns to his concern about the Golah (Exile) and the devastating implications it holds for the future of Israel. Gabriel is convinced the major is making him pay for his "crime" of living in the Diaspora by sending him to his death. Grimly, the major loads him down with equipment, including a bazooka, and, commandeering the Morris, personally drives him to the front. Carrying a case of maps of the Middle East, he is the embodiment of the new Israeli warrior, a demiurgical brother dragon to the aggressive company commander of Yehoshua's earlier story "The Last Commander." Like that figure, he departs only when he is satisfied that he has whipped his charge into a competent fighting machine.

Caught now in the throes of war, Gabriel endures a heavy bombardment while the unit he is attached to waits for orders to advance. Explicitly, Yehoshua has Gabriel define his temporal condition: "And in that same place, still deployed in advance formation, we waited two days, as if frozen where we stood. And personal, linear time, the time that we knew, was blown to bits. And a different, collective time was smeared over us like sticky dough" (298). It is the "sticky dough" of relativity, in its displacement of linear time, that Yehoshua has pressed into service too.

But Gabriel has no intention of remaining frozen in the impersonal, anonymous construct of war, exposed to a possible death. He deserts, posing as a Hasid, recovers the Morris, and makes his way out of the Sinai desert headed for Jerusalem where he enters the ranks of the ultraright orthodox community, hiding out in the Mea Shearim district. The Morris is painted black, and used by the ultrarightists for their own purposes. Gabriel is listed as missing in action. Certain that he is alive somewhere, Adam takes his tow truck all over Israel, night after night, searching for him. The Morris is the key to finding him. Through an accident involving the Morris, Adam locates Gabriel and brings him back to Haifa.

Interwoven into this plot are the tribulations of Adam's adolescent daughter Dafi, a venturesome insomniac, and Na'im, an Arab youth who works for Adam and falls in love with Dafi. Subconsciously, Adam continually places Na'im in compromising home situations, as though he wants to provide a lover for his daughter just as he has done for her mother. It is bizarre but if not acceptable conduct, it is at least explainable, for Adam, like the engineer of "A Long Hot Day," has a suppressed incestuous attraction to this child-woman. The attraction finds its expression indirectly through the thoughtless encouragement and freedom he gives the young couple, and directly through his even more bizarre seduction of willing-unwilling Tali, one of Dafi's schoolmates, an unstable, fatherless girl whom he beds on an iron cot in an intensive-care room of the geriatric hospital where Veducha has been a patient. Earlier, Veducha had recovered consciousness and gone home. Adam sends Na'im to look after her. Subsequently, Veducha dies. Yehoshua's message is that in this crazy world in which we find ourselves, the basic acts of life go on in the midst of the dying.

Yehoshua's six characters in *The Lover*, as real and as believable as they are, function simultaneously as symbols for the author's political and social concerns. For example, Veducha is a symbol of Zionism, a once youthful pioneering spirit, now drifting into decline. Her 1947 Morris is the symbol of the 1948 War of Independence and the resulting freedom it brought to the Jews in Israel. The novel itself, with its emphasis upon coma, insomnia, somnambulism, and escape into a dreamworld, emerges as a symbolic warning to the Israelis to wake up and rediscover their true direction—which lies not in an outmoded Zionist idealism, or military aggression, or right wing orthodoxy, all false lures— if apocalypse is to be avoided. The novel reflects the universal soul-searching that preoccupied Israel after the Yom Kippur War, soul-searching very similar to what Israel has more recently experienced since the beginning of the Palestinian uprising in the occupied territories. Yehoshua's achievement in *The Lover* lies in his capacity to transform into art all these compelling realities of Israeli life.

Pirandello-like, Yehoshua accomplishes this transformation by presenting his six characters in a series of monologues. The action in which they are all involved is thus commented on and interpreted subjectively from each individual's point of view. This technique must inevitably involve some repetition. For Warren Bargad these "recapitulations," while useful in giving "the reader-viewer a second look [and] an opportunity to perceive nuances which may have been missed the first time around," nonetheless "appear artificial and forced," constituting a "ploy [that] eventually works against itself," leading to irresolution, over-schematization and tendentiousness.[19]

These same strictures were leveled against Lawrence Durrell's *Alexandria Quartet* when *Justine* (1957) and *Balthazar* (1958), the first two volumes of the tetralogy, appeared, structured as they were on a "soup-mix" time-space continuum based on relativity theory that functions in fiction on a different logic from that of traditional space and time usage, dependent as it is upon three dimensions of space and an exclusive dimension of time. It is a logic in which everything is viewed subjectively and interiorized, linear movement becomes cyclical, simultaneity is the norm, causality breaks down and indeterminacy, the incapacity to gauge any phenomena or occurrence accurately, reigns supreme. The result is a reality that is disordered, fragmented and repetitive. Although this is the direction in which the modern serious novel has been moving from the time of Joyce and Faulkner, it was still being resisted by readers and critics when the *Alexandria Quartet* appeared, and even at this late point in the twentieth century, only an all too small number of critics have accepted this shift into the fourth dimension.[20] That Yehoshua is comfortable with the fourth dimension is confirmed in general by the cyclical, subjective structure of *The Lover*, and, in particular, by his explicit statement to that effect in Gabriel's view of reality at the Front, quoted above. Once the reader understands Yehoshua's use of relativity, the charges of artificiality and tendentious over-schematization in the construction of the novel lose their meaning. Probably Yehoshua came to his own understanding of the cyclical, subjective approach through his close study of Faulkner.

Pirandello apart, Faulkner is Yehoshua's more immediate model. His novel *As I Lay Dying*, aside from providing Yehoshua with a modern monologual narrative format, is one in which everything is relative. Veducha's commentary consists of silent monologues as she lies dying. Faulkner's well known technique of the unpunctuated stream-of-consciousness is modified by Yehoshua into a *stream-of-unconsciousness* and this innovation succeeds because, in another technique Yehoshua garnered from Faulkner, it is spectacularly lyrical. Unconscious, she possesses an indomitable will to survive, and must make her way back through revolutionary metaphorical stages of stone, plant, and animal. She does recover but only to die, for as a symbol of a now outworn Zionist ideal, she is a dire warning to an Israel debilitated by the exigencies of frequent warfare in an age of missiles and atomic warheads, a warning that survival is possible only if the nation turns toward other expectations.

In this regard, the theme, too, is Faulknerian. It has to do with the decline of a tightly knit society through the ravages of war and the abandonment of love. Yehoshua views the shredding fabric of Israeli society in much the same way that Faulkner described the disintegration of the post-bellum American South. In *A Late Divorce*, Yehoshua came to extend still further his reliance on Faulknerian structures and themes.

Faulkner's presence is everywhere felt in *A Late Divorce*.[21] It is a presence that both exhilarates and depresses, so sustained is the emotional intensity of the story. It is structured in a more closely knit fashion to what many regard as Faulkner's single most important work, *The Sound and the Fury*, than is *The Lover* to *As I Lay Dying*. Though both of Yehoshua's novels are Faulknerian tours de force, they are far from being simply derivative, displaying an enormous power in their originality, enabling them to function organically and soundly in their own right.

Like *The Sound and the Fury*, *A Late Divorce* opens in a puzzling way. At the outset of each chapter one has to determine who is reporting the action. The plot is not just handed over; readers are literally set adrift to construct it from the relationship of the characters and the actions in which they are involved. While this technique in both Faulkner and Yehoshua is somewhat disconcerting to the unsuspecting reader, it has become almost commonplace to devotees of modern serious fiction that the distance between writer and reader has been telescoped into an interlocking relationship in which an elaborate game of detection is undertaken. No one any longer expects to have the plot handed over without a struggle, but it is a richly rewarding struggle for the reader predisposed to immersion into the subjective consciousness of the characters. Nor are things ever what they seem, for there are multiple sides to every question. Pondering, speculating and puzzling are the basic requirements for solving the narrative riddles that are presently the illuminating mirrors to interiorized human experience.

The puzzling over required of the reader by *A Late Divorce* is similar to the suspense that develops in a detective novel, and if it is momentarily distracting, it is compensated for by the sheer lyrical quality of Yehoshua's prose, a poetic accomplishment that we have already observed in Veducha's monologues in *The Lover*. Like Faulkner's, Yehoshua's prose functions somewhat as poetry does in communicating on an emotional level, making it easy for the reader to relate to the characters and to respond to their actions.

Yet, despite the elaborate guessing game that goes on, Yehoshua's plot emerges smoothly enough. Yehuda Kaminka, aged 64, an Israeli teacher living in Minneapolis, returns just before Passover to his homeland to divorce his wife Naomi, committed several years earlier to a mental hospital following her attempt to lodge a breadknife in Kaminka's chest. Schizophrenic though his wife obviously is, Kaminka is no less paranoid. He needs the divorce in order to marry his American Jewish friend Connie who is about to give birth to his child. Kaminka's three children by Naomi are grown, two of them married, one living in Haifa, a second one in Tel Aviv and the third one in Jerusalem. Their turbulent, nerve-wracked lives are further unhinged by Kaminka's reappearance and the family hostility that resurfaces around the divorce proceedings.

At stake in those proceedings is the ownership of the family apartment, a valuable piece of real estate. In the end, Kaminka gives up the property in return for the divorce. At the last minute, he decides that he wants back his share in the house. He makes an unauthorized entry into the women's dormitory of the mental institution, where much of the action is centered, and rifles Naomi's effects to locate and destroy the papers. To make his escape from the mental hospital, he disguises himself in her dress and heads for a hole in the fence. As he reaches it, he is accosted by a huge, mute guard with a pitchfork in his hand, and the story ends, as Southern gothic novels frequently do, in horror, as the guard goes berserk and kills Kaminka with the pitchfork.

What do these middle-class Israelis have to do either with Southern gothicism or the once aristocratic Compsons of *The Sound and the Fury*? For one thing, like the Compsons they are degenerating into the Snopeses of Israel. For another, they are no different from any human beings under extreme stress in a sophisticated but demoralized society. For still another, the Kaminkas and the Compsons live on the edges of madness, though this is more overtly rendered in Yehoshua's book than it is, except for Quentin's condition, in Faulkner's story. Much of the action in *A Late Divorce* takes place on the grounds of the mental hospital to which Naomi has been committed, but the actions of visitors are sufficiently irrational to suggest that those on the outside are no different from those on the inside. That irrationality is effectively illustrated in a number of instances, a memorable one being the bizarre interrogation by the rabbinical authorities who make up the divorce court. The hearings, appropriately are conducted inside the hospital.

Following the structure of *The Lover*, *A Late Divorce* is arranged in a series of nine monologues, each one devoted over the nine days of Kaminka's visit to Israel to each of the nine main characters: Gaddi, Kaminka's young grandson; Kedmi, his aggressive, insensitive attorney son-in-law; Dina, his daughter-in-law, an aspiring writer who is frigid; Asa, Dina's husband, a lecturer in history who is impotent; Tsvi, another son who is a homosexual; Refa'el, the homosexual son's aging and much-exploited lover; Ya'el, a daughter marked by her generosity of spirit, unfortunately married to the crass attorney; the insane Naomi; and, finally, Kaminka himself. Aside from the child, normalcy is found in only one adult, Kaminka's long-suffering daughter, Ya'el, who accepts, loves, and cares for everyone unequivocally, much like Caddie in *The Sound and the Fury*. Even the family's dog, Horatio, is a *meshugganah* who is driven wild and killed in the road.

Yehoshua invokes Faulkner at the book's outset, hinting broadly (but imprecisely, on purpose) at its grisly end in his use of an epigraph to the first chapter, taken from *The Sound and the Fury*: "Benjy knew it when Damuddy died." Damuddy is Benjy's grandmother. It is not she, but Gaddi's grandfather who is marked for death. Benjy, of course, is the thirty-three year old idiot son of the Compsons. Gaddi, though a bright child, seven and one-half years old—still a bed wetter, recalling the opening to Joyce's *Portrait of the Artist as a Young Man*—is modeled after Benjy, whose mental capacity is only that of a small child. Naomi is patterned after Caroline Compson, the unloving, hypochondrical mother. Ya'el, as noted above, is Faulkner's Caddie. Asa, the brilliant historian, derives directly from Caddie's brother, Quentin, the third Compson child, a bright but unhinged abstractionist who commits suicide after his first year at Harvard, obsessed, as Asa is, over a problem of virginity, sufficient in its magnitude to wreck his life as it does Asa's. Tsvi, the third Kaminka child, is modeled after Jason, the fourth Compson child. While Jason is heterosexual, both he and Tsvi are dominated by their cruel willingness to apply their cold, inhumane logic to all their relationships. They are alike also in their total dishonesty; and of all the Compson and Kaminka children only these two purposely cultivate their sick mothers for their selfish gain.

Yehoshua imitates Faulkner further by naming his chapters for days of the week just as Faulkner used dates for his chapter headings; and the books of both authors end on holidays of corresponding seasonal significance, Yehoshua's on the first day of Passover, Faulkner's on Easter Sunday. Just as Faulkner did, Yehoshua makes it clear by implication that redemptive religious and moral values are everywhere present but are either ignored entirely or merely paid lip service by people bent on their own destruction. Finally, the basic themes of the books are identical. Each demonstrates for us the impact of the loss of love within the family unit, and the devastating effect this loss has, first on the children, and in time on society as a whole. Yehoshua warns us that this is a lesson every generation must learn anew whether it lives in the turn of the century American South or in modern day Israel.

For all of the parallels with Faulkner, Yehoshua's *A Late Divorce* also carries the same themes, messages, and warnings we are already familiar with from his earlier works: marriage is fraught with disaster in modern society, generational conflict is increasingly destructive, ultraright wing orthodoxy is a hypocritical and sinister threat, the trench mentality of the Israelis is a corruption, and the Golah, as long as it persists, endangers the survival of the Jewish Homeland. Like Gabriel, Kaminka is an escaped Israeli, a deserter, who comes home briefly, not to give but to take. Finally, the display of the grotesque, the bizarre and the phantasmagoric confirms the mental sickness of the contemporary human condition in which the barbaric urges of the unconscious are given free rein.

Except for Ya'el's loving nature, for which she is constantly humiliated, there is no redeeming grace. There may be some distant hope for Israel in the future, if one is to take seriously the fact that Kaminka's lover's son will, after his death be born and become a stutterer named Moses. Whether he will lead the Jews of the Diaspora, principally the American Jews, back to the Promised Land is open to question. More than just a ploy and a long-range hope, the true meaning of this stuttering Moses is in our recognition that the opportunity for making Aliyah, like the example of the biblical exodus, is always present.

After Yehoshua finished *A Late Divorce* he began a play, not yet translated into English, which, as he notes in the interview, contained, for the first time in his work, some autobiographical elements. Having completed it, he turned his attention to a historical novel. He put that project aside because "he couldn't catch the basic background for it." He then wrote his third novel *Five Seasons*, translated by Hillel Halkin and published in the United States by Doubleday in 1989. Though he was writing it at the time I interviewed him, he was understandably reluctant to discuss it. He mentioned it because, as he told me in the interview, "coincidentally with your own life, it is about a man in his fifties after the death of his wife."

I had lost my (first) wife in 1980, her death coming after four years of viral cirrhosis. Her suffering and precipitous decline parallels closely the suffering and decline of the protagonist's wife in *Five Seasons* during her terminal illness from cancer. Moreover, like the protagonist, Molkho, I became a widower with three children, two of college age, one in high school. When I first read an advance proof copy of *Five Seasons* in the autumn of 1988, a few months before the book was published in 1989, I was astonished by the thoroughgoing insight Yehoshua had into the condition of a husband and father desperately watching his wife slowly die, unable to reverse the illness, working day and night administering medications, attempting to maintain a semblance of family order, providing moral and other supports to reinforce the children and allay their concerns, and subsequently being confronted with the complex problems of putting together a new life for himself while helping his children restabilize their lives and move them forward.

Though I therefore have more than a residual personal involvement with the tragic substance of *Five Seasons* and have found the novel enormously moving because of it, I have, nonetheless, been able to detach my reading of it from my family experience of eight to twelve years ago and can view it objectively. It seems to me superior to *The Lover* and *A Late Divorce*, representing another move, another advance on Yehoshua's part, despite the grimness of the subject matter, into a more mellowed sophistication and a greater self-reliance in controlling and exploiting his narrative capabilities.

To be sure, Yehoshua's major themes and concerns are once again articulated: generational conflict; the decrepitude of old age; the sterility of an outmoded idealism; the aimlessness and indirection of contemporary Israeli middle-class life; the destructiveness of the ultraorthodox; the competition, tension, despair and malaise of marriages coming apart (though here it is the specter of terminal illness rather than weariness and contempt that accelerates and modifies the disengagement, so that while the onset of cancer keeps the couple together, it dehumanizes the previously unhappy wife into an angry, helpless victim, and the frustrated, bewildered husband into a beleaguered, put-upon caretaker); the trench mentality of the characters (the enemy here is the cancer, not the Arabs); sexual separation and impotence; the husband's subsequent infatuation with a child-woman, and the failure of Aliyah.

In technique, the symbolism is in the main less pronounced but consistent with Yehoshua's earlier practice; and the use of the bizarre is attenuated as well, manifesting itself more in the effect a terminal disease has on the psychology of those intimately involved with it than the unanticipated, outrageous surfacing of a primitive unconscious urge or impulse on the part of one or more of the characters. There is no obvious reliance on Faulknerian or Joycean structures though the novel is completely westernized. Finally, its temporal and spatial patterns are familiarly linear rather than relative: the plot glides smoothly along the changing temperatures of the five successive seasons into which are set Molkho's travels from his home in Haifa to Jerusalem and the Galilee, to Paris, West Berlin, Vienna, and East Berlin.

Though Molkho, a Levantine accountant with the Ministry of the Interior, based in Haifa, is on center stage throughout the story, the novel is dominated by women, in much the same way that they dominate and control the action in Saul Bellow's *The Dean's December*. As in that book, it is the protagonist's wife and his mother-in-law, Frau Starkman, who govern Molkho's life and thoughts. This is particularly true of his wife, both before and after her death. The book opens with her death and closes with the death a year later of Frau Starkman who lives nearby in an old age home exclusively for well-to-do German Jews. She is knowledgeable about music, widely read, gracious but nettlesome, independent, superior, tough. Neither she nor her fellow inhabitants of the old age home have attempted to integrate themselves into Israeli society, though she has been in Palestine and Israel since her husband's suicide and her subsequent escape from Germany in the 1930s with her small child, the daughter who grew up to marry Molkho. To a lesser extent, Molkho's mother, a widow living in Jerusalem, still orders him around, holding to outmoded standards that she inflicts on her diffident son as if he were still a small boy.

Once Molkho has buried his wife and gone through a month's mourning, he begins slowly to reorganize his life. He rearranges his bedroom, disposing of the accumulated hospital fixtures. Because his wife's prolonged illness cost the family so much money, he ponders at length the disposition of a large quantity of expensive unused but nonreturnable medications. He goes back to work full time, and gets his financial affairs in order. He looks after his academically weak son, a high school student, the only one of the three children still at home, a likable wayward lad unable to confront his mother's death. An older son lives at the university, and an older daughter is in the army.

Apart from meeting his children's needs, Molkho's concerns turn inward. He has not had sex for the seven years of his wife's illness, and sexual desire within him is dead. This becomes a major concern complicated by the dangers a long married, always faithful middle-aged widower knows he must face when he begins going out again with women. Torn between his loneliness, his still tender feelings for his dead wife and his continuing ties to her, and his need for the company of women in the hope that it will stimulate sexual desire, he allows himself to become passively involved with a number of women, none of whom are suitable. His passivity, of course, is a mistake. Women interpret it as deep depression and sense that he is not sufficiently independent to remarry. The only active move he makes, an entirely safe one, is to buy a new car, a fancy Citroen, to which he is drawn, as he describes it, by its femininity. He treats it like a lover. For the time being, it becomes a comfortable symbolic sexual substitute, his feeling for it reminiscent of the sexual solace the engineer in "A Long Hot Day" obtains from sleeping in his car while his marriage is disintegrating.

Refusing to take control of his life by choosing the women he wants to be with, he is taken in hand first by a widowed woman attorney his age who works in the ministry, an intellectual, as was his wife (he is not an intellectual and while he is intelligent, he has, in fact, been a little slow-witted, a persisting bone of contention in his marriage) who intimidates him from the start. She invites him to a small family gathering where he is surrounded and outclassed by brighter people. All of them are interested in music, and music plays a commanding symbolic role throughout the novel. Though Molkho is a novice, the attorney sees music as a bridge to their friendship, and she asks Molkho to meet her in Berlin for two nights at the opera.

Molkho is a pragmatist, yet he is also a romantic, and he views the trip as a means to resurrect his sex life. Still, he lacks confidence in his own capacity to perform and is fearful that the prospective intimate encounter will turn into a disaster. Coming out of the opera house the first night they are in Berlin, the couple finds an icy rain pouring down and a shortage of cabs. When Molkho runs to get one, the attorney rushes after him, and tumbles down the stairs, badly bruising an ankle. From this point on, the situation turns comic. Molkho's romantic expectations are dashed: ironically, instead of sexual renewal, he spends most of the night tending another sick woman, who overdoses on a strong pain-killer he has gone out to get for her; and she sleeps through the night and all day as well. This is the first of three occasions when Molkho finds himself alone with a complacent woman, potentially willing to yield, but each time he hesitates and loses not only the opportunity to become sexually active again, but also respect as well.

The whole episode is neatly framed within the context of the operas. The work they see the first night is a 1930's German expressionistic opera with a cacophonous score that reminds Molkho in a disturbing way of one of his wife's major surgeries. It is not enough that she was born in Berlin and that it was there that her father committed suicide, he must also contend with the memories of her more recent suffering, so that to have come to Berlin was a mistake in the first place. Molkho feels the connection with the music, but he can't assimilate it into his consciousness. In what is probably a comic spoof on himself, Yehoshua gives us this exchange between the couple during the operatic performance:

> Feeling her eyes on him, he smiled at her dolefully. "Tell me if you understand anything," he whispered. "It's symbolic," she told him. "It's really very symbolic." "Yes, I can see that myself," he replied, "but of what?" (102)

In the interview, as we noted previously, Yehoshua indicated that he wanted to examine human relationships shorn of symbolism. That symbolism continues to be an essential element in his fiction is clear from its use here. While Molkho is too close to the situation to be able to discern its meaning for himself, we perceive immediately that the cacophonous sounds, sights, and actions of the opera stand for the disharmonies of his own life. The symbolism is made even more explicit in the second night's operas (there are two, one substituted for the other), and elsewhere in the novel. Yet, however serious Yehoshua is in using the technique to give us insights into Molkho's problems, he is at this stage in his career more relaxed and playful with it, somewhat in the manner of Saul Bellow in the novelist's spoof on symbolism, *Henderson the Rain King*.

The attorney remains too drugged to accompany Molkho to the second night's performance, but he is excited about attending it since the company is presenting one of his favorite operas, Mozart's *Don Giovanni*. When he arrives at the opera house, he learns to his dismay that *Don Giovanni* has been canceled and Gluck's *Orpheus and Eurydice* has been substituted. Disappointed, he stays for the presentation, astonished that a female is singing the role of Orpheus. It is for the reader to put the symbolism into context: Molkho in his role as the lover Don Juan has been canceled, and replaced with a figure closer to his own reality, a passive female-like Molkho-Orpheus who will be torn to pieces by the furies because he can't keep from looking back, from being overwhelmed by memories of his wife. And he is torn to pieces by the furies. After Molkho returns to the hotel, the attorney rouses herself to have a late dinner, and in the beer hall they visit, she all but castrates him, beginning by urging him to talk about his wife:

> "She was an intellectual," said Molkho, seizing on the first word that came to mind while looking at the legal adviser, who returned his gaze steadily. "She was very honest ... I mean, very critical ... of herself too. An intellectual. Nothing was ever good enough for her. She never felt fulfilled or happy. And maybe she never even wanted to be. Although ..." He stopped in midsentence because just then there came a sound of thumping from upstairs, followed by such loud singing that he couldn't hear himself think. "And I'm not an intellectual at all," he concluded, though it wasn't what he'd started out to say. "Yes, I've noticed that," she said gently, regarding him with a newborn affection that only made him feel more certain that the coup de grace was imminent. ... Suddenly he missed his wife so badly that it hurt. The legal adviser bent toward him, leaning so far across the table that he felt her hair brush his face, in her eyes a cold, intellectual glitter. "And so," she whispered, "you killed her little by little—I only realized that today. ..." For a second he felt his blood curdle. ... Slowly his eyes met hers. The thought was not new. "You're killing me," his wife used to say to him, although it was odd that the two women should think the same thing when they never met (138).

Molkho is devastated by the attorney's remark. Perceptively, Yehoshua raises the problem of guilt that frequently is part of a situation where one spouse must preside over the slow death of the other. With all the goodwill in the world, one nonetheless becomes the unwitting accomplice to the doctor's orders, to the administration of drugs, to making decisions that strip the diseased individual of identity, and becomes a guard in addition to being a guardian, all of it demeaning and played out in a ritual of failure that is inevitable. The bitterness of the victim is increased by the growing distinction between the healthy spouse's assured survival and the diseased spouse's rush toward death. The better the job that the healthy spouse does, the more that spouse is vulnerable to reproach. It is a strange irony and a true one, but it is one that Molkho is far from resolving. He knows, of course, to avoid the legal adviser in the future and he does.

Molkho is instructed by his superiors to investigate the accounts of some villagers in the Galilee, and he makes several trips to Zeru'a to determine if state funds have been misappropriated. The town manager is elusive and evasive, and Molkho has to wait him out at the home of the village's sick treasurer, an Indian Jew who has a pregnant wife and an eleven-year-old daughter. The daughter becomes Molkho's guide. Being both a child and a woman, innocent, a naif, much as Molkho has himself become a naif, the girl leads him around. He becomes infatuated with her, particularly after her father turns her bed over to Molkho for a nap. Though Molkho does not allow this fantasy to get out of hand, his yearning for the child-woman is sufficiently strong to reveal how far he is from achieving a stable, appropriate relationship.

Molkho's next encounter with a mature woman is as bizarre as his fantasies about the Indian girl. The woman is Ya'ara, an old schoolmate with whom Molkho believes himself to have been in love at one time. She has long been married to Molkho's school-counselor, a poor intellectual now turned orthodox. Ya'ara has remained barren, and the school-counselor's right wing orthodox mentors have told him that he cannot be fulfilled without children. They want him to divorce his wife and marry a rabbi's young widow. Ya'ara and her husband love one another, but she has been backward and passive all her life, and he has allowed his mentors to usurp his judgment. He won't abandon Ya'ara until a husband has been found for her. Molkho is the intended sacrificial goat. He knows the idea is crazy, and he even finds the woman unattractive. She is an insomniac, she smokes compulsively, wears no makeup, needs to shave her legs, wears her clothes like sacks, eats voraciously, watches television endlessly and is hardly communicative. Nonetheless, he convinces himself that the arrangement might work, and that if he was in love with her once, he could learn to love her again. They agree to have her spend a weekend with Molkho in his home when his son is away on a hike. The husband telephones frequently to find out if anything has happened, but even though Ya'ara expects Molkho to make love to her, he doesn't, being too timid. Ya'ara rejects Molkho and, like the attorney, devastates him by telling him contemptuously how depressed he is.

Molkho's final encounter is with a young, plump Russian immigrant whose mother was a childhood friend of Frau Starkman. Arriving in Israel nearly a year before, the mother has made a good adjustment and is content to remain there, but the daughter, unable to master the most rudimentary elements of Hebrew, is determined to return to the Soviet Union. Frau Starkman asks Molkho to take the young woman to Vienna in the hope that the Russians will allow her to reenter the Soviet Union. The Russians refuse, but Molkho is determined to succeed in this mission, and he takes the woman to Berlin. There, he returns to the same hotel he stayed in with the attorney, but arriving late, he finds they have only one room. Unable to communicate with the young woman because she knows no Hebrew, he makes it clear to her that they have no choice but to sleep in the same bed. This, too, becomes comic. Again, Molkho is timid, and he never finds out whether a sexual liaison is in the offing. Crossing over to East Berlin, he takes the woman to Communist headquarters where she is given permission to return. Molkho returns to find his aged mother-in-law in the hospital dying from pneumonia. He realizes that with her death, he is at last free from both his wife and her mother, and, perhaps, he can find the way to make a meaningful life for himself with a woman "realer" than the ones who have occupied his life.

It remains only to be observed that the several relationships Molkho pursues in *Five Seasons* give us insight into various facets of Israeli life, becoming targets for those aspects of it to which he objects. The view of the Ministry of the Interior is one of bureaucratic rigidity; the evasions of the youthful village manager at Zeru'a confirm the breakdown of the bureaucracy and the misdirection of the young, the efforts of the ultraorthodox to destroy a loving marriage because it is childless illustrate their propensity for mental cruelty and destruction; and, perhaps most damaging of all, the episode in which Molkho goes out of his way to help the young woman return to Russia is a ringing indictment of not just the failure of Aliyah but also of the careless and costly indifference of the Israelis to their future and the future of the Jewish people. For the Israelis to send a Jew back to the Soviet Union is unthinkable. In reconfirming the Golah it reflects a total breakdown of Israeli values and a rejection of the Jewish dream of freedom. And ultimately, Yehoshua is telling us that however hard life is, we cannot as human beings live it passively, waiting for love to be doled out to us. If we want it, we must strive for it. Without it, life becomes meaningless.[22]

In the interview with Yehoshua, he distinguishes between what he calls "world" writers and "subject" writers, that is, those who people an entire world that the reader can always locate and identify with, and those who move from subject to subject. His best examples of world writers are Appelfeld and Faulkner; his choices of examples of subject writers include Bellow, Dostoevsky and Camus. Yehoshua's preference is for the world writers whose universes become totalities. He would prefer to be a world writer, but as the interview makes clear, he sees himself as a subject writer. Yet in retrospect, it seems to me that Yehoshua has consistently built a universe as special to his world view as Appelfield's and Faulkner's universes are to their world views. He has, I would argue, moved from being a subject writer, if ever he was one, to being a world writer. Yehoshua's world is twofold: contemporary Israel and the consciousness of the human being as it is reflected through the Israeli experience. This twofold world is consistent in its imagery, its reality, and its meaning; the characters who people it are understandable, terribly human, and very similar to each other; they are characters with whom we can relate, identify, sympathize. We can either accept them or reject them, but they are not ones to whom we can remain indifferent. Because there is so much throbbing life in Yehoshua's narratives, and because they are presented to us with so much variety, color, depth, and profundity, in a masterful blending of Israeli and modern Western contexts replete with symbolic meaning, taken together they constitute a unique and important literary achievement.

Interview 2   A. B. Yehoshua

March 7, 1985

JC: Your family and forebears have been in Israel for a long time. Tell me about them.

ABY: My father belonged to an old Sephardic community in Jerusalem. His forebears had settled in Palestine long before the Zionists came. My father was an Orientalist and an authority on the Palestinian Press in the early part of this century. He published twelve books in the seventeen years before his death on the subjects of old Jerusalem, the Sephardic community and its relations to the Arabs. He knew Arabic very well, not just how to speak it but to write it, too. When he was still a boy his father sent him to study with an Arab sheik. He was not like those perfect German Orientalists who know all the mysteries of the Koran but are unable to go to an Arab village and ask for a coffee. He was thoroughly acquainted with the Arab world and he had many Arab friends. He was not dovish like I am. It's peculiar. Even though he had extremely warm relations with the Arabs—and before the Six Day War they were always passing messages to him through the lines—he used to argue with me about what he considered to be my naivete about Arabs. "You don't know what you are saying," he would tell me, "you don't know the mentality of these people." At the time I began to publish my books, he was working as an official in the government. "What's happening here?" he said, "My son is publishing books, but I never did," so he started to write his own books.

JC: In your novel *A Late Divorce* the protagonist is an elderly Israeli who lives in America but returns to Israel to negotiate a complex divorce from his demented wife. While he's there, he dies. Is any of the material of that book autobiographical?

ABY: Not in any literal sense. *A Late Divorce* has no direct autobiographical elements. The first time I used personal elements in my writing was immediately after my father's death. I was blocked for a time and I could not write. Subsequently, I did write a play about a family after the death of the father. It was really very personal. As a rule, I only use scattered elements from my biography, nothing recognizable. But the first draft of that play sounds as if I had tape-recorded conversations with my mother. The play was produced in Haifa. After I finished the play, I began work on a historical novel with a plot divided into five episodes covering a century and a half in the successive generations of one family. It was difficult to catch the basic background for it. If a Londoner wants to write about nineteenth-century London, he can find all the traces and elements of nineteenth-century London life he wants. That's not true with Israel and Jewish history because so much has been destroyed, and one has to start from the new. For the time being, I've abandoned that novel and am working on something else.

JC: This new one is not historical?

ABY: No.

JC: Is it set in contemporary Israel?

ABY: Yes.

JC: I gather that like most writers you would prefer not to discuss your works in progress.

ABY: That's so. I mention it because coincidentally with your own life, it is about a man in his fifties after the death of his wife.

JC: Curiously, a novel was recently published that follows in general the outline of the historical romance you've set aside. It's called *The Brothers* and is by Bernice Rubens, a Welsh Jewish writer who lives in London. *The Brothers* covers five generations of the same family in episodic form. They go from Russia to Wales to Germany and back to Russia again. It was cleverly done.

ABY: Were there lapses of many years between episodes?

JC: No. Rubens would start out with one generation and trace its history. Then when the members of that generation died or were killed off, she would pick up with a young son or daughter or niece or nephew and carry the story forward.

ABY: In Israel that plot arrangement would be a problem.

JC: Before we get too far removed from your own family's history, tell me where your father's forebears came from originally?

ABY: Salonika, then in Greece, now Turkey.

JC: And your mother's family?

ABY: From Morocco. After her mother's death, her father came to Palestine in the 1930s for religious reasons, bringing with him his two young daughters. He died several years afterward, and my mother stayed in Israel, detached from her family—in Morocco. I visited them in the 1950s when the French were still in power there—I have from my mother's side 50 to 60 cousins, and I saw all these great families sitting together as though nothing would ever change their lives. By the time my mother was grown, she saw that the important element emerging in Israel was the Ashkenazic Zionists, and she subsequently steered my sister and me towards them. So in a way I am a sort of assimilated Sephardi.

JC: With your father's family coming from Greece and your mother's family from Morocco, there is a strong Mediterranean component in your background, is there not?

ABY: Yes. I think that "Mediterranean" is a key word in understanding and talking about Israel. In the early days, people argued the question whether Israel would be western or oriental. Some of us realized that Israel would have to integrate into the region. Our region is not the Middle East so much as it is a region of the Mediterranean. It is Greece and Italy and Egypt and Malta and Turkey. That is our true environment. We don't have to visualize ourselves in the context of Iraq or Iran or Saudi Arabia. They are not our true neighbors.

JC: Your natural element, then, is the sea and the sand of the Mediterranean, the blues, the greens, and the whites, like the Chagall colors.

ABY: Yes, exactly, and along with them the colors that you see in the southern part of Italy. That area is not typically a Western civilization but it is not its opposite either. It is a special melange, a special mixture, and Israel can fit into it properly not as a stranger but as another element in this milieu.

JC: Our mentioning the sea and the sand of the Mediterranean brings Lawrence Durrell to mind, and his *Alexandria Quartet*. Do you consider it to be an important work?

ABY: Yes, it is cosmopolitan, and I admire these novels that give Jews such important roles. Israel has a whole body of literature that deals with the Levantine societies before and during the two wars. Perhaps, now, with peace between Israel and Egypt more novels of this kind will appear. In the 1920s, my father and his family spent three or four years in Egypt. He studied law while he was there. My grandfather had been nominated as Chief Rabbi of Egypt. When I went to Egypt about two years ago, it turned out to be the most exciting visit I've ever had to a foreign country. It opened a whole new dimension in my understanding of my own life as an Israeli. It was an opening to some different aspects of the East. That is why I am so eager to have peace in the Middle East. Continuing peace with Egypt will help Israel to find its proper balance between its western element and its eastern element. *The Alexandria Quartet* helps us to understand the entire region. Moreover, it is a very nice work; the smells and colors of its world are the smells and colors of my world.

JC: What is your view of the situation of the writers in Israel today?

ABY: A dramatic change is occurring. There used to be a kind of structured Zionist, socialist center and writers wrote comfortably from within its boundaries. They were very much concerned with what we would call the "national experience." It placed a lot of responsibility on those writers who wanted to express not only their personal experience but also the experience of the nation in general, relating it to the use of the Hebrew language. Hebrew contributed to the awareness of a national consciousness. This has long been a trend. From the beginning, Hebrew literature wasn't detached as are other literatures. It is analogous to the concern for national problems one finds in Tolstoy, Dostoevsky, and even Chekhov who were always probing the Russian condition. In a way, this concern with the national experience gave direction to Israeli writing. Each of us placed himself at a certain angle to this central consciousness, saying, "this I accept, this I reject." This center has now collapsed and we cannot act as if it still exists. In the coming years we will have to find our way in an Israel that no longer has a center. The goal of the Israeli writer may be to return to the mother's womb and to be reborn again without the father. There is a need to return to something stable but today expectations are diminished. The center has broken down and it makes it impossible to present a comprehensively ordered picture of Israeli society. We have to find a new way today of expressing the Israeli experience.

JC: In what direction do you think Israeli writing is going?

ABY: Ethnic concerns are emerging. The oriental Jews who came to Israel in the 1950s and 1960s did not express themselves back then about the traumas they were undergoing in their adjustment to life in Israel. Subsequently, their problems were widely discussed in the newspapers, in political debates and in lectures where the claim was made that they were not well received or that they were discriminated against because of cultural differences. It was all elaborated in the journals, what was happening to a whole community of Jews from the Arab countries, what their problems were in confronting a Zionist state, how they went through a triple shock, moving from their native countries to Israel, from restricted lives in the Diaspora to independence, and from oriental culture to western culture. The subject of their settlement is starting now to be elaborated by writers emerging from their own community. This ethnic writing is more local. I think there will be less panoramic writing that tries to, or pretends to try, to speak on behalf of the whole society and more of the local kind of writing that deals with the experience of a certain group and digging, perhaps, more deeply into those experiences.

JC: In what direction is your writing going?

ABY: I am moving toward using more experimental language. All of us have treated language not as an instrument but as a goal unto itself. Still, the subject matter has commanded our attention, it has loomed larger than the aesthetic forms, larger than the language because the subject matter grips us. Despite that pull, I have to go for innovation in the language, for innovation in the aesthetic forms. This is one direction. A second direction for me is probing more into psychology and human relationships without putting it into a symbolic context. It may emerge as a sort of mystical writing, or an escape from reality. People like to escape from reality. If they realize there is no longer a center, as we were saying before, they may turn to mystical solutions. These mystical solutions will be tested in literature.

JC: Would you say that the emphasis on forms, in the aesthetics of the writing are an advance over what's been published in the past since there was so much intensity of feeling about the national experience, and that now there is more detachment and objectivity?

ABY: Objectivity was always there. We always kept our critical sense. That is especially true of my generation. Amichai and I were very critical along the way. The criticism was possible because we were sure there was a center that could be criticized. There was something there. There was a consensus, so one could speak out against the consensus. If there is no consensus, as is presently the case, there is nothing to criticize. There was a time when one's criticism was important. The people toward whom it was directed were shocked or moved by it, but that time has passed. If you write criticism today it may not have any relevance because your opponents no longer use the same frames of reference.

JC: Everybody is moving in different directions and at different speeds. What you anticipate happening is different from what Agnon did in the past, and what other writers who settled in Israel but who came out of a different culture have done, different even from what Appelfeld has been doing.

ABY: I always divide writers into two groups: writers of the "world" and writers of the subject. Writers of the "world"—Faulkner is a good example—create and people a world, and in their stories their characters live in that world, and you always know precisely where you are with them. Appelfeld is a world writer in that sense; he has created a certain "world" of the Holocaust, and he has a commitment to it. He has to write about it. It has taken courage to do it, and he took a lot of risks, but now it has payed off. It was a long shot because he was doing his own version of the Holocaust. Already in the 1960s and the 1970s, people were saying "Enough, Appelfeld, write about Israel, write something about what is going on around you." But he continued in those years to pay homage to a world recreated in his imagination because in the years in which his novels were set he was a child between the ages of eight and thirteen and he was not in a concentration camp, he was all the time hiding, so that the Holocaust is for him something he has imagined. That was not without its problems because he had also to hide his identity, and there was a question as to whether his identity would survive. From that question, he has constructed a very interesting world in all its details and with all its possibilities. Yet, it is all hypothetical, but his commitment to it is total. He's not alone, of course. These writers have their own worlds. They are not affected by anything that is changing, they have their commitment to their worlds and in this sense, they are lucky. The other group into which I place writers is composed of writers of the "subject." Subject writers have a commitment only to the subject of a given book. They have their craft, they have a certain biographical image of themselves, and what they want is to find a subject onto which they can project their own inner world, arranging, as it were, a kind of confrontation of themselves with the craft of writing. They are always in search of a subject. Take, for example, Saul Bellow. He moves from one subject to another. Even though he locates his scenes in a familiar world, often Chicago, he nonetheless moves from subject to subject. *Humboldt's Gift* deals with the question of the way the poet acts in American society, *Mr. Sammler's Planet's* subject is the Holocaust and confrontation with the New Left, *Herzog* examines the personal trauma within. Of course, there are linking threads that go through the novels, but you cannot sense that there is the "world" of Saul Bellow. There is a world but it doesn't exist in the way that Faulkner's world exists. Faulkner could take a character and continue to write about him after a particular novel was finished and tell you all there is to know about him in his own setting. He exemplifies the best of the world writers. I think it is unfortunate that in the modern world, there are more subject writers than world writers. But it is no longer possible to close off a universe the way Faulkner did. Faulkner could take a Joe Christmas in *Light In August* and move him around for thirty years through many cities, but he always has him going back to his hometown, going back to his sources, his beginnings, even committing murder, and it all happens in a closed off world. Christmas doesn't want to watch television or listen to the radio, he simply stays in his closed world. No one can close off a world like that today.

JC: Apart from Saul Bellow, who else comes to mind as a subject writer?

ABY: Dostoevsky is a good example, too. *Crime And Punishment* is *one* subject. Of course, there are some linkages in Dostoevsky's novels, too, but the subject dominates. He uses his characters to elaborate upon his intellectual concerns. Proust, on the other hand, is a typical world writer. He wrote about his childhood and his memories constitute his world. He sets out to describe all the inner relations of his world. This is not a subject. Many intellectual subjects surface from his description but his main commitment is to the world that he knows. He defined the borders of that world in terms of family and time. Joyce is a mixture, but his tendency is toward world rather than toward subject. His world is the world of Dublin, a simple world. He had to go to Trieste in order to see his commitment to Dublin as a "world." Camus is a typical subject writer. He writes about the here and the now, his characters are in various places, his locales can be the Second World War, or anywhere. His short stories all take different subjects. All of it together doesn't have the smell of world writing. With Faulkner you get that smell on the opening page of his novels, you know who his characters are, you are accustomed to seeing them in earlier novels and you have only to renew the acquaintances. This kind of writing is now less and less possible.

JC: In which camp do you place yourself?

ABY: I am a writer of the "subject." I would be happy if I had a world, but I don't. The problem today is to find a subject capable of filling the void of a "world" that is no longer there. That vacuum is being filled by what I call "international writing." Books like D. H. Thomas's *The White Hotel* and William Styron's *Sophie's Choice* move from continent to continent with ease. Bits and pieces are taken from the world and manipulated into forming a subject. In *Sophie's Choice,* Styron takes elements from the concentration camps and puts them in New York. I don't like *Sophie's Choice.* I don't mean to attack it, I am just uncomfortable with the technique of pulling elements from the world in this mode to formulate subjects. Continuity is missing. Again, I return to Faulkner. The actions in his novels can occur within a three mile radius, there are all those family connections, and other kinds of connections, such as those between *Absalom, Absalom* and *The Sound And The Fury.* Faulkner doesn't hesitate to have his character Quentin tell the story of *Absalom, Absalom* even after he has committed suicide in *The Sound And The Fury.* In Faulkner's world, Quentin is a real person, not merely a literary figure.

JC: Where do you place Philip Roth's novels?

ABY: To me Philip Roth is a subject writer. He started out writing about
      family matters in *Goodbye Columbus,* and with his neurotic rebellious
      Jew in *Portnoy's Complaint,* and afterward he switched to writing about
      what was happening to him as a writer. In my opinion, when a writer
      starts to write all the time about writers it is a bad sign, because it is as
      if he doesn't have any other thoughts or inspiration. All one gets is the
      problems of the writer with his editor and his publisher, his money and
      his readers. I realize that writing about writers has become the subject
      of many modern writers, but I think it is a sign of weakness. The writer
      doesn't have to scratch his head and ask himself what will be the sub-
      ject of his new book, or how he will renew himself? After awhile it gets
      monotonous and repetitive. Faulkner repeats himself in many of his
      books. But when he is finished, he has constructed a world; you have
      the houses of Faulkner, not the houses of Henry James, places one can
      touch, locations and people. You can get on a bus and know you are
      travelling through Dixie. If you said to Faulkner, "you repeat yourself,"
      I think his reply would have been, "So what, my characters are here,
      and they are the same characters, what is the problem?"

JC: Let me ask you about a couple of American Jewish writers. In the past
      few years, Cynthia Ozick has emerged as a major American writer. What
      do you think about her work?

ABY: She represents a new advance in Jewish writing. She has gotten beyond
      the classical Jewish question of the limits, the content of Jewish iden-
      tity that for so long has obsessed Philip Roth, beyond, for example, the
      questions Roth's characters confront with their guilt feelings about their
      fathers. She accepts Jewish identity as a fact, and her work is positive
      for that reason.

JC: How do you regard Chaim Potok's fiction?

ABY: I don't know his novels as well as I know Cynthia Ozick's stories. I
      wouldn't place him on the same level as Cynthia Ozick. His novels don't
      seem to have the same depth. He is doing for American readers what
      our early Hebrew writers did in Palestine, writing about religious Jews
      in conflict with secular society. Hebrew literature is filled with this sub-
      ject. I know of many classical novels that deal far better with this sub-
      ject than does Potok's books.

JC: Who do you respect the most among contemporary Israeli writers?

ABY: I respect Appelfeld a lot. He and I started together. We were friends in
      the university. I remember very well the time he read to me his first

story. I respect his devotion to the world that he is creating and the way in which he has introduced aesthetics into writing on the Holocaust. Up to Appelfeld, the Holocaust had produced a lousy literature; it was very bad.

JC: Why was it bad?

ABY: The situation of the Holocaust was always one of black and white. There was no possibility of using humor. Reality always outstripped the wise fantasy of the writer. It outstripped the imagination, because the reality was far greater than anything the imagination could create. Holocaust writing was always "victim" literature, the accusers and the killers, the confrontation between the Germans and the Jews. It did not deal with the relations between the Jews themselves. Appelfeld dealt with those relations and opened up new possibilities for treating the Holocaust in literature. And he found the proper style to do it.

JC: What other writers are you close to?

ABY: Amos Oz. Though our writing is different, we are closest friends. We have the same ideological beliefs about the Diaspora, and Israel as a topic in our writing, but we write independently. We were born two streets away from each other—he is three years younger than me—so we feel like brothers to one another. That is not to say that I approve unequivocally of everything he writes, but I approve much of his work, and I read every word he writes. He is, by the same token, my censor, and he reads every word that I write. He sends his drafts to me and I send my drafts to him. It is really a very close, warm relationship.

JC: What about women writers?

ABY: We have now quite a number of women writers and the best of them is Amalia Kahana-Carmon, a short story writer and novelist. Her work is fine and delicate: she has a special style and a kind of technique like Virginia Woolf's. Because she is so sensitive and knowledgeable about languages, including English, she has not yet approved any translations of her short stories and novels, and, therefore, she's not known in America and that's a pity. Another fine writer was Yacov Shabtai. Unfortunately, he died about three years ago. His first book was widely acclaimed when it appeared. It is called *Past Continuous*. It has been translated into English and published by the Jewish Publication Society. He died when he was forty-eight years old. He had a collection of short stories and two novels. He completed the manuscript of the second novel before his death, and it has been edited by his wife. It is called *Past Perfect*, a wonderful novel and I hope it, too, will be translated into English.

JC: How do you feel about Amichai's poetry?

ABY: Amichai is an excellent poet, I like very much his poetry. I hope that if we have another Nobel prize awarded to an Israeli writer, he will be the man to get it.

JC: Who else do you consider important?

ABY: There is a writer, now seventy years old, and unknown in America. His name is Samech Yizhar. His *Days of Tiklag* is a masterpiece. It is a novel about the War of Independence, and is one of the masterpieces of war literature of all time. I regard it as unique, and I think it is the single most important Israeli work we have. It is of the size and scope of *War And Peace.* Yizhar uses a collective stream-of-consciousness style, doing for groups what Joyce did for the individual. The book is an attempt to understand in a detailed way the collective consciousness undergoing the experience of war. It is marvelous in the feats of language Yizhar develops in order to describe all the little nuances in the minds of the people and their experiences in war. The several groups he writes about were carrying the war on their shoulders. People in America don't appreciate the real danger Israel was in, the absolutely crucial moment in our history between 1947 and 1949. Few Americans knew what was really happening in Palestine. Of course, they know what's going on today, and there is an outcry over every little thing that happens. Back in those days a community of 600,000 people faced an onslaught from seven Arab countries. They had only a minute force to fight a terrible war that was erupting everywhere, not just at the front.

JC: And there was of course, the problems with the British as well. . . .

ABY: And the British as well. The Jews were being inundated, they didn't even have arms.

JC: Yizhar's novel has never been translated?

ABY: No. He has written short stories and a long novella, and some of these works have been translated, though not the *Days of Tiklag.* It will require a superior translator who knows English and Hebrew equally well. It will be a goal not unlike the effort to translate *Ulysses* into Hebrew. That translation took twenty years to do, and it has only recently been completed.

JC: Speaking of translations, were you satisfied with the English translation by Hillel Halkin of *A Late Divorce?*

ABY: Yes, I was quite satisfied. I don't check English translations of my work as meticulously as some other writers. What I read of it, the echoes I got from it, were very, very good.

JC: Your recent speech entitled "Diaspora—The Neurotic Solution" to the Board of Governors of the American Jewish Committee convened in Israel has been widely reported in the American-Jewish press, and it has attracted a lot of attention. How did you come to object so strongly to Jews' living outside of Israel?

ABY: Sometime ago I wrote a book on Zionism called *Between Right and Right*. It is now out of print. It tries to analyze the phenomenon of Diaspora. I have been obsessed with the question of exile for a long time, trying to understand why it has dominated Jewish history. In my research, I discovered that exile had never been forced and that over history Jews went by their own will into the Diaspora. The phenomenon of exile is, of course, ancient and biblical. We think of Abraham and Jacob. I was astonished to realize that dispersion was not forced but undertaken voluntarily. This started as far back as Babylon when after Cyrus' declaration many Jews did not return. By the time of the Second Temple, half of the Jews were in the Diaspora. What is more, the Romans didn't force the Jews into exile. Titus took the leaders and some of the people to Rome but there were plenty of Jews left; over the centuries countless numbers of them have moved around in the Diaspora by their own choice. The Jews have been everywhere in the Diaspora during their two thousand years of exile, but in Eretz Israel they were few in number. I am anxious not for the survival of the Diaspora— even the Diaspora is losing people all the time by assimilation, and I know that in the twenty-third century in colonies in space Jews will be sitting around saying "Next year in Jerusalem"—but for the survival of Israel. For me Diaspora is the great failure of the Jewish people; I regard the Holocaust as a consequence of the Diaspora. We have paid too much for it, and we will go on paying through the continuous loss of our people. We are doomed to lose more and more. People keep saying "I want to return to Eretz Israel," and "Next year in Jerusalem," but they don't come to the Jewish homeland. It is not a matter of money or of danger; it is a pathological separation, and my diagnosis of it is that Jews in the Diaspora have a fear of being locked into a total Jewish situation. It is an independence for which Jews have not been trained, and our culture and our civilization perhaps even reject it. Israelis, too, are not free from this disease which I call "the genetic elements of the Diaspora in our blood." My concern is for Israel and for its survival. We need people to survive. We need them more in peacetime than in war-time. We are surrounded by millions of Arabs. From the Jordan to the sea there are now more Arab children than there are Jewish children. The Arabs have a higher birthrate. If we are to survive, those who say "Next year in Jerusalem" should either come to Eretz Israel or quit saying it. There is, moreover, so much talent among Diaspora Jews that we want them in Israel creating with us in order to have Jewish creation in all aspects of our life. As I said, it is not a question of money or economics, or even a question of immigration, the capacity of the Jews to move from one place to another was established a long time ago. So I will not stop insisting to the Jews that they must come and settle in Israel. I think they are cheating themselves by their ambivalence, talking about Israel but refusing to move there. They are deluding themselves thinking they can do more for Israel by staying in America. That's simply not true, and they get upset with me when I tell them they cannot do the best for us by their political activity in behalf of Israel. America is a nation of 230 million people, and the American government will do what is good for 230 million Americans and not what is good for 5 million Jews. I hope that future relations between Israel and America will not depend upon the ability of a Jewish senator to put pressure on whatever administration is in power. I hope that one day the American Jews will come, and be with us and create with us.

JC: On this eloquent note, we will bring our talk to a close. Thank you.

Chapter 3

T. Carmi

T. Carmi, as Carmi Charny calls himself, is a native of New York, born December 31, 1925. After obtaining a bachelor's degree at Yeshiva University in 1946, followed by a short period of graduate study at Columbia, he went to France, attended courses at the Sorbonne and worked in orphanages serving Jewish children whose parents had been killed in the Holocaust. He moved to Israel in 1947. His first volume of poems *Mum Vahalom* (Blemish and Dream) was published by Mahbarot Lesifrut in Tel Aviv in 1951. Since then, thirteen more books of poetry have followed. His fourth volume, *Hayam ha'Aharon* (The Last Sea), also published in Tel Aviv by Mahbarot Lesifrut in 1958, earned for Carmi the Shlonsky Prize. His eighth collection, *Davar Aher* (Another Version, Selected Poems and Translations, 1951-1969) published in Tel Aviv by Am Oved in 1970, won the Brenner Prize.

Although Carmi has long been established in Israel as a poet, translator, and editor, and is well-known in the West, only four volumes of his poetry have been translated into English. All four were distributed in Great Britain, but only two have been available in the United States. These are *The Brass Serpent* (Nehash Hanehoshet) translated by Dom Moraes and published by the Ohio University Press, Athens, in 1964; and *At The Stone Of Losses* (Leyad Even Hato'im), translated by Grace Schulman and published jointly in 1983 by the Jewish Publication Society and the University of California Press. Various other poems have appeared from time to time in translation in anthologies.[1]

The Brass Serpent and *At The Stone Of Losses* give us the essential Carmi, a poet naturally familiar with American, British, and Irish literature, and also with other Western literature, particularly French. Carmi notes in the interview here that in his student years he was attracted to W. B. Yeats, T. S. Eliot, Ezra Pound and Marianne Moore. Simultaneously, he was steeping himself in medieval and early modern Hebrew poetry. Two early objectives were to find the means of relating modern themes to the structures of classical Hebrew poetry, and, more specifically, as he says in the interview, "figure out how to do in Hebrew what Eliot was doing in English." While Eliot did not influence Carmi ideologically, as Carmi notes, he was an attractive model in the latter's pursuit of the modernist idiom, style, and technique. Carmi's poetry thematically reflects that modernist approach in its emphasis upon loss, its sense of resignation, its laconic, and occasionally sardonic view of human failings, especially in love relationships. At the same time, this nega- tivism is strongly counterpointed by an affirmatively passionate exaltation of life and sexual love, both of them infused with primordial energizing forces in nature and endowed with mystical meaning. In his introduction to the British Penguin edition of *T. Carmi and Dan Pagis, Selected Poems,* trans- lated by Stephen Mitchell, and published in London in 1976, the American poet, M. L. Rosenthal, describes Carmi as an "Israeli [D. H.] Lawrence."[2]

Carmi's poetry is Lawrentian in some basic respects. The two poets share the techniques of investing animate and inanimate objects with strangely primitive powers, personifying them, and emphasizing the presence of a stir- ring force within the human being that in Lawrence's work is often referred to as "blood consciousness." Both poets discern mysterious presences and meanings in the universe, particularly in human relationships; and both are more inclined to concentrate on and write, though not exclusively, about private or personal affairs between themselves and others, usually the women with whom they are at that time involved, than to explore public issues. They differ, however, in these respects: Lawrence's context for mystery is largely druidic and Greek, Carmi's is kabbalistic; and where Lawrence demeans the intellect in favor of his emphasis on the "blood consciousness," Carmi does not favor one over the other but rather achieves a balance between them.

Several of the poems in *The Brass Serpent* have connections to Lawrence's *Birds, Beasts And Flowers,* first published in London in 1923. These include one of Carmi's best known poems "To A Pomegranate Tree," which relates to Lawrence's "Pomegranate," and Carmi's title poem "The Brass Serpent," which has some affinities with Lawrence's poem "Snake." No doubt, there are others. The poems in Lawrence's *Birds, Beasts and Flowers* were largely composed in Tuscany and Sicily with the Mediterranean Sea and the warm sunshine never far away, in settings that parallel Carmi's Israeli habitat. Both Carmi's and Lawrence's pomegranate poems emphasize the tree's colors: Carmi's "Green, I said/ To your branches bowing in the wind/ And red red red"[3] recalling Lawrence's lines ". . . the pomegranate trees in flower,/ Oh so red, and such a lot of them," and "Pomegranates like bright green stone."[4]

Beyond the parallel references to colors the poems are similar in present- ing their speakers as vulnerable to the trees' impact on their consciousness, employing that image and impact metaphorically to represent an ambivalent involvement with the persons addressed, who have similarly invaded the poet's private domain. Both poets invite these persons, clearly a lover in Carmi's poem and presumably a similar figure in Lawrence's poem, to look at the pomegranate, that is, to visualize the relationship between the lovers but not to usurp it. Carmi writes, "Come, my love, and see. . . . Have a look at this odd tree" (9) while Lawrence says "And, if you dare, the fissure!/ Do you mean to tell me you will see no fissure?/ Do you prefer to look on the plain side?"[5] The similarity of the metaphor in both poems points to the ambivalently disturbing elements in the erotic relationships, where desire is in conflict with the singular reserve of the speakers. The invasion of the lovers, like the impact of the trees, cannot be controlled by the speakers of the poems and is therefore threatening.

In "Snake," Lawrence describes an encounter in Sicily with a venomous golden snake. Both have come to a water trough to drink, the snake arriving just ahead of the man. He is filled with fear and loathing for the reptile and, at the same time, with that age-old fascination humans feel for snakes, conscious of its beauty and its concealed natural power, of its vital life. He hears voices urging him to kill the snake but he cannot bring himself to take a stick and dispatch it. As it leaves the water trough to enter a fissure in the earth, the speaker hurls a log at the water trough and, alarmed and writhing "like lightning,"[6] the serpent disappears into the bowels of the earth. Ashamed of his action, the speaker lauds the snake "as a king in exile, uncrowned in the underworld,/ Now due to be crowned again . . . one of the lords/ of life."[7] Carmi's "The Brass Serpent," a much longer poem than "Snake," shares with Lawrence's work the images of fear mingled with adoration, of serpent and water, of the vital power of the snake, of the burnished color of brass equivalent to the yellow-brown golden serpent, of the need to lash out at the snake, of lightning movement, of caverns and fissures, and the recognition of the snake as a symbol of power and vitality.

Of course, these images grow out of the ways in which human beings experience snakes and describe them, but a parallel reading of the two works suggests that Carmi was to some degree influenced by Lawrence's poem. Where Lawrence is explicit about the serpent's role as king of the underworld, Carmi elaborates on the snake's power by inference, as the snake speaks, reminding humankind that it has "smuggled pain into the womb"(43), and "marred men's flesh with thorns of sweat"(43). That is, the snake is the catalyst of mortality, not so much in the limited sense of its fatal bite and in its actions but in its role in the loss of innocence in the Garden of Eden, imposing terrible burdens upon adults for all time: the travail of labor during childbirth for women and the curse upon Adam that his progeny would be forced to obtain their bread by the sweat of their brow. Yet Lawrence's and Carmi's perceptions of the ancient ambivalent bond between man and snake are alike. So close is the bond between human and serpent in Carmi's poem that some characteristics of Satan in the biblical guise of the snake are seen as intrinsic to the nature of man, who will "feed between tombs of lust"(40).

Carmi's poem moves back and forth between the Satanic serpent and the more immediately dangerous vipers the Israelites encountered during their forty years in the desert. He takes his text from Num. 21:8, quoting it as the first of two epigraphs to his poem: *"And the LORD said unto Moses, Make thee a fiery serpent and set it upon a pole: and it shall come to pass, that every one that is bitten, when he looketh upon it, shall live. And Moses made a serpent of brass."*(39) It is not, however, the biblical text that informs Carmi's "The Brass Serpent"; it is a related commentary from *The Zohar*,[8] which is much more elaborate and expansive in its potential interpretations. The second epigraph reads: *"Three voices are there which are never lost ... the voice of a woman in labour, when she mounts the chair of pain: that voice floats from end to end of the world: the voice of a man when his soul departs from his body: that voice floats from end to end of the world: the voice of a serpent when he sheds his skin."*(39) Just as the Zoharic passage expands the biblical verse, so Carmi's poem expands the Zoharic passage, emphasizing in its seven sections not so much "the voices that are never lost" but the eternally shared relationship principally between the serpent and man and woman. Between birth (the woman s perpetuation of life) and death (the man's consequently succumbing to mortality) the snake symbolizes the ongoing process of existence, fueled by the mysterious energizing forces of nature. In "Vigils," the third section of the poem, the speaker acknowledges the presence of this energizing force:

> The moon like a squinting lizard bobs at me.
> I am tired, very tired. My bride, how shall we fly
> Upon the belly of our frayed love: by
> What miracle? And how can we be free
>
> If we do not dare to lift our eyes to the power
> That stands in the heart of the sky, serpent and flower?
>   (41)

In Section five, "The Serpent Speaks," the voice of the snake directly acknowledges its role as the symbol of the life-force:

> They call me the eater of dirt, the crawler, the kneeless.
> Yes.
> But have you seen, in the spring,
> My chrysalis burst into the miracle
> Of a seraph's wing?
> Restless ones, look up at me.
> You will flower, you will flower.
>
> Not by riddles, not by those, but by what you see above,
> I shall tempt you to live. (44)

And because the same power, akin to Dylan Thomas's "force that through the green fuse drives the flower"[9] fuels plant, animal and man, the kinship between the human being and the reptile is strong enough for one to take on the characteristics of the other. In section six, "The Man Speaks," the voice describes its acquisition of serpentine features:

> I know further that my fingers are scaly,
> Reptilian, old. I know that the rod
> Of the reeking serpent once flowered within the wall
> Of the tabernacle of God.
> What would I do with my hands if they flowered and dew
>   fell?
>
>   . . . . .
>
> I look. I look. My eyes,
> Nervous reptilian heads, draw in
> And out, grubbing for darkness from above.
> I look, and it is the earth at which I am looking.
> I feel my blood flowing. (44-45)

By relating all living things, flower, snake, man, and woman to each other through the shared life-force, the relationship between the reptile and the human being is made positive. On the literal level Carmi affirms the intention of the biblical passage, that by looking upon the brass serpent Moses made, the Israelites in the desert who were snake-bitten would recover. On a symbolic level, the poet seeks to establish the kabbalistic notion of the interconnectedness of all things in the universe by linking the eternal voices of the woman giving birth, the man dying, the snake's cyclical renewal of its life in the shedding of its skin, and in the common participation of all living things in the same mysterious energy. Ultimately, the kabbalistic objective is to restore harmony to this universe in order to restore harmony to the divine universe, long since put in jeopardy by the disobedience of Adam and Eve, continued by their progeny down to the present day.

Although Carmi's poem would seem to be far removed from Lawrence's poem, curiously it is closer than one might think. Carmi's exaltation of interconnectedness is an acknowledgement of the need to restore harmony to the universe. This restoration can come about only in the identification of all living creatures with one other. In the closing lines of "Snake," Lawrence writes, "And I thought of the albatross,/ And I wished he would come back, my snake."[10] The allusion is to Coleridge's "The Rime of the Ancient Mariner," with its message that the mariner, and, by extension, humankind, cannot be redeemed until they acknowledge the interconnectedness of all of God's creatures. The mariner must learn to love and bless the water snakes. Coleridge's approach, obviously not kabbalistic, puts the emphasis on the love of all living things. This approach is endorsed by Lawrence. Carmi's emphasis on interconnectedness and the implied necessity of achieving harmony is the equivalent of Lawrence's emphasis upon the need to extend love. The closures of the two poems are also similar. In "Miriam," the final section of Carmi's poem, the narrator's voice calls upon Moses's sister to instruct him in blessing all things. In "Snake" the narrator at the end recognizes that he has missed an opportunity to "bless" the snake and that he must expiate his pettiness.

Through the use of kabbalistic materials, Carmi is able to achieve a multilayered effect that is a kind of hallmark of his poetry. The layers of meaning are literal, symbolic in a non-kabbalistic context, and kabbalistic. "The Brass Serpent" is a good example. On the literal level, Carmi draws simply upon our mixed loathing, fear and fascination with reptiles to suggest that humans can exhibit characteristics that are reptilian, and that in the myths and legends known to us all, reptiles can exhibit characteristics that are human. At the non-kabbalistic symbolic level, Carmi deals with the implications of the Lord's instruction to Moses to make a brass serpent to save the snake-bitten: that one must have faith in God's restorative powers. At the kabbalistic level, the poem's function is to teach humankind to seek harmony with all of life.

A companion poem to "The Brass Serpent" is entitled "I Said A Familiar Name." It is based on several related ideas from *The Zohar,* including the belief that the voices of a man when his soul departs and that of a snake when it sheds its skin are never lost, the assertion that thirty days before a man dies he loses his echo and his reflection in a mirror, and a belief that is expressed as an epigraph to the poem: *"A man calls out in a field or in a different place and a different voice returns which is unknown . . ."* (35). The possibilities for ascertaining which voice is heard, and whether or not it is an echo are rich in the speaker's apprehensive contemplation of the nearness of his own end. The idea articulated in the epigraph is presented first in the poem's opening section:

> I said a familiar name
> And a different voice came back
>
> From a different place in the ground
> And its sound was no strange sound.
>
> I said a familiar name:
> Has it now found a place in the ground
>
> To awaken in afterdays
> As the sound of a different voice? (35)

The second section incorporates the imagery of "The Brass Serpent," focusing primarily on "the voice of the serpent when it sheds its skin" and the connection between the serpent and death. The connection is made in the two closing stanzas of the section:

Widen your eyes to see the earth: and hear.
For there is no escape: the time draws near

When it will strike your head. Hold up your head.
Once more the skins of serpents are being shed. (36)

While the time of death may be approaching, it has not yet arrived. In the
third section, the speaker can still hear his echo:

It was not you I called
I called   called

I said a different name.
Name   name

(I must be very careful.)
Be very   very careful

The time is not yet here
Here   here

And on the day I call?

The day I call from my despair? (36)

Reassured that it is his echo—notice that there is no closing punctuation at
the end of the echo lines—the speaker is still keenly aware that one day his
call may disconcertingly be responded to by a different, unknown voice, or,
more alarmingly, that there will be no echo at all. In section four, in a style
and cadence that is strongly reminiscent of Yeats, Carmi puts into verse the
images of the Zoharic precursors of death:

Thirty days before his disappearance,
Between new moon and new moon,
Man loses his semblance.

The mirror is masked.

Thirty days before he turns to ghost,
Between half moon and half moon,
Man's echo is lost.

The question is asked.

Thirty days before he is closed like an eye,
Between full moon and no moon,
Man lets his dream fall loosely by.

The night is hushed.

But when his soul flies high,
Flies to the new moon,
His voice will arise and forever remain. (36-37)

That death will come is certain, and it can be anticipated by the loss thirty days earlier of the audible and visual presences of the man. About those losses he can do nothing, but at least there is consolation in knowing that the sound of his voice when his soul does depart will never be lost. The question the speaker keeps asking is when his death will occur. The concluding section provides an answer but it simultaneously poses another question:

> No words at all came from me.
>
> I raised my head to the sky
> To work out how many days there would be.
>
> No words came at all from me.
> I raised my head to the sky
>
> And the voice came back   came back to me. (37)

The speaker asks silently when his time will come. By not speaking, he precludes the possibility of an echo, and, yet, in the concluding line, he hears an echo. This tells him his time is still in the future. The question left for the reader to resolve is how there could be an echo to an unarticulated sound. Carmi doesn't explain it, but perhaps the text itself does. Kabbalistic exchanges are not grounded in logic or in pragmatism. They are based on faith. If one has sufficient faith, the question silently asked is certain to be answered in some way. The voice of the serpent when shedding its skin is never lost but it is also never heard. Hence, it is possible for a "silent" echo to come back to a "silent" voice. Another possibility is that the voice that comes back is the voice that will be heard when the man's soul does depart. Since that time hasn't come, the voice is owned by the man, but his death-cry is not necessarily in his possession since it belongs to the future.

Although "The Brass Serpent" and "I Said A Familiar Name" are concerned with death, Carmi chiefly writes about the vicissitudes and uncertainties of modern love. At the literal level, his poems on love express the concerns lovers have about pleasure and pain, ecstasy, fidelity, separation, and loss. His treatment of these concerns is sufficiently well done for the poems to be read and appreciated without probing for deeper meanings. However, some of these poems are illuminated by kabbalistic ideas and are thereby given a richer density. Carmi will often return to the use of the same kabbalistic idea in poems with widely varying subjects. For example, the idea of the echo and the mirror used as precursors of death in "I Said A Familiar Name," is found also in a much later poem, "I Say 'Love'", from *At The Stone Of Losses*. The second section of the poem connects the lover's fear of a commitment to love with this foreknowledge of death:

> This need to say
> I love you,

to see the furrows
vanish from your forehead,

to hear my body
in you, silent,

this fear of saying
I love you,

and let the night hear
a voice without echo,

a mirror ask where is your face,
this need, this fear

of saying the sea is transparent,
and it is yours

if it goes dry before my eyes
and it is mine.[11]

The stanza's meaning is enveloped in the paradox of the compulsion to risk everything in love, held back by the fear of loss. On the surface, the fear expressed here would ordinarily be interpreted as apprehension over any one of a number of normal hazards that may terminate love affairs; but from the inclusion of the precursory images of the *The Zohar*, we know that the fear is actually that death will bring the relationship to a tragic end. Only by knowing the source of the images employed can the depth of the paradox be understood: this particular love is a matter of life and death.

Kabbalah is obviously of the first importance to Carmi and he says as much in the interview. Unlike Amichai, who observed in his interview with me that he had little patience with Jewish Mysticism, adding that "it didn't do anything for [him]" it does a lot for Carmi. His use of its resources operates to move his poems from simplicity to complexity, although it places an additional burden on his translators, a burden mitigated somewhat by the fact that English is Carmi's native, although second, language—he spoke Hebrew first—and he is well equipped to collaborate with them. Occasionally, the imagery in Carmi's poems invite kabbalistic interpretation even where non-kabbalistic biblical allusions seem dominant.

An early poem entitled "René's Songs" provides a useful example. These lyrics are found in *Eyn Prahim Shehorim* (There Are No Black Flowers), Carmi's volume of poems, published by Mahbarot Lesifrut in Tel Aviv in 1953. "René's Songs" has been translated into English by Ruth F. Mintz and is included in her *Modern Hebrew Poetry A Bilingual Anthology*. René is a French orphan whose family has perished in the Holocaust, and his "songs" are both lamentions upon his losses and an affirmation of life. In the opening lines the child defines himself in terms of the oppositional aspects of white and black, of light and dark:

> Bright-haired am I, my face and body white.
> Bright as my mother's hair;
> White as my father's silence;
> The day he ascended in the smoky chariots,
> Why did Lo-Imi whisper in the frosty light that hour!
> —René, you are the black flower.[12]

To understand this hauntingly beautiful poem, the reader needs three pieces of information. These Mintz provides, as follows: The line "There are no black flowers," which becomes a refrain in the songs, Carmi obtained from Karl Marx's essay "On Style." Mintz quotes the pertinent passage as follows: ". . . the essential form of the spirit is gaiety and light, and you make shadows its only manifestation; it must be dressed only in black and there are no black flowers. . . ."[13] The name "Lo-Imi" is René's term for the director of the orphanage and means "not my mother," an adaptation by Carmi of the term "Lo Ami," (not my people), from Hosea, chapter 19.[14] The reference to "the smoky chariots" can allude either to Elijah's ascent (Second Kings, 2), that is traditionally biblical, or Ezekiel's ascent (Ezek. 1), that is at the heart of Merkabah mysticism.[15] Carmi's immediate reference is to the smoking chimneys of the crematoria where René's father perished, and suggests his ascension into heaven in glory like both Elijah and Ezekiel.

Using this combined imagery, we can see that on the literal level, Carmi establishes the child's loneliness and his bitterness over his orphaned state, along with his antipathy to his surrogate mother. At the symbolic level, Carmi indirectly moves the child's lament from individualized anguish to a moment of *Yizkor* (the remembrance of the dead), in which we all participate in private and public memorials for the six million perished Jews. At the kabbalistic level, Carmi assuages both the personal and the universalized grief somewhat freeing the soul of the deceased for its glorious reunion with God. Finally, in the paradoxical image of the nonexistent black flower, Carmi grapples with the problem that René, with his decayed teeth, his bad lung, his horrible memories, and his residual fears *is* a black flower, despite the fact that there can be none. The problem is simultaneously aesthetic and metaphysical. In Marx's term, René is only a shadow. Carmi resolves the aesthetic and the metaphysical incongruities through the child's refusal to accept his portrayal in terms of shadows and blackness. His will to live moves him into kabbalistic luminosity with the coming of spring and a renewal of life. At the close of the poem, he observes signs of spring evident in the backyard of the orphanage, and sings:

Lo-Imi, my mother!
Please come to the veranda
Look at me here in the garden.
Listen to the fragrance of the tiding.

When the pipes break forth
From the tender bamboo trunk
Swaying in the wind;
When the Chevreaux valley
Sparkles like a many-colored vase;

When the shining bud sings
I fasten my mouth
To the pipe
And spring melodies break forth and rise
Out of this damaged lung of mine
From between my decaying teeth—
My mother, my mother!
Like the almond tree I burst in Spring's heart
Into the heart of Springtime with lively pipes.

(336, 338)

The Zoharic imagery of luminosity abounds in Carmi's verses, images of light and fire are pervasive throughout his work. In the interview, Carmi discusses the story from *The Zohar* of Simeon ben Yohai's instruction to his son to cover the mouth of one of his disciples who had just come into his house and was unaccustomed to seeing the curtain of fire there. The question posed is why the son wasn't instructed instead to cover the man's eyes. Carmi suggests that "the man needed to be reassured, and the human touch, the hand over the mouth, would accomplish that, would keep the man from screaming. It turns into a synesthetic moment." Like the poem, "I say 'Love'", a section of which was analyzed above, Carmi's earlier poem "Awakening" from *The Brass Serpent,* employs the same theme of the lover's fear that the relationship may be sundered by death, but in this poem he draws not upon the Zoharic precursory images of death, the echo and mirror, but upon the story about Simeon ben Yohai and his disciple. In understructuring his poem with this story, Carmi is able to make more emphatic his theme that love is so fragile that it needs the constant reassurance of caresses:

Please pass your hand across my lips.
I'm not accustomed to this light.

Batlike our love in flight bangs round through dark.
It does not miss its mark: and your face shapes
My hands for me. What shall I learn in light?
Quick, pass your hand across me.

Your childhood (what's the time?) slept in my arms.
It's ten o'clock between the sea and night:
Midnight between us: seven between the blinds—
Oh no, I'm not accustomed to this light

Which comes to make cold slits of both my eyes,
Opening like gunsights. On those scales I weigh
My blind eyes, and the terror of your clay.
Quick, pass your hand through me.

Face to face, I'll have no face, perhaps.
Perhaps I'll stay quiet, or perhaps I'll talk.
Please pass your hand across my lips.
I'm not accustomed to this light. (21)

Love is Carmi's home territory. For love he will fight. Because love commands his attention, the other chief subject of the poet, war, is portrayed as a distraction. He has no yearning to fight. That isn't to say that he underestimates war's destructiveness or undervalues the role it has played in modern Israel's history. It can't be ignored, but it can be given a reduced priority. For example, in Carmi's poem "Diary Entry" in *At The Stone Of Losses,* a poem composed on March 16, 1978, when Israel invaded Lebanon in the Litani operation, the speaker insists on keeping "to his schedule" (53). He visits in turn his accountant, his tailor, the copy center and his lover, iterating over and over "I keep to my schedule," on the grounds that continuing to do the simple things is best:

The sages would conclude
with comforting words
(they were right, of course).
The accountant must calculate,
the tailor must sew,
the child must cry.
When everything becomes a metaphor
one should say simple things. (55)

Yet, despite the fact that the impact of the distant military action is played down, its tragedies must be acknowledged, and with a grim irony that twists and turns his own words back upon the speaker, he says in this section's concluding lines:

I've just been told
that a friend's nephew
from a kibbutz in the North
fell among the cedars of Lebanon.

What could be simpler than that? (55)

Acknowledging the destructiveness of war, Carmi wants to mitigate its horrors and spare those who can be spared. The language of his war poems is filled with what his translator, Grace Schulman, calls "a kind of hysterical calm" in her introduction to *At The Stone Of Losses.*[16] In "Author's Apology" the section entitled "Order of the Day" tells us to

> Keep the children happy!
> Keep the children happy!
>
> Don't let them hear the hoarse screams in our throats,
> or see the forest of antennae growing out of our heads,
> or hear the shredding sounds on all sides—clothes, paper,
>   sheets, sky;
> don't let them hear the neighbor's eyes triggered behind
>   the shutters,
> or see the camouflage colors beneath the skins of our
>   faces,
> or hear the wireless networks crackling in our bodies.
>
> We have to invent a code for grownups
> to speak of a
>   distant bell (he fell)
>   green pine (missing in action)
>   small cloud (captured)
>   bird's nest (wounded) (71)

The code is then incorporated into a radio message:

> This is your commanding officer:
> "A bird's nest, carried on a small cloud,
> comes to rest in a green pine
> to the sound of a distant bell.
> Good night. Over and out." (71)

The simple narrative, a bare outline of what could be a story for children, is told calmly. Behind the ironical facade lies the hysterical truth, the troops have suffered all the major disasters of war. But the important thing to do is to

> Keep the children happy!
> Keep the children happy! (71)

As small as Israel is and therefore vulnerable to both ground and air missile attacks, everyone, children included, are potential victims. Keeping "the children happy," that is, safe, Carmi suggests, is so much wishful thinking. This unrealistic hope contrasts starkly with the portrait of Amos Oz's twelve-year-olds overwhelmed by their fantasies of battle in *The Hill of Evil Counsel*, and of Appelfeld's youths confronting the Nazi terror in *Tzili The Story of a Life* and *To the Land of the Cattails*.

However hopeful the speaker of "Order of the Day" is about the children's safety, the adults are always vulnerable. In his elegy to a fallen soldier, "Military Funeral at High Noon," Carmi describes the impact of a soldier's burial on the parents of the deceased:

> The angel who made them forget
> all the womb's wisdom
> when they saw the light of day,
> strikes them again.[17]
>
> Everything is ground down, razed, forgotten.
>
> A different forgetting alters
> the father's bone-structure,
> the veins' routes,
> the whites of the eyes.
>
> A different forgetting alters
> the composition of the mother's blood,
> her skin color,
> the blacks of her eyes.
>
> They will have to replace
> all their documents.
> Today, they become strangers
> in a new country.
>
> Immigrants in the land of the living. (63, 65)

A life has been cut off in its prime, and its after effects are devastating for the soldier's parents. The grief and the poignance of the poem are genuine, the metaphor of being forced to start out anew in old age by the grim circumstance of their soldier-son's death is tellingly effective. As the soldier's comrades-in-arms prepare to fire a final salute and with their "barrels aim at heaven" (67), there is no hint here of anger at God, as there would be in Amichai's poetry, and no implied suggestion that the soldiers are shooting at God in retaliation.

Since Amichai is the only other poet to be included in this book, there is some value, however limited it may be because there are many fine poets at work in Israel today, in comparing Carmi and Amichai. In terms of style, Amichai tends to be more expansive, writing in a wide range of verse forms. He is equally at home in the short lyric and the long narrative poem. Sometimes he employs formal cadences; at other times he uses colloquial speech patterns. He achieves a sense of gravity without ever seeming to be grave. Carmi, on the other hand, is more constrained, finding the power and beauty of his poems principally in the short lyric that tends to be terse, epigrammatic and almost always colloquial.

Unlike Amichai, Carmi has no monumental battle waging with God. His struggle is against time and its relentless decimation of lovers. Where Amichai is often light-hearted in his cynicism about sexual love, Carmi is far more grave, striking a note of dead seriousness in his celebration of physical passion. The opening section to his "Platform No. 8" is a good example:

> To shine on your hair;
> to flame around your face;
>
> to light up your hand
> and see through it;
>
> to be on all sides of you
> at once;
>
> to press my forehead
> against your sleeping eye;
>
> to leave the shells of my hands
> on your breasts,
>
> my breath imprinted
> on your white cheek,
>
> and to see in you, always
> my true face,
>
> and my gravity. (43)

Carmi's true face is his gravity. Love matters a great deal to both Amichai and Carmi, but Carmi seems as obsessively grave about love as Amichai is about God's insensitivity.

Another difference, one that I have commented on above, needs to be mentioned again in closing. While Amichai's poetry is rich in its use of biblical imagery, figures, and history, Carmi's verses are suffused with the elements of *Kabbalah*. The uses of Jewish Mysticism are widespread in modern literature, and apart from Carmi, writers as diverse as W. B. Yeats, Henry Roth, Malcolm Lowry, Lawrence Durrell, Isaac Bashevis Singer, Chaim Potok, Thomas Pynchon, and Cynthia Ozick have employed its subject matter effectively, some with more subtlety (which invites mystery!) than others. From its storehouse of vision, knowledge and wonder, and with its myriad of metaphors for luminosity, Jewish Mysticism can and does provide a vast resource. The use of its essence of mystery requires a certain obliquity and indirection, a turning away from the obvious if it is to be used advantageously. To put it more directly, mystery must be conveyed mysteriously if its transformative quality and its hidden meanings are to be invoked successfully. Carmi has become a master in his respect. He maintains the appropriate aesthetic distance, is subtle and indirect, and, as a result, his poetry conveys the sense of wonder and mystery that are crucial to the sophisticated portrayal of his real and luminous worlds.

Interview 3   T. Carmi

March 11, 1986

JC: Tell me something about your background. Where did your parents come from?

TC: My mother was from Poland. She came from a small town called Demblin, near Warsaw. My father came from Petrikov in the Ukraine. He was ordained in a well-known yeshiva and is today living in Tel Aviv.

JC: When did your parents leave Eastern Europe and where did they go?

TC: They left in the early 1920s, going first to Paris—my mother knew French—and then to upstate New York. My father decided to make a living teaching Hebrew. After I was born in 1925, Hebrew became my first language even though I am a native American. My parents were ardent Zionists and their intention was to settle in Palestine. Hebrew, Hebrew literature, and Palestine were the mainstreams of their lives.

JC: When did your family go to Palestine?

TC: Actually, they didn't in that sense. My mother took my younger brother and me to Tel Aviv in 1931. We stayed three years. My father remained in the United States. It had something to do with a family matter but more to do with our education. When we got to Palestine the students and teachers laughed at me because of my Ashkenazi pronunciation of Hebrew. I picked up the standard Sephardic fast. When we returned to New York, the students and teachers laughed at me because of my Sephardic pronunciation. Again, I made a fast switch. I made Aliyah in 1947. My brother, who is a psychologist, came to Israel later, and my father still later.

JC: When did you first begin writing poetry?

TC: Around the age of fifteen. Before that I wrote some short stories. They were bad. One I submitted to the *Bitzaron Quarterly*. It was accepted, but when the editors discovered the author was fifteen years old they decided not to publish it. That's when I switched to writing poetry. My first Hebrew poem appeared in *Hadoar*. The editor tampered with one of the lines so I never printed anything there again.

JC: Over the years what has been your approach to writing Hebrew poetry?

TC: I try not to think about myself in terms of critical approaches. I'm a great believer in letting the subconscious do its work. Still, one can't avoid the question entirely. On the one hand, I had a traditional background, orthodox schools, synagogue training and a lot of exposure to classical Hebrew poetry. I studied medieval and early modern Hebrew poetry, Bialik and company as well. On the other hand, I was devouring modern American and English poetry during my high school and college years. In that formative period I wanted to bridge the two. I found nothing in Hebrew literature that was the equivalent of the poetry I encountered in American anthologies. That isn't to say modern Hebrew poetry wasn't being composed. Those were the war years and modern Hebrew writing was not yet reaching the States. I knew nothing at the time of Nathan Alterman's "imagist" poetry, of Avot Yeshurun's idiosyncratic ironies and elegies, of Amir Gilboa's experiments combining traditional elements with colloquial usages and personal concerns with national motifs. I came across the poetry of these writers first in Paris. I was there for a year in 1946, working in childrens' homes. The children were camp survivors, orphans and those whose parents were unable to care for them. From Paris I went to Palestine. There, of course, I encountered more modern Hebrew poetry. In New York the Hebrew poets I had admired most were Simon Halkin and Gabriel Preil. Preil is a very good poet. A new selection of his work has just been published. There was a program in his honor in New York last week. I had written the preface for his new book, and I delivered a talk about his poetry. Curiously in 1945, I was editing a Hebrew journal and in it I printed my first and almost my last piece of criticism. It was a review of Preil's first book of Hebrew poems and now, a little more the forty years later, we are together again in New York and in the same book. It was a touching moment.

JC: When you were growing up, who were the English and American poets you were attracted to the most?

TC: It would be pretty much the usual list. Yeats, Eliot, Pound and Marianne Moore. I was especially attracted to Yeats. Allen Mandelbaum, who now edits the Jewish Poetry Series for the JPS, and I translated Yeats's "Sailing to Byzantium" into Hebrew while we were still in college.

JC: Did Eliot's and Pound's politics interfere with your enjoyment of their poetry?

TC: No, not at the time. My constant concern was how do I do what they are doing in Hebrew poetry?

JC: You were saying last night that your poetry tended not to be optimistic, that it was marked by sadness. Your poem "Story" in the recently translated collection *At The Stone Of Losses* bears this out:

> When the woman in the fishing village told me
> of her husband who had disappeared
> and of the sea that returns and dies
> at her doorstep every evening
> I was silent.
> I couldn't say to the shells of her eyes
> your love will return
> or the sea will live again.
>
> (There are days when I cannot
> find one word
> to tell you.)[1]

There are other examples as well. The sense of loss seems pervasive. Were you influenced in your youth by the nihilism of Pound and Eliot?

TC: I don't think Pound is nihilistic. There are those early lyrics that are optimistic, and lovely, not at all ideological or philosophical or religious.

JC: I had in mind Eliot's *The Wasteland* and his other early poems that emphasize the disintegration of Western civilization in the twentieth century.

TC: Eliot's poetry probably was not an influence in an ideological respect, certainly not consciously, because in my waking life I was optimistic. The desire to settle and live in Palestine and to be part of a Jewish cultural revival there suggests considerable optimism. No, my only thought was to figure out how to do in Hebrew what Eliot was doing in English. I tried to fuse—I don't know that I succeeded—the techniques of modern poetry in English with the rhythms of spoken Hebrew. I don't think I was able to do that until I had spent ten years in Israel. The problem was that my Hebrew was too good, in a classical sense. It had not been tested by daily life, buying groceries, having an argument, or dreaming.

JC: Yes, though a good poet will exercise restraint and will discipline himself whether he is expressing optimism, pessimism, nihilism or, what have you.

TC: There is always the need for discipline. I'm not convinced that the categories "optimism/pessimism" mean much. When people say to me Samuel Beckett is pessimistic, I don't feel that way at all because the very act of writing, of structuring words artistically, goes beyond those categories. It brings about an equilibrium, it brings order out of chaos. That's more liberating, not less so, which would be pessimistic.

JC: In reading your poems, I find a good many specific Zoharic and other kabbalistic allusions and images. One thinks readily of "An Israeli Abroad" with its reference to the opening of "Ezekiel" and the "Merkabah," or great chariot vision, which is one of the pre-Zoharic cornerstones of *Kabbalah*; of "The Song of Thanks," which also alludes to "Ezekiel," Chapter One; of "I Say Love"; and the fifth section of "Author's Apology" with its adaptation of passages from the Zohar. One would have to conclude that your use of *Kabbalah* is conscious and deliberate. Is that the case?

TC: Yes, I do use *Kabbalah* consciously and deliberately. I find the material from *Kabbalah* stimulating. I'm not formally religious in any way, but I find the Jewish mystical tradition attractive. For example, there is a story that Simeon ben Yohai had a curtain of fire in his house. One day one of his disciples came to see him. As the man entered, Simeon ben Yohai told his son to go over to him and put his hand over the disciple's mouth because he was not accustomed to seeing so bright a light. Now, a story like that really gets me going. Why didn't Simeon ben Yohai instruct his son to go over and cover the man's eyes? That's what you would expect. The point was that the man needed to be reassured, and the human touch, the hand over the mouth, would accomplish that, would keep the man from screaming. It turns into a synesthetic moment. There is a lot of material in *Kabbalah* like that, and for one reason or another it means a great deal to me. It has nothing to do with the kabbalistic religious system. I have transferred much of this material into psychological categories from which I get images for my poems. I suppose that makes me a pirate. Let me give you another example. A disciple of Abraham Abulafia[2] describes a moment of ecstasy when a body of fire emerged from his body and faced him like a mirror. This is the height of the miraculous. It's a way of going to meet your metaphor. It has something to do with the great objectivity that's there when you are writing even though you're being entirely subjective. There's the sense that something else is coming into being and facing you as a result of what you're doing. It's like having that same kabbalistic experience, but since something else is being created, I guess it really isn't piracy.

JC: I have observed that there are numerous images of fire in your poems, and they have an aura of mysticism about them. I see now where you are coming from. One I find especially appealing is "From This Day On":

> The earth has taken over.
> When I break out of the zone of your silence,
> fire greets me with seventy tongues.
> I cherish several samples:
> the wisp of hair on your forehead;

> your shoulder's glow before the grate;
> your breath at the edge of my lips.
> That's all there is.
> But now I anticipate
> years of research and deciphering.
> It's not every day that a man grows
> wings of fire and water. (31)

This is a charming love poem, a tribute to the beloved, and it can be read for that meaning alone; however, when I first encountered it, all kinds of images from the *Sefer Yetsirah*[3] seemed to leap out at me. And, of course, I am reading the English translation, so I am arbitrarily one step removed from the Hebrew. I think perhaps that poses less of a problem since you mentioned in your poetry reading last night that you had collaborated with your translator. And you do a lot of translating yourself. What basic principle do you follow when you are translating another writer's works?

TC: My ideal can be summed up in a quotation from Robert Graves that goes "Subdue your pen to his until it prove as natural to sign his name as yours." That is the ideal, but it's not often achieved. You have to ask yourself if you were writing this poem or this play in your native language how would you say what is to be said. If you ask that question, you often arrive at solutions, I find, which are not literal but which are closer than a literal translation, because you are there translating in terms of your cultural values and the history of your language. I translate primarily on invitation of the theater. Mainly, I do translations of plays, sometimes plays in verse. They are then staged in Israel and published there. I've translated *Beaux' Stratagem* and *Rosenkrantz and Guildenstern Are Dead,* and, in recent years, I've been spending a lot of time doing Shakespeare's plays. Translating Shakespeare into Hebrew is impossible, but it is marvelous. Of course, some of Shakespeare's plays have been translated before. There is a tradition of translating Shakespeare that goes back over a hundred years. There was a translator named I. E. Salkinson who did some great translations over a century ago. He also translated the New Testament into Hebrew. He converted. He was a very curious man. He did all his translations before Hebrew was revived as a spoken language and his translations are still of interest. There is a history of iambic pentameter in Hebrew so that you find yourself working in the same metrical system as English, whereas when you are translating from the French, as I recently did *Cyrano de Bergerac,* you have the problem of translating syllabic metrics into tonal or accentual metrics. There were other problems, too. It took me a long time because it is all in rhymed couplets.

JC: Did you translate it into Hebrew in rhymed couplets?

TC: Yes. But capturing Rostand's wit and elegance was not easy. As difficult as it was, it was a rest from doing Shakespeare. Still, I enjoyed translating Rostand. There's nothing more difficult than translating Shakespeare. That accounts for the fact that not all of his plays have been translated. *Measure For Measure* has never been translated. If anyone did it earlier, I don't know about it. *A Midsummer Night's Dream, Hamlet* and *Much Ado About Nothing* have been translated. The rate of obsolescence of Hebrew in the theater is frightful. The changes in the language, the changes in theatrical convention and the changes in the idiom of modern poetry altogether make translations that were done as recently as twenty years ago sound unnatural.

JC: So the life of a translated play in Israel these days is fairly short.

TC: I wouldn't put it that way because I think the rate of obsolescence is straightening out, slowing down. It's no longer the way it was, and there are good historical reasons for the change. The earlier translators in Israel, Nathan Alterman and Abraham Shlonsky, were the first ones to introduce the rhythms of speech into Hebrew poetry. Alterman more than Shlonsky. Those rhythms are more apparent in Alterman's translation of *Othello* than in Shlonsky's translation of *King Lear*. But even Alterman's *Othello* today sounds too classical. One way I have of knowing that the curve, the rate of obsolescence, is straightening out—and I don't mean to blow my horn about this—is that my translation of *A Midsummer Night's Dream,* which was commissioned by the theater and first produced in 1965, has since been produced four times by other theaters in Israel, and I haven't had to change a syllable. But I don't think it has to do with an objective phenomenon. Patterns of speech in Israel have become better stabilized. You get a clearer picture today of how taxi drivers talk, of how people in the marketplace talk, how people in the bars talk and how professors talk.

JC: How would you describe the situation of literature in Israel today?

TC: It's in a chaotic state.

JC: When A. B. Yehoshua was in New Orleans, he said that in the early years, in the 1920s and 1930s, the pioneering days in Palestine, it was the socialist Zionist core of thought that sustained Jewish writing but after the War of Independence that core collapsed and the writers in Israel had to scurry around to find new ways of dealing with the Jewish experience in Israel. Do you agree with Yehoshua's view, or would you characterize the past as it has led up to the present differently?

TC: I don't know that I would put it as drastically as Yehoshua did. After all, one of Yehoshua's great concerns today is that Israel should be Jewish and that the Jewish people in the Diaspora should come to Israel. If that's not Zionism, I don't know what Zionism is. Apparently, Yehoshua is still motivated by it. In the 1920s and 1930s there were in Palestine mature writers who had done most of their writing in Europe, and they were going through the throes of transition from Europe to Palestine. After Bialik came to Palestine he hardly wrote a single work of poetry. No one has ever explained his famous period of silence, but I suspect one of the reasons for it was simply the change in pronunciation. His oldest poetry was composed in Ashkenazi Hebrew. In Palestine he heard only Sephardic Hebrew. Now, those are two different sets of music. Bialik was an instinctive craftsman but he was also a very delicate one, and he couldn't make the change. After coming to Palestine some poets tried to transpose their earlier books from Ashkenazi to Sephardic, which meant changing some of the rhythms and changing the meters. It was almost always a failure because it was an exercise in artificial transposition. Yehoshua was right about the scurrying around that occurred. There's a famous line by Chaim Gouri that was written around the time of the War of Liberation. The line says everybody spoke in the first person plural; that is, your "I" was a "we." To a certain extent the "we" crumbled in the years following the War of Liberation. The poets became much more individualistic, antidogmatic. That the old models didn't serve as well anymore is, I think, true.

JC: How would you describe the situation of poetry in Israel today. What might we expect in the coming decade?

TC: There's an old Talmudic saying that ever since the Temple was destroyed the gift of prophecy was given to fools and children. I don't know what to expect. Poetry is very much a part of the fabric of Hebrew literature. It's not hermetic. There is and has been experimentation but it has not been radical experimentation. There is a neoclassical school of poetry that writes in an "archaic pre-biblical" style, inspired by Canaanite mythology and Ugaritic epics. At the other extreme, there is poetry that limits itself almost consciously to street Hebrew. Amichai once said in a poem "I use only half the words in a dictionary." I don't think this self-imposed limitation is true of him today, but he thought it was in the past. His generation couldn't draw on the models of their predecessors because in the early days the main models were from Russian poetry. Abraham Shlonsky and Nathan Alterman drew on the models of Russian Futurism and Russian Symbolism, introducing Russian verse forms. An American influence came in the 1950s and 1960s and changed the whole picture. There has been, for example, one small group of poets who derived from William Carlos Williams. This group really tried to "Williamize" Hebrew, writing object poetry, employing minimalism. That is to say all the Israeli poets are very different, Amir Gilboa, Dan Pagis, Yehuda Amichai, Meir Wieseltier, but whatever the trends, the Israeli poets' dialogue, friendly or unfriendly, goes on with the long tradition of Hebrew poetry.

JC: Can you elaborate on that observation?

TC: In Amichai's poem "A Sort of Apocalypse," he writes

> The man under his fig tree telephoned the man under his vine:
> "Tonight they will surely come.
> Armour the leaves,
> Lock up the tree,
> Call home the dead and be prepared."[4]

Here Amichai has taken the famous biblical passage from Micah, chapter 4, "They shall sit every man under his vine and under his fig tree and none shall make them afraid," a passage of reassuring peace, and turned it into its opposite meaning, because the allusion is to camouflaged army men, awaiting an attack. In the allusion you get a balanced image from ancient and from modern Israel. Another good example of this blending of past and present is in Amir Gilboa's poem "Isaac," though here what is combined is the ancient story of the *Akedah* with a tone and technique that are not biblical but entirely modern:

> At dawn, the sun strolled in the forest
> together with me and father, and my
> right hand was in his left.
>
> Like lightning a knife flashed among
> the trees. And I am so afraid of my
> eyes' terror, faced by blood on the
> leaves.
>
> Father, father, quickly save Isaac so
> that no one will be missing at the
> midday meal.
>
> It is I who am being slaughtered, my
> son, and already my blood is on the
> leaves. And father's voice was
> smothered and his face was pale.
>
> And I wanted to scream, writhing not
> to believe, and tearing open my eyes.
> And I woke up.
>
> And my right hand was drained of
> blood.[5]

JC: What a marvelous contrast Gilboa's version is to the retelling of the *Akedah* in a famous poem by the World War I British poet, Wilfred Owen. His version goes as follows:

> So Abram rose, and clave the wood, and went,
> And took the fire with him, and a knife.
> And as they sojourned both of them together,
> Isaac the first-born spake and said, My Father,
> Behold the preparations, fire and iron,
> But where the lamb for this burnt-offering?
> Then Abram bound the youth with belts and straps,
> And builded parapets and trenches there,
> And stretched forth the knife to slay his son.
> When lo! an angel called him out of heaven,
> Saying, Lay not thy hand upon the lad,
> Neither do anything to him. Behold,
> A ram, caught in a thicket by its horns;
> Offer the Ram of Pride instead of him.
> But the old man would not so, but slew his son,
> And half the seed of Europe, one by one.[6]

In Gilboa's "Isaac" it is the father who is suffering. That's more Jewish. In Owen's poem, it is the son who suffers. That's more Christian. Of course, that approach was understandable in Owen, since he had been strongly influenced by a very religious mother, and for a time he was an upaid curate at a vicarage in Dunsden. His anger over the slaughter he had witnessed in the trenches also has a telling effect.

TC: I've known Owen's poem for a long time. He dealt with the real life he was experiencing in France. The same kind of preoccupation with the drama of everyday life is found in much contemporary Israeli poetry. Perhaps, too much of it is concerned with immediacy. Recently, criticism has been leveled at it because it deals too much with real life. It's not sufficiently philosophical, not sufficiently existential and this is probably true. You won't find demonstrations in Israel against nuclear weapons because the country is too preoccupied with its day-to-day problems, its immediate survival problems.

JC: Are you saying that the daily news is so pressing that there isn't any time for reflection or reflective verse, that Israeli poets can't get the objectivity or the distance they need?

TC: It's partly that, it's also partly that a good many of the poets face a sort of permanent conflict. On the one hand, they have to resist the immediate drama of everyday life which, in the nature of things in Israel, is always a potentially explosive subject, one that can be overly dramatic or sentimental, one that is capable of summoning reflexes that the poem cannot sustain. To put it another way, there is a desire to resist what you would call "national" poetry. There is very little of it written, very little patriotic poetry. On the other hand, there is also a strong feeling of being of one's time and place. All of these poets served in the reserves. Most of them have been through one or two or three wars. Most of them have had or have children in the army, so the pressures of everyday life are there. Israel is a nervous country. What did Shelley say, that poetry was an exposed nerve. In Israel it is a very exposed nerve.

JC: Do you read much fiction?

TC: No, I read quite a lot of poetry.

JC: What will your next project be?

TC: I haven't decided yet. At the moment, I'm very busy teaching at Yale. I recently finished translating *Cyrano de Bergerac,* which we talked about earlier, and one-half year ago, I brought out a new collection of poems in Hebrew.

JC: What is its title?

TC: It's sort of untranslatable. The Hebrew is *Ahat Hi Li.* It is an idiom in Hebrew which means "I don't care," but if you translate it literally it means "she's the only one for me." John Hollander suggested to me that I render the title "All One To Me."

JC: You've written a lot of love poetry.

TC: Yes, I have. I suppose most of my poetry is love poetry.

JC: How popular is poetry in Israel today? Do the people buy a lot of poetry?

TC: Oh yes. Generally, a lot of poetry is bought in Israel. Poems are read on the radio two or three times a day. And as we have only one television channel, the moment the writer is seen on television, he's had total exposure. Every newspaper has a literary supplement. That means every Friday six newspapers have to fill two pages with poetry and criticism, so a lot of nonsense is published, as well. Israeli poets don't have the trouble contacting their audience the way American poets do.

JC: What is the ordinary size of a printing of a volume of poetry?

TC: The size of the printing would be about a thousand copies. I'm not a best seller like Amichai or Gouri but my books sell well and steadily. All the books go out of print; some of them go into second editions. Every now and then a selected or collected edition will appear. But some of the Israeli poets sell in the thousands of copies.

JC: You're spending a good deal of time traveling all over America these days, reading your poems and lecturing. What's your impression of American Jews?

TC: I haven't actually spent that much time here to be able to comment. When I left in the 1940s I didn't return to the United States for fifteen years. I did spend a year at Stanford and another at Brandeis, but that's it except for some hit and run visits. One thing that has impressed me on this visit is the great upsurge in Jewish studies all over the place. Even at Yale they were surprised when I offered a seminar where Hebrew was a prerequisite. I don't know that this was so ten or twenty years ago. Everywhere there seems to be evidence that is symptomatic of this change. There appears to be a whole generation of young avid scholars. At least, these are my impressions.

JC: Thank you for gracing our Jewish Studies Program, and for all your impressions.

Chapter 4

❖ ❖ ❖

Aharon Appelfeld

Since 1962, Aharon Appelfeld has been well established in Israel as a writer. He is the author of fifteen books, including novellas, novels, collections of short stories, and a memoir (whose Hebrew title translated is *Essays in the First Person*). A familiar literary figure in his adopted land, it has only been since 1980 that his fiction has become known in the West. While in the interview following this essay he emphasizes that he has taken all of Jewish life as his subject and is involved in writing stories set in places and times other than central Europe just prior to and during the Holocaust, the American reader knows him only through his six novels of the Holocaust translated into English through 1988. These novels constitute a major achievement and their enthusiastic reception has facilitated Appelfeld's meteor-like rise to fame. Their attraction lies in the author's narrative power, his vision, and his broad range.

Underlying that power, vision, and range is Appelfeld's uncanny evocation of mood and his sense of time and place in reconstructing entirely the lost world of central European Jewry as it existed just before its extermination by Hitler's legions. Appelfeld's inventiveness brings back hauntingly the lives and outlooks of the segment of European Jewry that was so deeply immersed in German culture, so thoroughly assimilated and so materialistic that it had neither the capacity to envisage the tragedy that befell it or the resources to accommodate that tragedy by linking it to Jewish apocalyptic history. The possibility that the next chapter of that history would be written in this assimilated Jewish community's own blood was unthinkable.

Lacking an essential Jewish identity and glorying in pan-Germanism, these Jews went to the death camps with perhaps a dimension of shock additional to that suffered by their eastern European coreligionists. The monumental disparity between their view of their exalted status and their professed patriotism, and the chaos of Hitler's storm troopers bearing down on them, provided Appelfeld with one of his most effective tools, a wide-ranging irony that finds its forceful meaning in the distance between the invitingly deceptive appearance of things the assimilated Jews delude themselves about and the unperceived harsh realities of their darkening existence. Appelfeld has emerged as the supreme ironist of Holocaust writing, not because this was a conscious artistic goal, but because the self-delusions of the central European Jews and their refusal to face reality defined them in a context of irony, an irony that was both comic and tragic.

Using irony as his main stock-in-trade, Appelfeld concentrated his attention not directly upon the experience of the death camps themselves, as Eli Wiesel had done, but upon the life-styles and attitudes of the central European Jews in the years just before the death camps opened, and upon the lives of the survivors, who escaped death by hiding in the forests, or by going underground, or for those who were interned, by a combination of a strong will to live and sheer good luck in escaping the gas chambers. To a lesser extent Chaim Grade[1] and Primo Levi[2] had also begun to go beyond Eli Wiesel's pioneering efforts, broadening the treatment of the Holocaust, but Grade's subject was eastern European Jewry and Levi's was the Italian Jews who were not assimilated to the extent of their German and Austrian coreligionists, and who, under Mussolini, were for a time in a less desperate situation. Neither Grade nor Levi had any particular reason to employ irony as a major tool. Consequently, Appelfeld added a whole new, highly significant dimension to the literature of the Holocaust.

For Appelfeld the addition of that new dimension was not an accidental choice. As the interview makes clear, Appelfeld was himself a product of that assimilationist society, and since it is in fact irretrieveably lost, he has felt that it is his mission to recover it experientially, not only its positive manifestations but more importantly its negative psychological aspects, in order to provide himself with a precise sense of his own origins while creating, through his art, an adequate memorial to the society in which his origin took root.

The Holocaust was a particularized tragedy for Appelfeld, as it was for Wiesel, in that they were children when their worlds crumbled. Appelfeld was a child of eight when the Nazis killed his mother and interned him and his father in a forced labor camp in what was then the Rumanian-occupied sector of the Ukraine. In seeking to recover those losses by reconstituting the family life and society he knew as a child, he has used the Holocaust more as a gigantic backdrop than as the center stage for his tragic dramas. The sense of the Holocaust is always present and always menacing, but Appelfeld never allows it directly into our presence. That is to acknowledge that very early in his career as a writer he mastered the technique of aesthetic distancing. It gave him more flexibility and greater objectivity in treating his material. It was, furthermore, an essential component of irony, for without proper distancing between the writer and his subject, and the subject and its reader, irony becomes meaningless. Along with the proper aesthetic distancing, irony requires, moreover, a certain detachment, and in this respect Appelfeld brings to his writing the required disinterestedness.

Through detachment, Appelfeld has employed his imagination to best advantage in reconstructing from his memories the society into which he was born. Much of his work is certainly autobiographical, but it is not factually so. While his narratives achieve objectivity by correlating with our own common knowledge of the Holocaust and the circumstances of the Jews in Europe at the time, Appelfeld's artistic constructs are totally subjective. Just as our views of reality are individually unique, so Appelfeld's views of reality are uniquely his own. The best description of the technique of subjective reconstruction of which I am aware is by Lawrence Durrell, who has his protagonist Darley say at the outset of *The Alexandria Quartet* that

> The solace of such work as I do with brain and heart lies in this—that only *there*, in the silences of the painter or the writer can reality be reordered, reworked and made to show its significant side. Our common actions in reality are simply the sackcloth covering which hides the cloth-of-gold—the meaning of the pattern. For us artists there waits the joyous compromise through art with all that wounded or defeated us in daily life; in this way, not to evade destiny ... but to fulfil it in its true potential—the imagination. ... We [referring to the people he had most closely been involved with in the past] have all of us taken different paths now; but in this, the first great fragmentation of my maturity I feel the confines of my art and my living deepened immeasurably by the memory of them. In thought I achieve them anew; as if only here ... can I enrich them as they deserve.[3]

In getting to the "cloth-of-gold—the meaning of the pattern," Appelfeld has done for pre-Holocaust central European Jewry what Isaac Bashevis Singer did for eastern European Jewry. Reliving "the great fragmentation," not of his maturity but of his youth, he has "deepened immeasurably" his own life and that of his readers by utilizing his memory as a springboard for recreating the society that first nurtured him. To be sure, Appelfeld's motivation and need were different from Singer's motivation and need. It is certainly obvious that both communities of which they wrote, the central European Jewish community and the eastern European Jewish community, were swallowed up by the Holocaust; but the distinction between Appelfeld and Singer is that Appelfeld was immediately cut off in childhood from his culture by its destruction by the Nazis, whereas Singer left Poland in 1935 a grown man, well before the German invasion, and he brought his culture intact to America, where, at his leisure, he could span its centuries of existence in Warsaw, Cracow, Lublin, Goray and all the other towns, cities, and *shtetls* that constitute the locales for his work. Singer could take from that centuries-old culture whatever materials he wanted, reworking them through his imagination into whimsy, parable, folktale, raw comedy, mysticism, and fantasy. It was a culture particularly rich in mysticism, folklore, superstition, and earthiness; it was a *milieu* replete with a vast amount of human experience with which Singer felt very much at home.

On the contrary, Appelfeld's *milieu* has been one with which he is profoundly uncomfortable. Where Singer's Jewish *milieu* was expansive, Appelfeld's *milieu* had been systematically diminished. Singer's world was steeped in *Yiddishkeit* while Appelfeld's world had moved toward total assimilation. A positive Jew, who has repeatedly affirmed his Jewishness (and he does so again in the interview), Appelfeld has had to confront the fact that his parents, along with most of the Jews of Austria and Germany, had denied their Jewishness. *Yiddishkeit* was not only alien to them, it was abhorrent. In the denial of their Judaism and the delusions they practiced, in their misreading of the politics of pan-Germanism, they added a dimension of incredulity to their foredoomed lives. As distressing as this situation has been to Appelfeld, he has taken the denials, the delusions and the incredulity and enlarged upon their diminished dimensions to stock and enhance the core of his irony. These escapist stances lend themselves peculiarly and completely to that irony which, in their enlargement, encompasses grim tragedy and an absurdly black comedy out of which the most profound pathos arises.

Comic and tragic irony, aesthetic distancing, detachment, evocation of mood and subjective reconstruction are the narrative strategies of Appelfeld's fictions. By being aware of them, we are able to grasp "the meaning of the pattern" in his Holocaust novels. Whence do these strategies derive? Appelfeld discovered them primarily in his reading of Kafka and Proust and, to a lesser extent, Thomas Mann.[4] They were his chief mentors. From Kafka and Proust he came to understand the value of detachment; *negatively*, in a sense from Kafka through that writer's use of impersonal and anonymous abstractions—in *Badenheim 1939* the functioning of the Sanitation Department, a euphemism for the secret police, is a perfect example—and, *positively*, from Proust's use of symbols and objects to trigger the recall of remote but incisive incidents in a character's earlier life. Both writers provided Appelfeld with an appreciation of nature in the evocation of mood. Proust, moreover, gave Appelfeld a model of assimilated Jewish life in modern Europe, a context shot through with Jewish self-hate. And from Kafka, Appelfeld got an appreciation for eerie comedy, immersed in irony and the absurd. Equally important, he found in Kafka, as Gershon Shaked in The *Shadows Within* suggests, "the characterization of the anti-hero who is at the same time a Jewish victim."[5]

Like Amichai, Yehoshua and Oz, Appelfeld appears to be influenced by the relativity theory, also. To Kafka and Proust, we must add the teachings of Einstein. Appelfeld employs the literary adaptations of the relativity theory, simultaneity, the breakdown of causality and indeterminacy (the fullest treatment of these principles will be found in the discussion here of Oz's *Touch the Water Touch the Wind*) in escaping from linear reality, both spatial and temporal. Although Shaked maintains that Appelfeld's works "are always inextricably bound up with locale and time,"[6] this is true only in the generalized frames of central Europe between 1939 and 1945. The novels are not consistently locked into place names and specific dates. The names of some characters are abbreviated while other characters are not named at all. Past, present, and future are occasionally transformed into the singular "great moment" in which these arbitrary measurements are telescoped into transformative events that both change the course of the characters' lives and bind them psychologically to particular events forever.

This temporal and spatial configuration occurs in Appelfeld's *Badenheim 1939*, the first of his novels to appear in America, translated by Dalya Bilu and published by David R. Godine in Boston in 1980. The year "1939" was, perhaps unfortunately, added to the American version (it was not part of the Hebrew title *Badenhaym 'Ir Nofesh* [Badenheim, Holiday Resort], first printed in Tel Aviv as part of *Shanim vesha'ot* [Years and Hours] in 1975), because it identified the time of the novel too specifically with the world upheaval that got under way that year, thereby undermining Appelfeld's intention of avoiding temporal specificity. The setting is in a spa in central Europe, typical of the vacation resorts assimilated Jews frequented for the reputed restorative values of their mineral springs and for their music and theater festivals. These spas certainly existed as real places in real time, but no one of them is Appelfeld's "Badenheim." Appelfeld's "Badenheim" is a figment of his imagination, a subjective reconstruction in which delusions are substituted for reality, causality breaks down, and mistaken judgments run rampant. The "real" as we know it in linear terms of time and space gives way to an elaborate hallucination that unveils for us truths that would not otherwise be apparent.

For example, at the end of *Badenheim 1939*, when the Sanitation Department has rounded up all the Jews who have come to the spa as vacationers and brings up an engine pulling "four filthy freight cars,"[7] these Jews believe they are being transported to a paradise in Poland, to a never ending glorious holiday. In his delusion, Dr. Pappenheim, the spa's impressario, remarks, "If the coaches are so dirty it must mean that we have not far to go" (148). He misjudges the cattle cars for coaches, and thinks the trip will be a short one. In this breakdown of causality and the application of Heisenberg's principle that it is no longer possible to measure anything accurately, the irony is overwhelming. The reader knows all too well that the trip will indeed be short, and that these people are on their way to the crematoria in Auschwitz. The absurd and ridiculous assumptions and corresponding actions of the vacationers would make this scene and, for that matter, the entire book, hilariously funny if the truth were not so appallingly tragic.

Earlier we are given a subtle hint that the absurdity and ridiculousness of the situation is to be interpreted as the essence of the ironic mode. One of the assimilated vacationers, Professor Fussholdt, a controversial figure who had at one time given lectures discrediting Theodore Herzl (Jewish political destiny) and Martin Buber (Jewish philosphy and spirituality), sits in his room correcting the proofs for his magnum opus, a book thought to be about "satire, the only art form appropriate to our lives" (62). Irony is the chief form of satire. In light of the fact that in our century the magnitude of destruction is so great and genocide so widespread, we can only deal with its implications indirectly. Irony functions by indirection, and, in that sense, it "is the only art form appropriate to our lives." This context for irony came into existence in the poetry of protest articulated by the English soldier-poets of World War I, principally Siegfried Sassoon, Wilfred Owen, and Isaac Rosenberg. Though it has become a staple of modern literature, only Appelfeld among the novelists of the Holocaust has used it to advantage. It makes his approach to the subject unique.

The powerful satire displayed in that "great moment" at the conclusion of *Badenheim 1939* is merely the closing crescendo to the irony that pervades the book. This irony is immediately introduced at the outset of the novel, though it is only in retrospect (unless we take seriously the mention of the subject of Professor Fussholdt's book) that we become aware of its presence. In the novel's opening paragraphs, we meet the spa's pharmacist and his sick wife, Trude. She is terminally ill, and from time to time she wavers between conciousness and unconsciousness. She has hallucinations, she shouts and screams, she anticipates the impending catastrophe. Because she is sick, the physically healthy vacationers pay no attention to her. Since her forebodings are realistic and extend beyond her condition, we come to recognize that she is sane, and, in that sense, healthy. The vacationers, though they are functioning in a completely rational manner, allow themselves in their pleasure seeking to be duped and seduced by the anonymous inspectors of the Sanitation Department, a seduction that will turn out to be lethal. Their gullibility and escapism, in contrast to Trude's sanity, tells us that they are really the ones who are sick.

Yet their malaise is masked by the narrative's suffusion of charm and elegance. Everything seems benign and carefree. On the surface, the vacationers' lives epitomize the assimilationist cultural pinnacle they have achieved: they go to concerts, read Rainer Maria Rilke and Herman Hesse, worship Karl Kraus, examine each others' pedigrees and indulge themselves in the delectable delicacies of the rich. All the good things in life, particularly holidays and travel, are theirs for the asking. Even the Sanitation Department resembles a travel agency, promising happy vacations in Poland. Posters beckon with the slogans: "Labor Is Our Life ... The Air In Poland is Fresher ... Sail On The Vistula ... The Development Areas Need You ... Get To Know The Slavic Culture"(29-30). The delightfulness and amiability of the inspectors, the vacationers and the townspeople both broaden and deepen the chasm between the pleasure of the spa's pastimes and the pain that underlies its frivolity. About this superficial pleasantness Gabriele Annan has observed

> The most shocking thing [in] this novel is not its satirical humor ... but its charm. Appelfeld manages to treat his appalling theme with grace. The atmosphere is not so much tragic as imbued with a Watteau-like melancholy. The characters emerge like Gilles from their bosky setting: funny, sad, helpless *commedia dell 'arte* figures, touching but not to be taken quite seriously. Diverse as they are, most of them share a general dottiness, an endearing Donald Duck irritability quickly melting into good nature and sentiment.[8]

Appelfeld leaves it to the reader to ferret out the truth behind the ever present "good nature and sentiment" and discover the true "meaning of the pattern." It is a pattern marked by ironic reversal. The charm and the elegance continue to be dominant even while those concomitants of civilized conduct are being consistently undermined, with the vacationers turned into hostages, their spa converted into a prison. The ironic reversal in *Badenheim 1939* is analogous to Joseph Heller's exploitation of the technique in *Catch-22*. In both novels, death and destruction are the supreme business of the day. The value system of Western civilization has been turned on its head, the blood-lust of those in power is overwhelming, and the few voices of sanity, Trude's in *Badenheim 1939* and Yossarian's in *Catch-22* are derided as crazy.

Though "good nature and sentiment" are paramount, the vacationers, running from their Jewish past, are capable of viciousness toward the increasing number of *Ostjuden* in their midst. As Sander Gilman has demonstrated convincingly in his *Jewish Self-Hatred*[9] an ethnic group will mirror its contempt for itself in its attitude and treatment of the inferiors in its midst. These inferiors are the central European Jews' poor country cousins, the *Ostjuden*, the less well-educated, still orthodox eastern European Jews who have moved to Austria seeking political asylum, religious freedom, and economic opportunity. The vacationers blame the rise of anti-Semitism not on the propaganda of the National Socialist Party whose agents have infiltrated the Sanitation Department, but on the *Ostjuden*, who are charged by their assimilated brethren with destabilizing the community. It is a classic case of scapegoatism.

Yet at the same time the acculturated Jewish aristocrats in Badenheim are castigating the *Ostjuden*, they are ironically being "rehabilitated" into an acceptance of Jewish Poland. The Nazis' propaganda paints Poland as the ultimate vacationers' paradise. These Austrian Jews can't wait to get there. As Dr. Pappenheim intones, "There's nothing to be afraid of.... There are many Jews in Poland. In the last analysis, a man has to return to his origins" (89). Some begin to study Yiddish, others gaze at the map and read travel brochures in anticipation of entering paradise. Without realizing it, they have become what they hate most. Again, the irony finds its expression in reversal. Bigots themselves, the vacationers are blind to the monumental bigotry that will prove their undoing. Pro-German, they believe anything the Germans recommend has to be better than what they have. The scapegoaters become the scapegoats, and they do so willingly. Ultimately, they are most blind to the impossibility that, as Christopher Lehmann-Haupt has pointed out, "any Jew could survive unscathed."[10]

The same evocation of mood, detachment, aesthetic distancing, the mild suspension of time and space, and the reverse irony that are at the heart of *Badenheim 1939* are similarly employed by Appelfeld in the second of his Holocaust novels, The *Age of Wonders* (Tor haplaot, Tel Aviv, 1978) published in the United States by David R. Godine in 1981, in a translation by Dalya Bilu. One finds also the same themes: Jewish self-hatred, blindness, arrogant self-centeredness, equations that reverse sanity and insanity, irresponsibility, misplaced blame, grim gaiety, and pleasure-seeking. To these are added, in this substantially longer work, disillusionment and bitterness. The doomsayers, whose role in *Badenheim 1939* was muted, are more vociferous here, but they are ignored and persecuted: in the most compelling scene of the novel, when the proud Jewish anti-Semites are rounded up and locked overnight in the darkened synagogue before being transported to the death camps, they attack not the Nazis who brought them there, but the aged rabbi whom they regard as the cause of their torments. It is another of Appelfeld's "great moments" when past, present, and future come together. Here the sinister, omnipresent evil, unnamed, malignant, and incarnate is all but nailed to the reader's forehead.

But where *Badenheim 1939* is a symbolic parable, a stylized dance of blind fools on their way to their deaths, *The Age of Wonders* is concrete in its particularization of the world's disintegration as seen through the eyes of a twelve-year-old Jewish boy. This is the first of three translated novels that attempt to answer a fundamental and recurrent question in Appelfeld's work: what happens when one puts a catastrophe of the magnitude of the Holo- caust on the shoulders of an individual, in this instance, a child? It was, of course, the central question for Appelfeld himself—one that he addresses in the interview—for it was his childhood of which he was robbed, and his has been a lifelong search to find the "meaning of the pattern" of that disaster.

As the novel opens in the first person, the as yet unnamed boy, speaking through the man he was to become, perceptively recalls the moment when his world went awry. He and his mother have spent the summer in the Austrian countryside, away from the child's father, an acculturated anti-Semitic Austrian Jewish writer, intoxicated with his fame and too busy to join in the family's vacation. Just before their departure from their idyllic summer sojourn, the child says

> It was only on the last day, with all the pleasantness stripped, the two
> rustic beds exposed, and our suitcases ready for the journey that Mother
> burst into bitter, soundless weeping. I had knelt beside her and foolishly

tried to wipe her tears away. I knew that new waters had come into the river, that we had been expelled, without anyone having to say, "Go." And all that simple splendor, consisting of no more than black bread, fresh milk, and apples in an old basket—all that simple splendor beside the nameless brook was gone forever. Mother wept and I didn't know what to say; in my embarrassment I had knelt beside her and wiped her tears away.[11]

The prescience of the boy, his awareness of a devastating change in their lives, is told with cool detachment and a modulated pace that differs remarkably from the heightened tension of the characters' increasingly anxious verbal pitches in *Badenheim 1939*. The boy's articulation of a problem he recognizes but whose ramifications remain veiled isn't stylized; in the straightforward manner of its presentation it cogently reminds us of the awful knowledge that children can be made to suffer unaccountably in a world where adults have gone mad and have abdicated their responsibility to others.

Perhaps the key to the pathos that permeates *The Age of Wonders* lies precisely in the fact that the boy starts out as narrator not merely of his own tragic destiny but by extension also of the tragic destiny of all Jewish Europe. The story, Kafkaesque in its symbolism despite its concrete meaning, is set before us with a matter of fact directness, even though at the outset we don't know how old the young speaker is, or even his name. The exact location of the town in which he lives is veiled; it is somewhere between Vienna and Prague. All that is really important is his tragic circumstance and, by implication, the approaching danger to his community. In time we learn that the child's name is Bruno K, a name one directly associates with Kafka's Joseph K. The boy's father, the famous pan-Germanic writer, is a weak, pompous, insensitive, opportunistic, bigoted egomaniac, convinced that his pro-Aryan stance in his books will save him from the increasing humiliations to which the Jews are being subjected. Though he has written about Jews and is accused by a rival of Jewish parasitism, he no longer considers himself Jewish, and he has only contempt for those who remain true to the faith. Reviling the *Ostjuden*, he says that ever since they arrived "things had gone haywire. They must have brought evil spirits with them"(24). His delusion is identical to that of the vacationers in Badenheim, and his fate is as predictable as theirs.

Bruno's mother is long-suffering, sensitive, strong in adversity, strict but warmhearted, preoccupied, a thoroughly assimilated Jewish woman who extends her maternal instincts to charitable works—unconsciously becoming Jewish again—on behalf of the beleaguered Jewish community about which she knows nothing. Her burdens are compounded. As the political and social pressures build, Bruno's father, for all his pan-Germanism, is exposed for not being pan-Germanic enough, and with his career and reputation toppling, he deserts his wife and child and moves to Vienna hoping to recoup his professional losses among the fashionable Viennese intellectuals in a futile attempt to start a liberal journal. The time for such pleasantries is long since past. His self-deception will never end until he goes mad and dies in Theresienstadt.

Much of the family's time is spent on trains. At first, they travel in first class luxury on holiday trips. As their fortunes decline, they travel in less opulent accommodations on more somber journeys. One trip is to a convent to bury Bruno's young aunt, who had converted to Christianity; another trip is to visit a young sculptor, a friend of the family, who has become a Jew again, and has had himself circumcised, outraging Bruno's father. The conversion of the young aunt, now dead, is heartily applauded; the young sculptor's "conversion" is emphatically condemned. Lying sick and impoverished in a medieval Jewish almshouse, the sculptor becomes in this novel the ill but sane Trude of *Badenheim 1939*. He is the healthy one; Bruno's father, his relatives and his friends are the sick ones. Still another train trip is made to seek the protection of the father's childhood friend, a powerful member of the Austrian nobility. The nobleman turns his back on Bruno's father, refusing even to acknowledge his presence at his gate. The motivation behind the nobleman's rejection is apparent to everyone except the father.

The family's decline is told in the move from happy, carefree train trips to miserable ones, a directional downturn that anticipates the final trip in the hellish transports that carried the European Jews to the death camps. Throughout Appelfeld's novels, trains are imaged as the harbingers and the vehicles of death. They are transformed into one of the most menacing symbols of the Holocaust era. Beyond their symbolic use, trains, and horse drawn carriages too, moving across seemingly endless, unfamiliar open terrain, frequently in the darkness of night, function in the displacement of reality. Rarely on schedule, meandering, shuttling between isolated way stations—the way stations also serve symbolically as suspended platforms from which the security of the past has dropped away—the trains are not so much the means of normal transportation as they are agents of psychological distortion, capable of generating fear and anxiety, of accelerating the aging process, of impressing upon their passengers that they are not run by friendly conductors but have come under the command of far-off sinister powers. The trains and the way stations mirror the chaos of a once ordered civilization now turned upside down.

Two years elapse between the time Bruno K and his mother take the train home from their summer holiday until they are forced to board the camp transport at daybreak following their internment the previous night with all the remaining Jews of their community in the synagogue. The synagogue scene constitutes, as we observed above, another of Appelfeld's "great moments":

> One after another people were thrown inside. Some were hurt and others were wearing dressing gowns. Two children carried satchels. . . . The light pouring from the dome made us small. But no one went and banged on the

door to get out. Their anger was directed against the people sitting in the front rows—as if they were to blame for the catastrophe.

"Where's the rabbi? Where's that criminal?" shouted someone.

. . . . .

The door was locked with a bang and we were prisoners in this temple in which we had never before set foot. . . . And among the bitter words we heard were some that were like nails driven into us and our private disaster. Someone knew that father had abandoned us to go and live with a baroness in Vienna. Someone even mentioned the baroness by name. Someone else added meaningfully, "Of course! It's all because of the degenerates. The decadent artists."

. . . . .

But these voices were only a distraction. The anger aginst the rabbi increased. There was no longer any doubt. Tonight judgment would be passed.

. . . . .

And when light broke through the skylights the rabbi was lying on the floor, panting and bleeding. . . . The silence of an aftermath gathered the people together on the floor . . . . The alien hall was filled with vapors from the people's mouths. Someone lit a cigarette and his hand shook like a prisoner's. A woman vomited.

. . . . .

By the next day we were on the cattle train hurtling south. (172-174)

The stark closing passages, from which the above lines are taken, meld the Jews' past, present, and future together and, in this moment held in suspension, souls are bared, all debts come due, good and evil are juxtaposed and life and death hang in the balance. With compassion and subtle irony, Appelfeld reminds us of another "great moment" in the long history of persecution, the crucifixion of Jesus, in the image of nails being driven into living flesh. This synagogue scene comes as close as Appelfeld ever gets to the horror of the Holocaust itself.

Appelfeld is careful always to stop short of the catastrophe awaiting Jewish transportees at the other end of the line. Book One comes to its end with the cattle cars "hurtling south" and Book Two, entitled "Many Years Later When Everything Was Over" opens twenty years later with Bruno (no longer Bruno K) again on a train, going from Vienna to his former hometown, Knospen (now named) returning for his first visit. We are told nothing about his camp experience or how he survived. We learn only that he eventually made his way to Palestine, settled in Jerusalem and married a woman who was the daughter of camp survivors. After three miscarriages, the marriage is slowly unraveling. Bruno has not lived, he has simply persevered.

His visit to Knospen is prompted by his need to come to terms with his traumatic past, more specifically to find, if possible, some reconcilation with his dead father through involvement in the possible republication of his writings. Little is changed in Knospen, the old anti-Semitism is still there along with the same houses and streets; and even the old Jewish anti-Semitism remains, personified in another survivor, Brum, who infuriates Bruno with his bigoted remarks. When he says, "My hatred for Jews knows no bounds" (268), Bruno hits him in the face and knocks him down. Remorseful over having resorted to violence, Bruno at least knows he has struck a blow against the worst kind of intolerance he knows, that of Jew against Jew. We last see him on the station platform waiting for the train that will carry him back to Vienna for his return to Israel and to his empty, unfulfilled life because, for him, "everything was over." It was over twenty years earlier when he entered the cattle car.

Why in *The Age of Wonders* did Appelfeld purposely choose not to relate Bruno's camp experiences? I think there are two basic reasons: because, foremost, his subject is not the Holocaust but the self-deception and bigotry that leads to persecution of one's own people; and secondarily, because the all-encompassing tragedy of the Holocaust is more amenable to elucidation as the subject of apocalyptic history and personal autobiography than as imaginative fiction. Eli Wiesel and Primo Levi demonstrated that the camp experience could be directly rendered into art, but it is an art that is more dependent on autobiographical reportage than on the imagination.

In a very perceptive review of *The Age of Wonders*, Gabriel Josipovici maintains that Appelfeld's choice of silence over elaboration is an effort toward the demythologization of the tragedy:

> Implicitly, the way this book is written is a condemnation of those authors, Jewish and Gentile, who, in the past few years, have made use of the events of 1940-45 for their own private purposes. Appelfeld's silence admonishes them—and us. Each man of course must sort it out with his own conscience; Appelfeld is at least clear that the real difficulty, human and artistic, is how both not to write and not to pass over in silence. For to write a story about these terrible events, however admirable one's motives, debases them; to use those events for mythological purposes, as so many novelists seem to do, is to go on playing the Nazi game. Appelfeld's is an exercise in demythologizing, a making clear of the roots of responsibility before the terrible choices history imposes on us, not as groups or nations, but as individuals.[12]

In the context in which this statement is made, Josipovici is not, I am convinced, condemning writers like Eli Wiesel and Primo Levi. I see nothing controversial in his observation. On the contrary, the point he is making is that through the limitations Appelfeld chose to impose upon himself, he moves from the particular representation of these marked individuals, the characters in his book, in their pre-Holocaust setting to a universal conclusion applicable to the Holocaust, that only by our individual actions can we create a world where such a monumentally destructive tragedy cannot happen.

In *The Age of Wonders*, then, Bruno K's ordeal in the camps is passed over. The gap recalls Virginia Woolf's famous interlude in *To The Lighthouse* where the World War I years are condensed and traversed in a dream-like fugue in which events, mainly tragic, are reported in brackets.[13] Woolf's protagonist, Mrs. Ramsey, dies, a daughter marries and dies from an illness connected to childbirth, a son is blown apart in France. When Woolf returns to the novel proper, her purpose is to link the remaining son, the young James, to his past, to give him the opportunity to complete the trip to the lighthouse that had been planned and subsequently postponed at the time he was six years old. The trip, of course, is symbolic. As he reaches the lighthouse the lives of the surviving Ramsey family members, along with that of their artist friend, Lily Briscoe, become complete. More importantly, James is reconciled once and for all with the father whom he had come to hate as a boy.

Appelfeld's purpose is much the same as Woolf's: to link Bruno K's post-Holocaust years to his past in pre-Holocaust Austria, thereby figuratively permitting him to resume his life from the point of its interruption. Equally important, the effort is undertaken as an attempt to effect a reconciliation with the image of the hated father. In *The Age of Wonders*, however, the symbolic return is doomed to failure, for the Holocaust has made impossible the normal resumption of Bruno's life and the potential restoration of the father-son relationship. This option, open to Woolf's James, is closed to Bruno K. The former moves toward fulfillment, the latter moves away from it. To emphasize Bruno's inevitable slippage toward oblivion, Appelfeld switches from the first person of the first book of the novel, where Bruno K is vital enough to tell his own story, to the third person in the second book, where he has become little more than a walking shadow.

The Age of Wonders was, in the main, well received by the critics on its appearance.[14] Coming out a year after *Badenheim 1939*, it confirmed the critics' judgment that the first novel heralded the recognition in the West of a major talent. In retrospect, it appears now that of Appelfeld's six Holocaust novels translated into English it is the most substantial, and it may well be the most enduring of Appelfeld's works that reconstruct his lost world. Josipovici sees the novel as marking the coming of age of postwar writing, "for it," he says, "has grasped and made palpable for us the relation of the great modernist tradition of Kierkegaard, Nietzsche, Proust, and Kafka to the crucial events of modern times, and it has done so not by being clever but by being wise, not by numbing us with images and ideas but by looking quietly and steadily at what is central to our lives."[15]

No doubt Josipovici is correct in emphasizing the wisdom and the vision of *The Age of Wonders* as it sets before us, in a modern context, the age-old

lesson of Cain and Abel. In a time when genocide has become a too frequently employed instrument of governments and individuals filled with
hatred of their own people, we need to be reminded more than ever before
that we are our brother's keepers. But not everyone will share Josipovici's view
that the book marks the maturation of the contemporary novel. Only the
passage of time will give us sufficient perspective to assign the proper value
to this work. For now, it is sufficient to observe that it is of singular importance in its contribution to the fiction of the Holocaust and in its establish-
ment of Appelfeld's reputation as a writer not only of novels that are tours de
force as *Badenheim 1939* was, but also ones of depth and profundity as well.
Appelfeld's modest expectations and quiet humility being what they are, his
satisfaction in the work may have consisted primarily in the opportunity it
gave him to recapture fictionally one stage of his own childhood experience,
despite the despair and loss that marked that childhood.

If *The Age of Wonders* answers with despair the question of what happens to a child caught up in the Holocaust, the novel that followed, *Tzili The
Story of a Life*, translated by Dalya Bilu, and published in New York by E. P.
Dutton in 1983, answers that question with a prospect of hope. It addresses
the problem of survival of the child outside the death camp but on the run,
living an anonymous existence. Because it is a fictionalized account, as the
discussion in the interview with Appelfeld confirms, of the author's own survival as a child in the forests after he escaped from the labor camp in which
he and his father were interned, the techniques Appelfeld had used with such
telling effect in his earlier novels, particularly evocation of mood, displacement in time, and reverse irony, are not in evidence here. The narrative is
straightforward, factual, and strikingly reminiscent, though not derivative, of
a number of Western writers. One technique employed earlier, detachment,
becomes Appelfeld's basic strategy for putting his material into proper focus
for the presentation of his tale.

That detachment, which is crucial to this novel, is accomplished immediately in two masterful ways. The first step Appelfeld takes is to have his narrator entirely efface himself in the opening paragraph:

> Perhaps it would be better to leave the story of Tzili Kraus's life untold. Her
> fate was a cruel and inglorious one, and but for the fact that it actually
> happened we would never have been able to tell her story. We will tell it in all
> simplicity, and begin right away by saying: Tzili was not an only child; she
> had older brothers and sisters. The family was large, poor, and harassed, and
> Tzili grew up neglected among the abandoned objects in the yard.[16]

From this point forward, the narrator's "we" disappears. Appelfeld's second
step separates his narrative from his own childhood experience by making
Tzili a girl rather than a boy. This simple change, which obscures but does

not obviate the autobiographical aspect, provides Appelfeld with an unusual degree of freedom to involve his protagonist in an entirely different set of experiences from those a young male would have. This change of the protagonist's sex is a master stroke; while it insures Appelfeld the narrative freedom he needs to describe Tzili's life independently of his own life, it still allows him to place her into those situations of vulnerability that would have been common to either sex.

Tzili is the dull-witted child in her lower middle-class minimally Jewish family, living in an unnamed eastern European village at the time of the German invasion. Her lot in life is to be neglected and abused. She is ridiculed at home and at school. She is reminiscent of the retarded Jewish girl in Isaac Bashevis Singer's *Shosha*, and she is also like his Gimpel the Fool in that she absorbs her punishment unflinchingly, keeping hold of her small mite of unquenchable faith. Accepting her lot, she does not even question her abandonment by her family as the Nazis approach. Living from hand to mouth, she blends her tiny self into the countryside, occasionally moving into a peasant household to perform domestic chores and absorb the constant beatings that are her due. By accident she assumes the identity of one of the illegitimate daughters of Maria, the region's most notorious prostitute, an identity that provokes beatings and makes her an outcast but saves her life by beclouding her Jewish identity. Never able to remain in any household for long, she learns to survive in the forest, to avoid being raped, to forage for food.

The seasons pass. Tzili reaches puberty. When she first menstruates, she believes she is going to die. When she doesn't die she takes control of her life to the extent possible, walking barefoot, sleeping in deserted barns and stables, bathing in icy streams, learning to distinguish between edible berries and poisonous ones. Autumn comes on with its rain, hail, and frost; Tzili is forced to seek shelter. She is taken in by Katerina, another prostitute and an old friend of Maria's, who befriends her in order to force her into prostitution. Tzili remains with her for nearly a year at the end of which time Katerina is ready to seek a return on her investment. When Tzili refuses to submit to the first peasant Katerina procures for her, Katerina throws a knife at her and Tzili runs away. Appelfeld's use of prostitutes in his novel is, of course, not accidental. He acknowledges in the interview that he lived with them, a child doing errands, and that they were important to his survival.

Up to this point the Jewish content of the novel is minimal. Tzili has learned that the Jews of her village have been trapped and killed, their homes looted by the peasants. Katerina speaks frequently of the many Jewish clients she had in her youth, of their generosity and good manners. Because she likes Jews there is some irony in Katerina's plan to exploit Tzili sexually, believing her only to be one of Maria's available daughters. Escaping from Katerina, Tzili returns to the forests during the warm seasons and seeks shelter in the winter with a farmer whose wife beats her mercilessly. When the spring thaws come, she strikes out again. She is fourteen and has learned much about life. In the woods she meets Mark, a forty year old Jewish escapee, mildly deranged and guilt-ridden for having abandoned his wife and children to the Nazis. He is sensitive, gentle, and kindly but filled with fear and self-loathing. Conscious of his Jewishness, Tzili becomes more aware of herself as a Jew. They remain together into the winter, surviving in a deep bunker Mark has built in the woods. Consumed finally by his guilt, Mark sets out to find his expiation at the hands of the murderous peasants. Tzili is pregnant with his child. Losing him, she also suffers the loss of her unborn child. As the war comes to an end, she identifies with and joins a group of Jewish refugees on their way to Zagreb. As they disperse, she finds her way onto a boat headed for Palestine. Unlike Bruno K in *The Age of Wonders*, the Holocaust has not killed her spirit. She has grown stronger and will survive to live, just as Appelfeld has done, rather than merely to exist as the shell of what once was a human being. Despite all that she has experienced, her humanity is still intact, and her identity as a Jew is now clear.[17]

Rochelle Furstenberg, in a commentary on *Tzili The Story of a Life*, describes Tzili as "a brilliant agent, a *tabula rasa* for recording this primal world to which man is returned as a consequence of the Nazi evil."[18] Once in the woods, Furstenberg observes, Tzili first leads an "animal existence," marked by her resumption of "the protective coloring" of her surroundings.[19] By the time she meets Mark she is ready to move from the stage of "primal nature" to the more advanced one of "home and family," going, after Mark's disappearance, "to the next stage of human connection, the community" when she joins the Jews on their way to Zagreb.[20] By progressing from the primal state in nature to the stage of social organization, Tzili moves away from the primitivism and barbarism to which the Nazis had reduced Europe, toward civilized order. Powerless and vulnerable, a simpleton, she has through her experiences gained a basic knowledge of the world, and in knowing how to respond to it, she endures.

With consummate skill, Appelfeld defines the power inherent in Tzili's absolute powerlessness. She attracts us compellingly, and though she is exasperatingly slow, uncouth, and simple, her helplessness tugs at us constantly. Aware at first of her weaknesses and of her limitations, we come to see eventually that some of these serve as strengths in her bid for survival. Determined to survive without knowing why, like any brute animal, she does so, as we have already observed, by merging with nature, the appreciation of which is a constant motif throughout the book. Though the winters can be harsh and threatening, nature is presented to us basically as a cleansing and restorative agent that affirmatively affects both body and spirit. Appelfeld's use of the nature motif is reminiscent of Henry Roth's use of it in *Call It Sleep* where Genya, after her father condemns and rejects her upon the discovery of her premarital affair with Ludwig, the non-Jewish church organist, finds solace and the will to live in the beauty of a field of cornflowers.

Part of Tzili's capacity for survival is in her ability to "parrot" and "ape" the manners of the peasants with whom she stays. She seems a younger image of Isaac Bashevis Singer's Magda in *The Magician of Lublin*. Neither is insensitive, nor are they smart, for cunning and wariness become substitutes for intelligence. Cerebral, then, Tzili is not, but she understands and responds to the needs of others directly and entirely through her feelings. Often silent and passive, she communicates eloquently through her emotions in much the same way Roth's little protagonist, David Scherl, does in *Call It Sleep*. In both works, as in Bruno K's situation, a child is victimized by an adult world that is marked by indiscriminate violence, and the protagonists, too young and incapable of apprehending the meaning of their situations through understanding and reason, grasp the meaning emotionally. It is only through their emotions that they can seek the means of dealing with their problems. David Scherl becomes a seeker after light in terms of Jewish mystical experience, Tzili finds her spiritual sustenance in nature. Through mysticism and nature both of these children escape the fate of Jerzy Kosinski's child-martyr who is subjected to horrible brutalities by peasants in *The Painted Bird*.

As Patricia Blake has pointed out, Kosinski's "martyred child survives with nothing but rage and revenge."[21] But Tzili has no need to hurl her anger at the past. Contrary to the view expressed here that Tzili's story is at least minimally positive, Blake maintains that it is basically pessimistic: "One seeks in vain for some faint sign of hope in Appelfeld's enigmatic parable. Redemption through suffering? Renewal or rebirth? Tzili's baby dies in her womb."[22] Though terrible things happen to Tzili, one is inclined to accept more readily Joyce Carol Oates's view that "This is fiction in the service of a stern and highly moral vision, in which details yield to a larger design and individuals participate in a historical tapestry they cannot comprehend."[23] Aware that this is Appelfeld's story transformed into fiction, a story of transcendance over a tortured past, the "highly moral vision" of which Oates speaks is, I submit, more to be associated with hope than with hopelessness.

One of the novel's major attractions is its sheer allusiveness, recalling, in addition to Singer, Kosinski, and Roth, Ernest Hemingway's pantheistic adoration of nature and his insistence on its cleansing and restorative power. Yet, Appelfeld's work is not derivative, rather, it has a universality that makes inevitable these comparisons with other accomplished Western writers.

The Retreat, Appelfeld's fourth novel to be translated by Dalya Bilu, was published by E. P. Dutton in the United States in 1984. It returns to the pre-Holocaust Austria of *Badenheim, 1939* and *The Age of Wonders*. Here we encounter another group of assimilated Jews, pan-Germanic, self-hating, shopkeepers and housewives among them, all sharing two traits: a malaise originating in their self-hatred and a propensity for failure. The malaise perpetuates itself in a vicious cycle: hating themselves as Jews, they seek to become more assimilated; yet the more assimilated they become, the more they hate themselves because it intensifies the awareness of Jewishness. The fact that they have also failed to find fulfillment in the normal pursuits of life, in their careers and marriages, compounds their losses and deepens the malaise. They seek a cure for their sickness at a retreat not far from Vienna.

The retreat is a mountain lodge operated by Balaban, a Polish Jewish horse trader much into the out-of-doors life of European peasantry. While its regimen emphasizes the sports of the gentiles, horseback riding and hunting among others, the clientele is reminiscent of the residents of the sanitarium in Thomas Mann's *The Magic Mountain*. The lodge is intended to restore to good health those "sick" Jews who find their way to it, mainly middle-aged men and women who have either given up on life or been dismissed from it. Behind them they have collectively left a trail of broken dreams; ahead of them they deceptively anticipate that they will restore meaning and order to their lives by following a regimen designed to cure them of a disease not unlike the tuberculosis of Mann's novel in its psycho-pathology. Their "disease" is, as Michael F. Harper puts it, "rooted not in biology but in ideology"[24] and therefore one that is incurable unless they change their ideas about being Jewish. This they are not about to do. They see being Jewish as a malignancy and as a deformity. Though they are mobile and functioning, they regard themselves as convalescents. They are the vacationers of *Badenheim 1939* one step further into desperation and malaise, their domain a sanitarium instead of a spa. Badenheim was located on a plain, this retreat is high up on a mountain; the convalescents delude themselves into thinking that by ascending into the mountains they can escape the evil of the plains below.

Proust's Swann in *Remembrance of Things Past* also retreated into a sanitarium, but unlike Appelfeld's characters, he realized that he had to live his life on the plains of Sodom and Gommorah below. Like Proust, Appelfeld does not allow his characters to maintain the illusion that they can escape through ascension. It is no guarantor of purification. In *The Retreat* the evil of the plains is simply transferred to the mountain hideaway.

The regimen these convalescents follow is mimicry of the gentiles. These bourgeois Jews take instruction in imitating the behavior of rustic Austrian peasants, for the peasants are lower down the social scale than the Jews' bourgeois non-Jewish counterparts in the Austrian middle class and therefore more attractive as "goyish" models. Lotte Schloss, the central figure of the book, a failed actress; Herbert Zuntz, a forgotten journalist who was once a student and follower of Karl Kraus; Isadora Rotenberg, a spoiled aristocrat; and Betty Schlang, a frustrated divorcee, among others, persevere in the belief that assimilation is within their grasp and that the successful resumption of their lives on the plains below will follow naturally; but we know that their project is foredoomed. Bruno Rauch, a long-time resident of the lodge explains the premises behind the convalescents' thinking to Lotte shortly after her arrival.

He still remembered the retreat in the good old days, the bracing, disciplined days when they got up early and went to bed early, ate peasant bread and yogurt for breakfast and worked on their accents.

"Do you miss those days?" asked Lotte.

"Of course. They were great days, days of the reform of body and soul. But how could I possibly forget them."

"But they weren't easy, I think."

"Indeed they weren't. But they were days with a purpose. Once a man realizes that his body is weak and ugly, his nerves destroyed, his soul corrupt, that he bears within him a decayed inheritance, in short, that he is sick and, what is worse, that he is passing his sickness on to his children, what can he desire more deeply than reform."[25]

Rauch goes on to explain that the regimen he has followed has cured him of his weak nerves, a defect of Jewish origin, improved his posture, which makes him feel taller, and straightened his back. He has ascertained that Jews suffer from "two hundred defects" (104) and that they are mice and rats. "Not for nothing," he tells Lotte, "does the world regard them as animals of the rodent species," adding, "I myself, madam, what was I all those years but a rodent?" (104-105)

This vicious self-deception gives to Appelfeld's narrative the same formidable and relentless irony we observed previously at work in *Badenheim 1939* and *The Age of Wonders*. The more these people strive for assimilation as the story progresses, the harder their lives become, and the harder their lives become the more they are forced to rely upon and console one another. The irony is doubled here by the circumstance of the Nazi takeover of Austria. Before its residents' eyes, the mountain lodge turns into a retreat of a different kind. It becomes a besieged ghetto under assault from the common enemies of the plains, the Austrian peasants whose lives they want to "emulate." As the novel comes to its close, we see the inmates moving toward the humanization they had sought to eliminate from their lives. Herbert Zuntz makes a daily trip down to the village for supplies. As the anti-Semitic noose tightens,

Herbert now returned from the village beaten and wounded. Ruffians fell on him and beat him up. His appearance toward evening was excruciating in its silence. Betty tended his wounds with wet compresses.

The pain was cruel, the shame terrible, but Herbert got up every morning and went to endure his suffering. The provisions he brought back were scant, but nevertheless their meager meals were eaten in tranquillity. Later, they began to take turns, and Rauch and Lauffer would go down in his place. They too were beaten and their wounds were bandaged by Betty. The world seemed to be narrowing down to its simplest dimensions: breakfast, supper . . . . Sins were not pardoned, sentences were not commuted, but no one threw them in the face of his fellows . . . . At night, of course, people were afraid. But they helped one another. If a man fell or was beaten he was not abandoned. (163-164)

Instead of succeeding in their efforts to achieve assimilation, thereby distancing themselves from each other as Jews, the inmates, as they are aptly
termed, are forced to become more Jewish. Unknowingly, they reconfirm their
Jewishness through their acts of compassion and charity and their sense of
sharing a common fate.

The "stern and moral vision" which Joyce Carol Oates ascribed to *Tzili
The Story of a Life* is more pronounced in *The Retreat* than in any of the
novels preceding it. It is part and parcel of "the meaning of the pattern" of
Appelfeld's fiction. That is not to say that he is into conscious moralizing, for
his real purpose has been to reconstruct the lost society from which he came;
but it was a society losing touch with the humane principles that once
understructured the Jewish view of human relations it now sought to deny.
To convey his point of view, Appelfeld uses the now familiar reverse irony of
the earlier books, but as if that were not sufficient, he iterates increasingly
toward the end of this narrative the importance of self-sacrifice: the willingness of Zuntz, Rauch, and Lauffer to risk their lives to obtain food, the compassion displayed when they come back assaulted, and the universal sharing
in the common predicament. While Appelfeld maintains the same aesthetic
distance that marked the first novels that were translated into English, the
detachment is less obvious. The comic dimension of *Badenheim 1939* is
entirely gone from *The Retreat*. Instead, there is a need to capture an intense
moment of Kafkaesque *angst*, and to preserve it as a photographer would,
through the graphic clarity, the penetrating vision and the power of the cam-
era's eye, with an urgency that commands the reader to reflect upon its significance in perpetuity.

The reaction of the critics to *The Retreat* was mixed. For example, Walter
Goodman maintains that Appelfeld's "powerful vision . . . only flickers" in the
novel and that in the translation the book becomes a shop of second-hand
phrases."[26] Vivian Gornick says that *The Retreat* "provides neither textured
description nor interesting ideas nor even a serious working-out of the allegorical implication," going on to insinuate that the novel fails because "Jewish identity as such—Jewish outsidedness, Jewish crucifixion—can no longer
command the existential attention it commanded after the Second World
War."[27] The continued, indeed, growing interest in all forms of Holocaust
literature, and, particularly, in the imaginative portrayals of Jewish life crushed
by the Nazi heel, is evidence enough, I think to refute Gornick's contention.
The presence in *The Retreat* of Appelfeld's implicit moral imperative implores
all civilized peoples to remember the existential condition of the Jews in
order to banish genocide—something the human family has not been able to
do since World War II—for all time.

More positively, Michael F. Harper credits Appelfeld with having written
a narrative that "is a cool, unsparing yet compassionate critique of 'assimilation' ", its power residing in the author's "incisive depiction of the effects of

discrimination on the consciousness of its victims, and in his dissection of an ideology riddled with paradox and contradiction but nonetheless devastatingly effective."[28] Jakov Lind sees the novel as "a small masterpiece, the vision of a remarkable poet on a passage of our contemporary history, given in an unassuming little volume of elegant prose."[29] Whatever the critic's or the individual's response to *The Retreat*, we should bear in mind Appelfeld's compelling need, related in the interview here, to tell his stories about assimilated Jews: "They were my background. I belonged to them and I want to understand them." In his effort to understand the members of this particular segment of Jewry and to reconstruct their lives, we are all enriched.

Two years after the appearance of *The Retreat*, Appelfeld's *To The Land Of The Cattails* was published in New York by Weidenfeld & Nicholson in a translation by Jeffrey M. Green. It is the story of a beautiful 34 year old Jewish woman, Toni, assimilated and made financially comfortable by a legacy left by a departed lover, and her adolescent son, Rudi, the offspring of Toni's three-year marriage to a non-Jewish musician with whom she eloped when she was seventeen. The year is 1938, the summer following the Nazi Anschluss of Austria, a political event Appelfeld does not mention. Robert Alter observes that in removing his material from "historical actuality" Appelfeld is able to achieve "a sense of the bizarre, the inscrutable."[30] In order to make peace with her estranged parents and herself, and in a need to reassert her Jewish identity, Toni takes the boy, who is reluctant, argumentative, and totally ambivalent about his Jewishness, by train and horsecart eastward from Vienna through Ruthenia to the Bukovinian *shtetl* of her youth.

The trip begins in urban sophistication and progressively moves downward through rural coarseness toward faceless anonymity. It starts as a conscious fantasy, turns into a dream and then into a nightmare as the couple travels to the land of the cattails, oblivious of the fact that in both time and space they are headed toward the great gaping jaws of the Holocaust. Since they are totally absorbed in themselves and in their ambivalent relationship with each other, the reader must carry the burden of their flight toward death. The resulting irony is both wry and tragic, enveloped in suspense. The time and space configurations are those of the dream, of relativity, for the seemingly short trip takes an inordinately long time, during which Rudi matures chronologically but not emotionally. As they approach their destination mother and son are separated from each other and the novel comes to its close with Toni and her parents—we never see their reunion—swallowed up in the maelstrom while Rudi, unaware of the gravity of his situation, sits on a way station platform with a thirteen year old Jewish girl waiting for a train to take them to an unknown destination.

Because this narrative is discussed in the interview—its publication coincided with the author's visit to New Orleans—I will say little about it here, other than to emphasize that it employs the same techniques we have seen

Appelfeld use effectively in his other novels, principally tragic irony and displacement in time, and that it explores further the question of what happens
to a young person when a burden of the proportions of the Holocaust is laid
upon his shoulders. Rudi is not conditioned for survival as Tzili was. Half
gentile, he is a curious mixture of Jewish sensitivity and the peasant's brutish
violence. This allows Appelfeld to bring into play an entirely different set of
experiences, all of them designed to diminish Rudi and bring him progressively
to the brink of his destruction, a brink Tzili begins with and then distances
herself from in order to survive. *To The Land Of The Cattails* and *Tzili The
Story of a Life* complement one another in the way that mirrors facing each
other produce obverse images of the objects between them. Tzili and Rudi
represent the obverse optional directions in which Appelfeld's life might have
gone during his youth. But beyond any private fictional speculation, Appelfeld's
full attention is on the tragedy of Rudi's approaching demise. He apportions
life to Tzili and death to Rudi, but Rudi's end is, at least, not without redemption. Patrick Parrinder acknowledges Appelfeld's need to find and memorialize the true meaning of Rudi's life and death:

> Like Toni's familiar grumbling refrain, "A person is not an insect," everything
> in *To the Land of the Reeds* [the British title] points to one end, which is
> extermination. The beauty and pathos of the final sequence, in which Rudi
> gives in to his destiny and voluntarily joins the other deportees quietly wait-
> ing at the train station, invokes one of the appalling paradoxes of Holocaust
> literature. Here the persecution and defeat of the body are seen as stages in
> the renunciation of self and the purification of the spirit."[31]

All deaths are grievous, but particularly so the deaths of young people arbitrarily deprived of the chance for fulfillment and happiness. But the collective horror of the Holocaust arbitrarily deprived of fulfillment those whose
lives it spared just as it did those it executed. We observed earlier that Bruno
in *The Age of Wonders* was little more than a walking shadow; his life held no
meaning after his camp experience. For Bartfuss, the protagonist of Appelfeld's
The Immortal Bartfuss, translated by Jeffrey M. Green and published in New
York in 1988 by Weidenfeld & Nicholson, life also seems devoid of meaning
in terms of fulfillment, love, family, home and hearth, justice, mercy, dignity,
and peace of mind. It is the absence of these essences of fulfillment that
makes Bartfuss "immortal." His immortality has nothing to do with the belief
that "There are fifty bullets in his body,"[32] or that he will live forever, but with
the realization that he is existing in this life, alive, as though he were already
dead. His actions are those of the living, but they are filled with the substance
of the dead, of shadows, of ghosts, of gestures trapped below the threshhold
of conception, of the emptiness of T.S. Eliot's "hollow men."

But Bartfuss is Appelfeld's hollow man, not Eliot's character, whose
hollowness is a metaphor for the emptiness of life in the present as a result of

Western civilization's voluntary dissociation from the spiritual values of its past. Appelfeld's "hollow" man has an empty existence because he *couldn't* dissociate himself from the spiritual values of his past, even when, as we have seen with most of the author's assimilated protagonists, they had rendered those values meaningless and despicable. Confronted with a disaster as great as the Holocaust while possessed only of an unwanted spiritual heritage, the Jews who survived the death camps were doubly vulnerable to emptiness. Divested of their past and robbed of their present at the time of internment, they emerged deprived of a future.

Of course, Bartfuss goes through the motions of the living. The motions are trivial or are trivialized: he smokes endless cigarettes, drinks endless cups of coffee, loiters in dirty resturants, walks all over Jaffa, takes aimless bus trips to the outskirts, accepts in silence the hostility of his all but estranged wife and two daughters, occasionally indulges in casual sex, gloats over his cunning in keeping his money hidden from his wife, and looks for ways to befriend his retarded daughter, Bridget, though in this effort he is usually thwarted. Having sworn himself to silence during his days of smuggling and racketeering in Italy after being released from the concentration camp and before coming to Palestine, he further constricts the possibilities of communication so that while he has acquaintances he has no friends.

Bartfuss remains uninformed about the meaning of his life as a survivor. On one occasion he makes a halfhearted effort to explore that meaning. He attends the funeral of a woman named Sylvia, his lover many years earlier when they were still in Italy, and afterward he sits in a cafe talking to Sylvia's ex-husband. The conversation is composed largely of irrelevancies. Among them is this exchange. Bartfuss says,

> "What have we Holocaust survivors done? Has our great experience changed us at all?"
> "What can you do?" The man opened his round eyes.
> Bartfuss was surprised by that question and said, "I expect generosity of them."
> "I don't understand you."
> "I expect"—Bartfuss raised his voice—"greatness of soul from people who underwent the Holocaust."
> The man lowered his head, and on his lips was a skeptical smile of hidden wisdom.
> "I don't understand 'generosity'?"
> The man rose to his feet, and with an arrogant movement he turned away, as though offering his place to someone. The short movement silenced Bartfuss. (p. 107)

Stingy with his wife, Bartfuss follows his principle of generosity by offering sums of money to other survivors whom he knew in the old days, now down on their luck. But the Holocaust has taken away his compassion. He forces his gifts on people without a rationale for giving and resorts to violence to make people accept his gifts. What he doesn't understand is that in place of generosity, of *Tsedakah*, he has substituted authority and humiliation, degrading these survivors just as the Germans did. Needing the money, they still have no alternative under the circumstances but to reject both it and him. Lacking "greatness of soul," his good intentions and the responses to them become hyperbolically distorted. The meaning of Bartfuss' life lies collapsed underneath this frenzied, crazy-quilted pattern.

At the time *The Immortal Bartfuss* was published, Philip Roth in an interview with Appelfeld asked him the same question Bartfuss asked Sylvia's ex-husband: "What have the Holocaust survivors done and in what ways were they ineluctably changed?"[33] Appelfeld replied that he had tried to answer that question in *The Immortal Bartfuss*, adding that "The Holocaust belongs to the type of enormous experience which reduces one to silence. Any utterance, any statement, any 'answer' is tiny, meaningless and occasionally ridiculous. Even the greatest of answers seem petty." He then offered two examples and a concluding statement, which, because of their relevance and insight into the fundamental question underlying the novel, deserve to be fully quoted here:

> The first [example] is Zionism. Without doubt life in Israel gives the survivors not only a place of refuge but also a feeling that the entire world is not evil. Though the tree has been chopped down, the root has not withered—despite everything we continue living. Yet that satisfaction cannot take away the survivor's feeling that he or she must do something with this life that was saved. The survivors have undergone experiences that no one else has undergone, and others expect some message from them, some key to understanding the human world—a human example. But they, of course, cannot begin to fulfill the great tasks imposed upon them, so theirs are clandestine lives of flight and hiding. The trouble is that no more hiding places are available. One has a feeling of guilt that grows from year to year and becomes, as in Kafka, an accusation. The wound is too deep and bandages won't help. Not even a bandage such as the Jewish state.
>
> The second example is the religious stance. Paradoxically, as a gesture toward their murdered parents, not a few survivors have adopted religious faith. I know what inner struggles that paradoxical stance entails, and I respect it. But that stance is born of despair. I won't deny the truth of despair. But it's a suffocating position, a kind of Jewish monasticism and indirect self-punishment. My book offers its survivors neither Zionist nor religious consolation. The survivor, Bartfuss, has swallowed the Holocaust whole, and he walks about with it in all his limbs. He drinks the "black milk" of the poet Paul Celan, morning, noon and night. He has no advantage over anyone else, but he still hasn't lost his human face. That isn't a great deal, but it's something.[34]

Appelfeld's statement emphasizes the peculiar conditions that impose their limitations on the survivors, limitations Appelfeld accepts and respects in his effort to render precisely the meaning of what it is to be a survivor. If we expect anything more of Bartfuss, or from Appelfeld, for that matter, we should know that there isn't anything more to be had.

What we should appreciate finally in respect to Appelfeld's Holocaust novels is his remarkable achievement in combining wisdom and insight with a substantial range of lyrical and narrative talents and strategies to reconstruct powerfully the lost world of his youth. In that reconstruction and in his depiction of the lives of the survivors of that world, tortured in the fire and flame of the Holocaust, he has uncovered what Durrell's Darley called "the cloth-of-gold" to expose "the meaning of the pattern" of his experience. In articulating it, he has given us a memorial to the fallen Jews of Europe, both the pious ones and the irreverent ones, and has opened windows of universal significance on the human condition in some of its darkest hours.

Interview 4   Aharon Appelfeld

September 25, 1986

JC: How did you survive in the forest when you were only eight years old?

AA: After escaping from the labor camp I wandered from place to place. I was lucky because my features were not Jewish. The peasants were hostile, even the decent ones would not accept a Jewish child. So I lived with prostitutes and horse thieves. They took care of me. I would take the horses to the pasture to feed. If I was with a prostitute I would run errands, and bring supplies, bread, vodka. She would allow me to sleep in the house.

JC: How long did you live that way?

AA: I was with these people from 1941 to 1944. In 1944 the Russians liberated the Ukraine, and I joined their army as a kitchen boy. They protected me, they loved me, and I stayed with the army for two years as it moved from the Ukraine across country to Yugoslavia. I went to Italy after the war where I was picked up by the Jewish Brigade and brought to Palestine.

JC: The settings of your novels are mainly in central Europe before the War, and you seem to be more closely identified with the Jews of Austria and the German language that they used than with the East European Jews and Yiddish. What was your background?

AA: I came from a very assimilated Jewish family, with a lot of mixed marriages. German was my mother language because Bukovina where I was born was then part of the Austro-Hungarian Empire. My grandparents still spoke Yiddish, but at home we used German. My parents cultivated it deeply, but after what happened, I was always ambivalent about it. As a child I had no formal schooling. After I came to Israel, Hebrew became my mother language, and I studied Yiddish to avoid German. I know it now, but I am still ambivalent. On one side I have an affinity for it, on the other side, I have a complex about it.

JC: Paradoxes and ambivalences of that kind are not uncommon among Holocaust and war survivors. Then there was the move to Israel. How did you accommodate all the changes?

AA: Coming to Israel was lucky for me. When I first arrived I was disoriented, not knowing exactly what had happened to me. I went as a child through much confusion. There were many questions: Why was I in Israel? What does it mean to me? What happened to me? What happened to my life? These were questions I could not answer. I was under considerable psychological pressure in not understanding the meaning of all that had happened to me. It would take me years to elaborate it. After I finished my first tour of army duty, I met a group of Jewish intellectuals who had escaped from Germany, from central Europe, Buber, Max Brod, Gershom Scholem—I studied under Buber and Scholem at Hebrew University—and these people gave me my first real schooling. These people were from my parents' background, and they had experienced the Second World War directly. Being around them helped me to understand my own life. A number of them had been friends of Kafka, and in time Kafka's works came to be enormously important to me.

JC: How did Buber influence your life?

AA: What Buber did for the German Jews he also did for the Israelis. He gave us a new perspective for today. Coming, as I did, from a very assimilated home, my early view of Judaism reflected all the old antagonisms. But suddenly Buber and Scholem opened new gates for me. It was a new life. All the good things that we had been lead to believe existed only in Socialism and in Marxism, and in Communism, too, we found to exist in our own tradition and at a more refined, civilized level. I came to realize that Judaism was not an archaic, primitive religion but a living religion of the highest level. It brought me back to myself and to my people.

JC: Yet most of the Jews in your novels translated into English are highly assimilated. Your characters are primarily central European Jews, middle-class Austrians whose lives are so assimilated most of them couldn't possibly find their way back to Judaism. A lot of them are headed toward more assimilation. In *The Retreat,* for example, the Jews believe that total assimilation is their only salvation. How is it that the majority of your Jews seem to endorse assimilation?

AA: I've published ten novels and five collections of short stories in Hebrew plus a volume of essays. There are many other manuscripts in progress. The five novels translated and published in America thus far happen to deal with assimilated Jews. They were my background. I belonged to them and I want to understand them. I have to be precise about them and not make them saints or super-Jews, I have to portray them as they were. But they are not my only Jewish subjects. Other novels yet untranslated, and some still unpublished, concern the lives of the orphans who settled after the war in Israel. I am also working on stories of Jewish life in eastern Europe sixty or seventy years ago. And I have done three novels on the lives of Jews living in the Middle Ages. My intention is to write about Jewish life in all of its manifestations. I have been preparing myself for years to do this. My preparation was twofold. On one side I studied Yiddish, Hebrew, and Aramaic, and the works of all the Jewish socialists. It took years to cover this ground, and I feel fortunate that I got to do it. In time, I read the Hebrew writers, Brenner, Agnon and others. On the other side, I learned from the German-Jewish writers, Kafka and Brod. I have been a student both of the German-Jewish tradition and the Jewish tradition. Now, I try to combine both of these traditions. I can relate to Kafka from both approaches. Kafka in his last years felt intuitively that he belonged to the Jews and that there was something very special in Jewish life. He studied Hebrew. Even when he was taken ill in Berlin he attended Jewish studies. His background, like mine, was very assimilated, but Judaism came to be extremely important to him. I feel the same way. Yet, there is a very big difference between us. Kafka didn't go through the Holocaust. I did, so I've had to deal with that experience first.

JC: Do you know Canetti's work?

AA: Of course, I'm familiar with Canetti. He belongs to my "family." I don't know why he isn't better known. To me, he is the most universal writer among the Jews who were in central Europe before the Holocaust.

JC: Are you moving in the same direction as Canetti, that is, a universal one or a more particular one?

AA: That's a question for others to answer. I want to understand what it means to be Jewish in Western civilization. I want to get to the heart of the phenomenon. I want to explore the kinds of roles Jews have played. That is why I have so many manuscripts in progress.

JC: Up until recently, Elie Wiesel's books seemed to have a monopoly on the subject of the Holocaust. With the translations of Primo Levi's novels and your novels that monopolization of the Holocaust has disappeared. How does your approach to writing about the Holocaust differ, say, from Elie Wiesel's approach?

AA: My approach to writing about the Holocaust is to explore its meaning through individuals. The question I have to confront is how to put a catastrophe of that magnitude on the shoulders of an individual.

JC: I've had the feeling in reading your novels that you were in fact reliving the tragedy of your family. Am I correct in believing that Tzili in *Tzili: The Story Of A Life,* though she is a girl, is really you yourself in your years in the forests?

AA: Yes. Tzili's problem was my problem. As a writer I wanted to examine the question of what it means to put a catastrophe of such proportions on the shoulders of a small child. In the same sense, I am speaking about myself in my newly translated novel *To The Land Of The Cattails.* Though it is a fictionalized account, I wanted to find out what it means for a Jew to return to his family's home in the midst of chaos. These people are saying "finally we are going home!" "wonderful to go home." But under the circumstances they have to ask, "Why are we going home?" observing that "it is not a home" or at best "a terrible one." And they learn, as your American writer Thomas Wolfe said, "you can't go home again."

JC: One can't go back into the past and recapture it.

AA: There is a deep human longing to do that, to go back and meet one's parents. That need to return and the effort made to return provided me with one of the psychological attitudes I wanted to examine in the novel. Part of the tension I wanted to generate grows out of the different attitudes Toni, the mother, and Rudi, the son, have about this meaning of the trip. Toni has to go back, Rudi resists it.

JC: Of course, there is a generational difference that gives Toni a sense of the past that Rudi knows only as foreboding. On the long trip home, both of them are totally absorbed in their individual problems and in their ambivalent feelings toward one another. Toni has to deal endlessly with her enormous guilt over having married Rudi's father out of the faith. To Rudi, her guilt is a bore. His energies are channeled into fueling his rebellious feelings against being forced to confront his Jewish heritage that is alien and uncomfortable for him. There is a wonderfully muted tragic irony that develops as the novel progresses. Toni and Rudi remain completely preoccupied with the vicissitudes of the trip, engrossed in their personal concerns and filled with various future expectations, yet the reader knows that in both time and space the two of them are traveling to their deaths in the Holocaust. That tragic irony provides us with a different dimension of insight into the horror of the Holocaust. I think that dimension functions effectively through your handling in the novel of time and space. The journey goes on and on and there are delays. One would think that going from Austria across Poland into the Ukraine even by horse and carriage would not take an infinite amount of time, and yet there is a sense of the infinite. Did the time sequences pose any problems for you?

AA: Yes, of course, because I wanted to emphasize not outer time but inner time. By the time Toni and Rudi got to the land of the cattails, to their home, they were not the same people. They were changed by their experiences on the road. The most profound changes were internal ones. Toni had had time to reflect on her life and what she had done with it. Her story becomes an inner account, not a confession, but an interiorized entity.

JC: That is to say that the inner time of which you speak has nothing to do with linear or chronological time.

AA: Exactly. Through the use of this suspended time, the nostalgia about going home becomes more poignant.

JC: And that sense of suspension and suspense is what gives substance to the tragic irony. A few minutes ago, you observed that both *Tzili* and *To The Land Of The Cattails* explored the question of the impact of the Holocaust on youngsters. Tzili and Rudi must both deal with it. Tzili survives, but Rudi, we know, won't. What was your purpose in diametrically opposing the outcome for these two characters?

AA: As you know, my works have come out of my deepest personal experiences. I never knew from day to day whether I would live or die. It could have gone one way as easily as the other. Rudi's experience is therefore as real to me as Tzili's experience. But he wasn't a survivor. He would not have been among those Jewish orphans who came to Israel after the war, and about whom I've written a novel not yet translated into English. It deals with their confrontations with the sunlight, the sand, their bodies and their memories, and what their experience in Israel does to them.

JC: You're mentioning the sand prompts me to observe that desert psychology has a prominent role in Israeli literature. In some of Amichai's poems and in Oz's *A Perfect Peace,* for example, the desert seems to impose itself on the protagonist's actions. Frequently, a character will go into the desert to find himself. Yonatan does this in *A Perfect Peace.* It is all very biblical. Has the desert infiltrated your work, too?

AA: It's there and it is a presence; however, it is not so much the desert that has had an impact on me as Israel itself. What Israel did for me is a miracle. It made me a free person. Psychologically free. I cannot imagine myself living, for example, in England or even in America and speaking so freely about my life.

JC: Why?

AA: Because when I came to Israel as a child, I was crippled with fear. In Europe during the Holocaust, all the world, all the people in it, became enemies. The Germans. Objects, too. The table, the trees, the grass. And then suddenly, I was among Jews, around people who received me warmly as a person, and later as an author. Israel gave me total freedom, freedom of every surrounding in which I found myself. Many people of my generation came to Israel, as visitors, as survivors. In Israel they became human beings again. Like them, I, too, became human. In Israel, they could speak freely about the past or the future.

JC: I take it you are talking about something that goes beyond ordinary experiences, ordinary freedom. Is it, perhaps, something unique?

AA: Yes, it is an openness to understand all phenomena. I want to emphasize that even though my roots were in central Europe, I was never a German writer. And I am not an Israeli writer in the sense of seeing all the world from an Israeli perspective. This openness is Jewish, and possessing it, I am, foremost, a Jewish writer.

JC: Are you suggesting that Jewish experience is central and universal?

AA: I think that the Jewish experience in the twentieth century is in all its manifestations, probably the deepest experience that human beings have had. I don't mean only the Holocaust. I am talking about all Jewish experience, religious, secularized, socialist, anarchic, liberal, nationalist. All the travels, all the illnesses, all the devotion. The range of this experience is a wonderful thing. It is what makes me so happy to be a Jew.

JC: I suspect it was not just Israel's gift to you. More likely, you earned it. In how many wars have you served?

AA: All of them.

JC: All?

AA: Yes. I was only sixteen when I was first mobilized. After the War of Independence I saw service in the Sinai Campaign, the Six Day War and the Yom Kippur War.

JC: In terms of your childhood experience in war torn Europe, did you have any ambivalent feeling over again being caught up in the throes of war?

AA: No, though war is always an unpleasant business. At first, I was in the infantry. By the time I was forty years old, I had become an officer in charge of culture. My assignment was to teach Jewish soldiers various subjects including Jewish philosophy, Jewish history, Jewish literature, even Jewish Mysticism. The army units were out in the desert. To give a lecture on Maimonides to troops out in the desert who are about to go into combat is a very moving experience.

JC: I don't think you would find that in any other army in the world.

AA: The questions the boys ask are good questions, challenging. And for years I have tried to answer them.

JC: Your positive feelings for Israel and all it means to you come through strongly. There is still a lot of trouble in the region. What do you think the prospects for peace are?

AA: There are ups and downs, of course, and these will continue, but there is peace with Egypt, the largest Arab country and the most cultivated one. Would anyone have said eight or ten years ago that there would be a peace with Egypt? We have peace with Egypt, we have done it. And I am sure the same thing will happen with Jordan. I am an optimistic person.

JC: What about Syria?

AA: Syria is problematical for us because there is in Syria an accumulation of fanatic elements and a buildup of Russian support. But I cannot see why we can't have peace. There is no reason why not. There is enough stone, sand, clay, and sun for all of us. Certainly, one can't ever be a prophet. We have a talmudic saying, that after the destruction of the temple all prophets are idiots. Still, we can hope. When you are in Jerusalem you will see Jews and Arabs living together; in Haifa, you see them walking in the streets together.

JC: The birthrate of the Arabs is higher than that of the Jews. Are you concerned that in time Israel could become an Arab state?

AA: Of course, it's a concern of mine. Israel need not become an Arab state, and the Jews should not dominate other people. They should rule themselves. As far as the occupied territories are concerned, we have to reach a fair compromise. The populated parts of the occupied territories should go to the Arabs, the non-populated areas should be ours. And we should populate them with Jews. I still believe Jews will come to Israel from every country. The quality of life must be made attractive to them. It will take time. Israel is a new country, filled with confusion. In Jerusalem alone we have about seventy different languages spoken, and many different dialects. It is a marvelous experience in Israel living together with Jews from so many different countries. For example, one of my neighbors is from Kurdestan. It is far away.

JC: In time as well as in space.

AA: I asked him if his life was very different. He replied that it was similar or better to life in Israel. How had he celebrated Succot, what did he do on Yom Kippur? His answers were similar. Yet he and his people were remote from other Jewish communities. Still, he had much in common with Jews from other parts of the world.

JC: Would you say that Israeli literature has reflected both that similarity and diversity?

AA: There has been in Israel a strong trend that set out to define the emergence of a new nation. A new type of Jew would come out of that experience. The Israeli would be different. That trend was common before the 1950s. My generation reached its prime after that time. Even when I was first becoming a writer, I had the feeling that that trend was a false one and that the Israelis would not turn out to be superman Jews, blond Jews, peasant Jews. You can give the people all kinds of experiences, but you cannot change the character of the nation. The Israeli writers I come into contact with now were all born in Israel. Their experience is the experience of Israel. I may be the only writer in Israel who declares that he is a "Jewish" writer. That is because I come out of a different background, and I have a different perspective. It tells me that Israel is not going to become the state of the "new" Jew, but it is to be the state of the Jewish people.

JC: Are you saying that the diversity resides, in a sense, in the similarity?

AA: Of course. It is all in the complexity of the peoples. Our literature is already a rich one, and we have a group of very nice writers, Amichai, Yehoshua, Oz. It's a group of very nice boys. In a country of only 3.5 million people, with many economic, political, and existential problems, there is still great creativity. And where you have great creativity, there is great hope.

JC: Well, it is certainly no accident that your books and those of Amichai, Yehoshua, Oz and others are being translated and read all over the world. That doesn't happen unless there is real substance in the writing.

AA: Exactly. It is not a miracle, you know. When I was young, I was fond of reading Jung. Now, I'm less so, but I continue to believe as Jung did, and as T. S. Eliot was to put it, that some writers possess a common memory of the people. It is not only the individual "I" that surfaces, it is also the common memory of the tribe. It's more than an "I."

JC: Speaking of Eliot, have you been attracted to American literature?

AA: Yes, mainly in the 1950s. I was attracted to Faulkner. He opened a lot of doors for me. But I've never gotten used to his style. His writing gives me the impression that it is unedited. When I read his books, I felt like a mountain was coming. His attitude to people, to death, to me was overwhelming. He is one of two American writers I loved to read. The other one was Thomas Wolfe. As for Jewish writers in America I love to read Bellow, Malamud, Philip Roth. Even if they define themselves as American writers, I define them as Jewish writers.

JC: I do, too. I don't think Bellow makes that kind of statement anymore. Roth still has some reservations about being a Jewish writer, but with every new novel he comes closer to accepting it. Malamud wrote out of an enormous sensitivity because he married an Italian Catholic, and a number of his stories are Jewish-Catholic and American-Italian equations.

AA: At the bottom all of them are Jewish, very Jewish. You cannot write a book like *Herzog,* a book like *The Assistant,* a book like *Goodbye Columbus* without a deep and profound Jewish experience.

JC: I would agree with that view. Yet Cynthia Ozick who is a fine writer and an astute critic, once claimed that they are not Jewish writers. Bellow she is willing to accept. Do you know Ozick's work?

AA: Yes. Apart from the fact that she is a good friend of mine, she is a miracle. She has worked hard to make herself into a Jewish writer. The others have sometimes been unwilling, she has made herself into a Jewish writer consciously. That is the distinction. I have been much moved by it. I know her uncle, a man named Reagelson. He was a Hebrew poet in Israel.

JC: Getting back to Israel, when a book of yours is published there, what is the size of the edition?

AA: The normal edition is about three or four thousand copies. My novels are taught in the high schools and in the universities.

JC: Have you been translated behind the Iron Curtain?

AA: Yes, in Rumania, and my books are being translated into Hungarian. In some parts of Europe, publishers have been a little apprehensive, a little afraid of my writing, because it is about the Holocaust. But then they realize that I'm not a political writer. I'm not accusatory. I am a political person because I live in a highly political society. One cannot escape this, but my life is mainly my fiction. Even in my essays, I'm not dealing with politics. I'm interested in the inner life.

JC: We touched on this matter briefly earlier, the process of writing about internalized experience. It is an approach that has come to dominate serious fiction. I'm thinking about Faulkner and Joyce. . . .

AA: Virginia Woolf . . .

JC: . . . D. H. Lawrence. What you do in your fiction is, in a sense, the same thing these writers did in theirs. Were you influenced by Joyce?

AA: I was much more attracted to Proust than to Joyce. I was struck by Proust's attitude toward the Jewish mother, and by his wonderful powers of observation. He was a half-Jew, but I count him as a full Jew. He had a deep understanding of Jews, their weaknesses, psychological and otherwise. And, in addition, there was an aspect of him that has long been very familiar to me. He had a kind of metaphysical attitude toward objects. There is a kind of worshipful attitude toward them, a kind of religiosity. I've tried to improve upon it, but I can't. I don't know where he picked it up. Some friends tell me he got it in the Orient. Perhaps, it was more than an essence of religiosity. Whatever it is, it has made me feel very close to him. I count myself as a religious person—even if I'm not attending synagogue—in the Proustian sense that there is a purpose to life.

JC: I suppose that in some respects your situation was similar to Proust. Both of you were assimilated, yet you had a Jewish reverence for things, if that is not overstating the case.

AA: After the Holocaust, I felt that I should not only identify myself with my parents who were assimilated Jews but with my grandparents who were believers. They are in me, too, and the presence of both sets is strong.

JC: Is there any tension between the two sets?

AA: No. When I am writing about assimilated Jews, I am totally assimilated. When I am writing about believers, I'm totally a believer. I have felt that I should understand all the variations in Jewish life and that nothing should be alien to me.

JC: On that universal note, we will bring our conversation to a close. I thank you for talking to me, and sharing so much of yourself so generously. Shalom.

AA: Shalom.

Chapter 5

Amos Oz

Among those Israeli writers to emerge in the post-Palmah New Wave generation, Amos Oz appears to have been peculiarly blessed. As the interview with him makes clear, he came from a family of intellectuals on his father's side, and in his mother's family there were poets. Bred to city life in Jerusalem, he joined Kibbutz Hulda, located between Tel Aviv and Jerusalem when he was fifteen years old, giving him the experience of communal socialist life. For three years, he was a student at Hebrew University. Thus, in moving back and forth between Kibbutz Hulda and the cities he has benefited from the best of both the rural and the urban Israeli experiences. Born in 1939, he knew Jerusalem when it was a divided city, and his early contacts with and observation of the Arabs close at hand no doubt have influenced his moderate political and humanitarian stance toward them, although having served in a tank unit in both the Six-Day War and the Yom Kippur War, he knows their brutality in war as well as their smoldering resentment in peace. His knowledge of Israeli life in an infinitude of ways is both intimate and extensive, and to its expression he has brought an engaging and powerful narrative capability.

That talent is far-ranging, original, and inventive. An excellent judge of his material, Oz is accomplished in determining which literary structure is best suited to its exploitation, and he is as comfortable with the novel as with the short story and the novella. More to the point, he casts his narratives in a variety of forms, using letters, telegrams, documents, reports, and journals with the same assurance as he uses interior and exterior monologues and dialogues. Close to nature, his descriptions of desert and mountain, of summer heat and winter cold, of birds and animals come alive as indeed do his city pavements and buildings. Whatever his focus is, his scenes teem with the velocity and passion of life, and this is never more true than when he is exploring the inner recesses of human consciousness. To his narrative constructs, he brings the sense of timing, the precision and the intense concentration of the dramatist and the lyrical virtuosity of the poet. Versatility is a hallmark of his work.

Like Yehoshua, Oz was quick to grasp Western techniques. While he pays his respects to his immediate Israeli forbears Berdyczewski, Brenner and Agnon, it is clear that the Russians, Tolstoy, Chekhov, and Dostoevsky have influenced him, and that figures as diverse as Melville, Flaubert and Sherwood Anderson have played significant roles in his literary maturation. Although the modernist themes of spiritual despair and sexual desperation pervade his stories, they nonetheless remain uniquely Israeli. Violence, irrationality, and malaise are often found, but unlike Yehoshua, Oz (despite the almost universal assumptions of his critics and readers) does not use his fictions directly to accommodate his political beliefs or to achieve desired political ends. That his stories do so indirectly is certain, but for him, as he iterates in the interview, the emphasis has always been on allowing the imagination free rein, and, in a sense, this is his guiding principle. In rejecting an ulterior sociopolitical motive, Oz releases his imagination to soar as it will, and soar it does to impressive lyrical and hallucinatory heights.

In my view, this uninhibited use of the imagination set into the besieged, austere Israeli landscape and mindscape with its sense of tragedy in the apocalyptic history of the Jews leading up to the Holocaust—a passage through time—and its desert mentality—a location in space—has produced a unique context for Oz's fiction. I would define that context as exotic realism. Having rejected the aspirational and exhortatory romanticism of the Hebrew writers who preceded him, he nonetheless has infused the reality of localized Israeli life with the exoticism of romantic literature: its traditional emphases on faraway places, strange practices, individualism, unpredictability (the breakdown of causality), madness, attraction to opposites, dreams, sensuousness, alchemy, sentimentalism, transcendence (levitation), rebellion, and escapism. His protagonists accept finite limits but they push against these boundaries—borders are everywhere present in the stories—as if infinity can be sensed if not realized.

Oz's career as a writer began in 1965, when he was twenty-six years old, with the publication in Israel of *Artzot Hatan* (*Where the Jackals Howl*), a collection of nine short stories. This was followed in 1966 by *Makom Acher* (*Elsewhere, Perhaps*), his first novel. His second novel and third work, *Michael Sheli* (*My Michael*) published in 1968 brought him to the forefront of Israeli writers and launched him on his already broad but still rapidly expanding international career. In Israel, *Michael Sheli* went into repeated printings, selling an unprecedented 50,000 copies. *My Michael* was the first of his books to be translated into English, by Nicholas de Lange, in collaboration with the author, and published by Alfred A. Knopf in 1972. My discussion of Oz's canon will begin with *My Michael* and follow the order of publication of his works in their appearances in English.

My Michael

In *My Michael* Oz undertook one of the most difficult tasks a male writer can ever set for himself: exploring and revealing a woman's psyche, and reporting his findings in the woman's own words. Few men have ever succeeded in this task—one thinks of Flaubert and Joyce—but Oz is remarkably successful in his portrayal of his protagonist, Hannah Gonen, who, over the ten years of her marriage, goes mad. Oz's book is the journal she keeps as she tells the story of her decline and fall in the first person. She is one of several highly memorable women who literally take over Oz's fiction, and while these women are not in control of themselves they certainly assert a controlling power in the evocation of their characters. In the interview, Oz explains his creative process as one in which he serves merely as a medium through whom the voices that come to him formulate themselves into characters. In that context, he has explained elsewhere the germinal development of Hannah, as follows:

> [Hannah] . . . nagged me for a long time. She did not give up. She said to me: "Look, I am here , I will not let you go. You will write what I am telling you [to write], or you will have no peace." And I argued back, I excused myself; I told her: "Look, I cannot [do it], go to somebody else. Go to some woman author; I am not a woman; I cannot write you in the first person; leave me alone." But no, she did not give up. And then, when I wrote, to get rid of her, and return somehow to my own life, she nevertheless continued to argue about every line, day and night. She wanted me to write in a certain way, and to expand the story. I said that was impossible, bad, extraneous, [I said] it was my novel—not hers, and that after all she was my *dybbuk* and not the other way around.[1]

When we first see Hannah, she is an avid first-year student of literature at Hebrew University. Going to class one day, she slips on a staircase and is saved from a fall by a stranger, Michael Gonen, a third-year geology major. The incident foreshadows all that is to come, though in the end Michael, whose last name means "protector," is unable to keep Hannah from a fall far more damaging than bruising an ankle. Becoming acquainted, their ensuing conversations and meetings are awkward: she is emotional, verbal, and imaginative, he is doggedly rational, often silent, unperceptive, and restrained. From the outset, she is thoroughly engaging, and she wins the reader's total sympathy and support, albeit unfairly at Michael's expense.

Though he is the soon-to-be geologist, she is the one who begins to probe and dig beneath his surfaces in an effort to find his ever-elusive inner core of being. He is a kindly, decent, responsible young man, but to her he becomes a rock whose history, composition, and meaning she can never fathom. When he takes her to class during their brief courtship to view a silent film on salt extraction (another incident of foreshadowing: salt rather than sugar will be their extraction from life) the ancient lecturer reminds her of "the dark woodcuts in *Moby Dick*."[2] Like Captain Ahab she will become a monomaniac obsessed with the destructive hunt for her own white whale, the beauty, the power, the grandeur and the freedom to be totally her own self. In her subsequent nightmare fantasies, she will roam the seas.

Against the advice of family, the couple rushes into marriage, hardly knowing one another. It is a trap from which neither escapes. Within three months
Hannah is pregnant. She gives up her literary studies and a potentially promising career in literature, which might have been her salvation. Subsequently,
she obtains a part time job in a kindergarten, but she has no interest in
children and when their son Yair is born, she has no love for him. Michael
begins graduate study, concentrating on erosion. The irony here is as poignant as it is obvious: the deeper Michael gets into his theoretical investigation
of erosion, the less is he capable of seeing the surface erosion of his marriage.

They endure and Michael perseveres, taking over more and more of the
household duties and child rearing, despite the ever increasing financial and
academic pressures on him. He maintains his calm and his patience, remains
dull and plodding, but he is good to Hannah and devoted to Yair, though his
training of the child is at times appalling. Hannah tries to be a good wife, but
she is bored and restless, and soon gives herself over to fantasies that enlarge
themselves into endless nightmares. She engages Michael in nightlong bouts
of sexual frenzy, in which she satiates herself through the exploitation of his
body, a betrayal of him for which she experiences sharp guilt, because the true
lovers who inhabit her fantasies in the dark of night are kept secret. In the
light of day, she longs for escape through disease. "I have fond memories,"
she says, "of an attack of diphtheria I suffered as a child of nine" (20). Being
sick, she recalls from her childhood, provided a temporary escape from
required routines, a measure of freedom and special attention. It was, as
Nehama Aschkenasy has pointed out, a way of thwarting time, for the "main
oppressor for Hannah is time in its existential and historical aspects."[3]

Her physical illnesses increase with the passing of time, but illness is
only one of several strategies Hannah employs to disrupt the relentless onrush
of her meaningless life, her immersion in "everydayness," to use Walker Percy's
term from *The Moviegoer*.[4] In common with Percy's protagonist, Binx Bolling,
Hannah is in despair, is suffering from malaise and is unable to decipher the
warnings in the messages whose presence she detects. In the days preceding
their wedding, Michael is preoccupied with an important paper and from
time to time she reads passages from it. His words, she records in her journal,
"made me shudder" (44). Among them are "Volcanic forces pressing outward.
Solidified lava. ... Gradual disintegration, sudden disintegration" (44). She
then observes that "I was startled by these words. I was being sent a message
in code. My life depended on it. But I didn't have the key" (44). Unlike Binx
Bolling, Hannah will have no counterpart to Kate Cutrer, another one of
modern literature's most engaging heroines teetering on the brink of insanity, to provide the key instruction in the meaning of the messages. Where
Binx was saved by understanding through Kate that he must move from the
"aesthetic" stage to the "ethical stage" in Søren Kierkegaard's paradigm for
salvation, Hannah will sink more deeply into malaise until the "volcanic forces"

building inside her in opposition to the "solidified lava" of Michael's dullness and restraint move her from "gradual" to "sudden disintegration."

To forestall her future disintegration, Hannah uses memory, the recall of the past as a second strategy for getting through the present. Repeatedly, she says, "I have not forgotten." It becomes the book's refrain, but rather than inhibiting time, it accelerates it, for her memories are increasingly those of her two closest childhood friends, the Arab twins, Halil and Aziz, with whom she used to wrestle furiously. "When I was twelve," she tells us, "I was in love with both of them" (28). A favorite game they played was called "Princess of the City." In it, "The twins acted the part of submissive subjects. Sometimes I made them act rebellious subjects, and then I would humble them relentlessly. It was an exquisite thrill" (18). The twins, now grown and now the enemy, are at the center of Hannah's sadomasochistic nightmare fantasies. These fantasies of rape and assault, of humiliation and dominance—she remains the Princess of her childhood game, both submitting to and rewarding them sexually for carrying out her terrorist attacks—are both attractive and repulsive to her, but she invites them since it is only this second half of the double life she is leading that holds any meaning for her.[5] In these respects, she is a typical example of the Oz protagonist, who combines exoticism with realism.

When the twins are not at the center of her nightmares, other characters from literature, Captain Nemo and principally the strongman Michael Strogoff, people her fantasies. She sees herself in different guises, a little girl in a blue dress, a dazzling Sephardic woman, Yvonne Azulai, seeking sexual thrills, and as the Ice Princess of Danzig—another divided city, like Jerusalem, both of them symbolically split and in conflict, reflecting herself. Fearfully, she welcomes these wild uncontrollable episodes, the worst ones occuring at the times when Michael is under the most pressure, finishing his dissertation and being called up for military duty during the 1956 war. Oz fits his prose to Hannah's several conditions. Milton Rugoff has observed that "when she is describing her daily life, the prose is flat and mechanical," when she is fantasizing, he writes, "it is lyrical and sensous."[6] Oz also uses stream-of-consciousness and telescoping to convey the sense of urgency in which Hannah's terrors envelop her. Convalescing from a sore throat she has rebelliously made worse by senselessly shouting, purposely straining her vocal chords, and taking a cold shower when she has fever, she slips into a prolonged assault fantasy of submission and dominance that concludes with this passage:

> We have searched the whole island most thoroughly and systematically and have not discovered who it is who is watching us out of the darkness with pale laughter on his face a silent presence watching unsensed behind our backs only his footprints appearing on the spongy pathway at dawn. Lurking and lying in wait in the murky shadow in the fog in the rain in the storm in the dark forest lurking beneath the surface of the earth lying hidden in wait

behind convent walls in the village of Ein Kerem a strange man lurking
relentlessly lying in wait. Let him come live and snarling hurl me to the
ground and thrust into my body he will growl and I will shriek in reply in a
rapture of horror and magic of horror and thrill I will scream burn and suck
like a vampire a madly whirling drunken ship in the night will I be when he
comes at me, singing and seething and floating I will be flooded I will be a
foam-flecked mare gliding through the night in the rain in the torrents will
rush down to flood Jerusalem the sky will come low clouds touching the
earth and the wild wind will ravage the city.

(214-215)

Of course, it is Michael, with the "my" in the book's title being ironic, whom
she wants to dominate, but that is never to be. In her fully conscious hours,
she ridicules him, hoping he will lose control and show some emotion, some
response, any response, other than his trite rock-like stolidity, but he never
does. It is interesting to note that the only untortured, happy fantasy Hannah
has occurs while they are on holiday at the kibbutz where her mother and her
brother's family live. Inordinately happy and for once a loving wife and devoted
mother in the countryside—Jerusalem is loathsome to her, suggesting her
sanity might not have come into question had she lived on a kibbutz—she
fantasizes about living "in Ashkelon. In Netanya. By the seaside, looking out
over the foam-capped waves. We would live in a little white bungalow, with a
red-tiled roof and four identical windows. Michael would be a mechanic"
(277-278). The fantasy presupposes Michael's failure as a geologist, which
would rob him of his career and his unflappable self-esteem, giving Hannah
the superiority she desperately seeks.

However, nothing changes, and the one-sided power struggle inside
Hannah's head continues. Michael remains composed even when Hannah, in
her conscious hours, buys dresses they can ill afford, and soon discards them,
and is extravagant and acts irresponsibly in other ways. Indulging herself,
she seems consumed with self-pity, seeking through her extravagances to
assuage her hurts. Self-pity, however, is predominately a rational weakness,
and Hannah is progressively irrational, her deep malaise propelling her finally
into a pathological state. Several critics, failing to make this distinction, have
faulted Oz for engaging the reader's sympathies in behalf of an unworthy
protagonist.[7] But she is far too complex to be dismissed on the grounds of
self-pity. Her extravagance, irresponsibility, escape fantasies, and her disdain
for her child and dissatisfaction with her husband make her a twentieth century Israeli Emma Bovary, a comparison critics have recognized.[8] Simpler than
Hannah, the protagonist of *Madame Bovary* did indulge in self-pity yet she
has escaped our scorn, and Hannah, for more significant reasons, should
escape it too. Despite some substantial differences from Flaubert's masterpiece—
Michael, unlike Charles Bovary, is neither obtuse nor a bore, and Hannah
does not literally commit suicide as Emma does—I am convinced Oz was

substantially influenced by the French author and that Hannah's characterization to some extent is modeled on Emma.

If Hannah shares some characteristics with Emma, she has other affinities with Lawrence Durrell's Justine in *The Alexandria Quartet* (1957-1960). Both are Jewish, spring from humble origins, are hysterical for psycho-political purposes and excessively libidinous. Both live in Middle Eastern cities that from their viewpoint have a sinister and pervasive influence over their lives, Hannah in Jerusalem and Justine in Alexandria. The adult actions of both women, irrational in Hannah's case and seemingly nymphomaniacal in Justine's, are motivated by the need to return to the past to unreleased childhood experiences: Hannah's "furious wrestling" with Halil and Aziz and Justine's rape by her uncle, the notorious Capodistria, when she is twelve years old, the same age Hannah was when she fell in love with the Arab twins. To find sexual satisfaction both women must continuously relive these encounters in their copulatory experiences. Both are engaged in violent plots, Hannah figuratively, in her final nightmare fantasy of using the terrorist twins to destroy Jerusalem's water supply, and Justine, literally, when she participates in the secret cabal designed to bring the Copts to power in Egypt when World War II begins. And in both instances, their only positive escapes from their hysteria and their troubles occur when they are safely ensconced on a kibbutz.

These are not the only literary associations one can make with Hannah. I believe she may have been partly inspired by the characterization of Yehuda Amichai's Mina in *Not of This Time, Not of This Place.* Amichai's novel was first published in Israel in 1963, just as Oz was beginning his career. Mina is a young Israeli suffering from bouts of insanity. She and her huband attempt to cover her increasingly frequent internments in mental institutions by giving her a second personality. After she has been committed, her friends receive postcards and letters from her, mailed from faraway places to suggest that she is on a prolonged, carefree vacation. Everyone sees through the elaborate ruse, but it is a way of ameliorating the shame of her condition. Her friend Joel, the protagonist of Amichai's novel, is also given a double personality. He both goes to Germany and remains in Jerusalem at one time. Moreover, he is an archaeologist whose life is hemmed in by a Jerusalem he does not like. I am tempted to believe that Oz may have chosen Hannah's husband's profession as a geologist because his professional interests are so close to Joel's, and Jerusalem is the most logical place to probe into the under surfaces of its ancient past. Two other suggestive links that would have been attractive to a beginning Israeli novelist are the splitting of Zechariah Siegfried Berger into two personalities, as we shall see in *Elsewhere, Perhaps,* Oz's second published novel in Israel, and the position both Amichai and Oz take about the futility of vengeance against Germany. It is difficult to believe that these associations are all merely coincidental.

Hannah's final nightmare fantasy in which she sends the terrorist twins to destroy Jerusalem's water supply sends her off the deep end. But while it signals her complete remove from sanity, it also squares her account with the native city she despises. Prior to the enactment of that fantasy she knows that her marriage is coming to an end. An old acquaintance and admirer of Michael's, Yardena, has enlisted his help in preparing for her geology examinations; in return she is typing Michael's doctoral dissertation. They spend a lot of time together. Though Hannah knows her replacement is standing in the wings, she is not disturbed, having come to regard Michael as a "worthless man" (284). So, in a sense, she has squared that account, too. "For some years now," she says, "Michael has been resting with his arms on the steering wheel, thinking or dozing. I bid him farewell. I am not involved. I have given in" (285). In a final silent speech to him, she acknowledges the end of the marital relationship, retreating into the anonymity of nature: "Please, Michael, stop smiling for once. Make an effort. Concentrate. Try to imagine the picture: You and me as brother and sister. There are so many possible relationships. A mother and her son. A hill and woods. A stone and water. A lake and a boat. Movement and shadow. Pine tree and wind" (285).

Hannah's final collapse and the ending of the marriage surprise no one, but her attack on the Jerusalem water tower is shocking. Jerusalem is at the center of the Zionist dream, the heartland of Jewish longing and hope, the Jewish dream of the ages. "Next year in Jerusalem," we say at Passover, and we sigh with the psalmist of ancient times and his present day counterpart who is still inspired by "Jerusalem the Golden." Oz is the first Jewish writer, so far as I am aware, to recognize and totally exploit the negative literary potential of Jerusalem. Once we get past assimilating this reversal of attitudes, we want to know what is behind Hannah's destructive act. Her violence can perhaps best be understood by reflecting upon her long-troubled relationship to her native city. In her conscious hours and her irrational ones, Jerusalem has from her earliest years terrified her. It has been her keeper, her jailer. It has bottled up her spirit just as her marriage has taken her identity from her; it "plays," as Hana Wirth-Nesher observes, "a dominant role in that its characteristics are intertwined with the psychology of [her] central consciousness."[9] These characteristics are those of "layers of walls—an outer city wall, the walls of a compound, the outer wall of a courtyard, and . . . the walls of a dwelling itself."[10] Wirth-Nesher emphasizes the sense of fear Jerusalemites experienced during the period of Hannah's youth, with the city surrounded on three sides by the formidable Judean hills then occupied by hostile Arabs, adding that to this fear Hannah, despite her familiarity with areas of the city, elicits a sense of being lost in a walled labyrinth that may have no openings.[11] She is isolated and alienated. She has nightmares about the city being swallowed up by earthquakes. Its menacing secrets lie hidden in its layers of earlier civilizations, secrets that are second nature to her but which her geologist husband will never discover in his study of the land's under-surfaces. Space then, the space Jerusalem occupies and its surrounding hills, like time, is Hannah's enemy and oppressor. In her claustrophobic response to Jerusalem, it becomes an objective correlative for her mental derangement. Her only means of breaking out of her confinement is through her nightmare fantasies. It is thus consistent with her deranged logic that the destruction of the water tower, spilling the lifeblood of the city, contributes to her final escape from the labyrinth.

In broader terms, Hannah may well symbolize the frustration the Israelis experienced in the post-Suez war years when life in Israel was austere and demanding, at a time the still infant Israeli government was trying to consolidate the nation, not knowing what to expect from its immediate enemies or from the Great Powers but determined to survive. In that respect, Michael represents the nation's will in his dogged effort to get on with his life in a nearly impossible situation. If these surmises are accurate, Hannah, in a still larger sense, represents the powder keg waiting to explode that Israel was, and, in some respects, still is. Oz's indirect sociopolitical message in *My Michael* becomes clear: there can be no peace and contentment until Israel gets beyond its hysteria over its enforced embrace with the Arabs and finds a means of "furious wrestling" with them that is less lethal than playful.

Elsewhere, Perhaps

In *Elsewhere, Perhaps* Oz's message about "furious wrestling" is made more explicit in the border turbulence that affects the lives of the settlers of Metsudat Ram, a kibbutz two miles from the frontier, nestling in a valley at the base of the Syrian mountains. The political ramifications of the siege existence, however, are muted as they are in *My Michael* because the Arab-Israeli conflict, however important, is not central to Oz's purpose. *Elsewhere, Perhaps* was Oz's first novel, entitled *Makom Acher*, published by Sifriat Hapoalim in Tel Aviv in 1966. The American edition is a revised, truncated version, issued by Harcourt Brace Jovanovich in 1973, a year after the appearance of *My Michael*. Along with the Arab-Israeli conflict, *Elsewhere, Perhaps* introduces a number of themes and techniques Oz would come to exploit more successfully in subsequent works, but the novel is remarkable in its own right for its melding of two traditional Western literary forms, the fairy tale and the morality play, for its insight into the psychological structure and functioning of two generations of kibbutzniks, the idealistic old-timers and their uninspired, restless offspring, and for its examination of the new Zion's deeply ambivalent, complexly unresolved relationship to Diaspora, more specifically, to its most deeply ambivalent relationship with the tragic manipulator of Jewish destiny, Germany.

Though there had been a tradition in Israel before the War of Independence of the constructivist kibbutz novel, extolling the pioneer spirit in reclaiming the land both geologically and politically as the Jewish birthright, emphasizing socialist equality and the necessity to put the collectivist experiment ahead of individual aspiration, Oz puts that approach aside, reverently but decisively, relegating it to the memories of the older settlers (though he effectively uses the still present moral strengths generated from the old idealism to resolve the protagonist's central dilemma), in favor of an examination of the human interplay, the stuff of life rather than of ideals, that makes up the days and nights of a diverse community of people no longer willing to subjugate or deny their personal feelings and needs to the collective good. In its worst aspect, the removal of restraints on human expression and action, in David Stern's view turns Metsudat Ram into "... just another small-town, an Israeli Peyton Place, one-third boredom, and two-thirds gossip."[12] But to view *Elsewhere, Perhaps* in so limited a focus is to miss the wealth of human experience Oz brings to his story and unnecessarily cheapen the value and meaning Oz still attaches to the kibbutz experiment. As recently as 1986 in an essay on kibbutz life, the author began by stating, "I have the feeling and belief that ... the kibbutz is the 'least bad' place to live, the 'least bad' of all the places I know—and I have been in all kinds of places."[13]

In this "least bad" of all places, the human relationships become seriously tangled. Reuven Harish, the kibbutz poet, tour guide and school teacher, a transplanted German Jew, deer-like, gentle, uncomplicated, and decent, is deserted early in their marriage by his wife Eva, who leaves him to rear their two children, Noga, and Gai, when she runs away to Munich with her cousin, Isaac Hambuger, a man to whom she was betrothed by her family as a child when they were still in Europe. The reason she gives is that Isaac needs to be purified and that only she can redeem him. The real explanation for her flight is that she is a high-spirited beauty, who is artistic, romantic, and Dionysian; she is frustrated and annoyed by Reuven's dullness and complacency and the severity of kibbutz living. In time, Reuven is seduced by Bronka Berger, another teacher at Metsudat Ram, the mother of two sons, and wife to Ezra Berger, the kibbutz truckdriver. The Bergers are Russian Jews, unrefined in the sense of Reuven's cultured background, and Ezra is stocky and hairy, a bear-like man given to reciting platitudes and the wisdom of the Bible.

Everyone at Metsudat Ram is aware of and shocked by the affair that continues uninterruptedly for a long period of time after Ezra doubles his truck runs and is away until 1:00 A.M. every night except for Shabbat. Around these central figures move the kibbutz inhabitants, who are introduced to us as considerably more than just stereotypes, each with his/her own sorrows and joys and point of view about the affair, their kibbutz assignments and their lives, past and present. No detail is left unattended, and the description of kibbutz life is thoroughgoing and penetrating, suggesting that Melville's expository influence in *Moby Dick* is present here as it is in the semi-technical geological explanations in *My Michael*. For example, the various work assignments, the daily routines, the committee structures, the layout of the kibbutz are all explained, as are the differences between a shtetl and a kibbutz. Even the old antagonisms between German Jews and Russian Jews are elaborated, the narrator of the novel observing early that in their schoolwork, the children of the German Jews "express themselves in carefully balanced phrases. Their writing is neat and tidy. The [children of the Russian Jews] let their imagination run riot. The former frequently suffer from dryness. The latter— from absolute chaos."[14]

There are other divisions based on age: the older settlers are still fervent about socialist Zionism but disillusioned over the secondary importance of their private lives and over growing old while the members of the young generation are wild and irresponsible and totally absorbed in themselves, frequently at odds with their elders. Cultural differences divide the settlers into music and poetry lovers as opposed to gardeners, sports enthusiasts and those for whom the pleasures of the mind hold no attractions. The nearness to the border and the occasional Arab ambushes divide the settlers into those who welcome an Israeli military presence into their midst and those who deplore the consequential militarization of their relatively peaceful valley.

Growing up in this divisional milieu is Noga, Reuven's tall and slender doe-like sixteen-year-old daughter who is just becoming aware of her beauty and her sexuality. Flaunting it, she is a torment to her denied boyfriend, the immature Rimi, soon to leave for military service, and a flirt to the adult men, a budding adventuress like her mother. In conflict with her father, who is filled with guilt and remorse over his adulterous behavior and the mixed message it is sending to his daughter, and given to nightmare visions of his approaching death, Noga rebukes him by seducing the sex-starved Ezra against his will in a still greater scandal to the kibbutz. Soon pregnant with Ezra's child, Noga stubbornly refuses to have an abortion, and the kibbutz is further divided now over what to do about her.

Into the midst of this turmoil comes Ezra's brother Zechariah Siegfried Berger, a wealthy bachelor and partner of Isaac Hamburger in the operation of cabarets in Germany. Like David Levinsky in Abraham Cahan's *The Rise of David Levinsky*, he is a lonely, unfulfilled, bitter man, unscrupulous in his business dealings, aggressive and yet possessed of warm instincts that fill his life with contradictions and make of it a mockery. He has come to Israel to visit his family, to whom he claims great devotion, and to find exotic talent for cabaret acts. His real purpose is to lure Noga into returning to Germany at the behest of her mother, and, no doubt, to turn her into his sexual slave. He is the devil incarnate, a despicable hypocrite who revels in casting abuse upon the Germans whom he grinds under his heel, exploiting them shamelessly and then glorying in the exploitation in the name of avenging the crimes of the Holocaust. During his prolonged stay at Metsudat Ram, he goes to Haifa every week to sleep with whores. Oz casts him in three guises: he is referred to as "Zechariah" when he is identified with the family and the kibbutz, as

"Zechariah Siegfried" when his stance is both Jewish and international, and as "Siegfried" when he is behaving like a vulgar deceitful German materialist. As Siegfried, he is a veritable Satan come to dangle the apple of travel, adventure, and an easy life before the mesmerized Noga, now disgraced as her mother Eva (Eve) was before her in this Garden of Eden.

The members of the kibbutz are divided into two camps over the disposition of Noga's case. Many want her to remain, while others vehemently argue that she must leave to rid their Eden of its corruption. Forceful, Faustian, persistent and persuasive, Siegried gains ground until Herbert Segal, the kibbutz secretary, openly opposes him in what becomes a battle for the girl's soul. Segal quells the turmoil in the kibbutz by insisting upon compassion and upon the necessity of Noga's remaining at Metsudat Ram. As Segal's victory over Siegfried becomes more certain at the novel's climax, the denouement follows rapidly. Reuven's guilt and his grief over his role in his daughter's downfall puts a stop to his affair with Bronka and brings him shortly thereafter to the death that has long stalked him. Noga's pregnancy and her refusal to have an abortion bring an end to her affair with Ezra. He gives up his nightly trip for supplies and returns to his wife. They are soon reconciled. Rimi's mother, Fruma, dies, and while Rimi is at the Kibbutz for her funeral Segal orchestrates a reconciliation between the two young people, who are quietly married shortly before Noga's daughter is born. Zechariah Siegried Berger leaves, his departure hastened by the outbreak of hostilities as the Arabs launch an attack on the kibbutz; the implication is that in addition to all his other vices, he is a coward as well. Peace returns to the kibbutz with the spring, and in a concluding paragraph describing the cosy scene in the Berger household with Noga and the baby present (a storybook close for which Oz has been both praised and censured) the narrator says:

> The armchair in the corner is ringed with light. No one is sitting in it. Do not fill it with men and women who belong elsewhere. You must listen to the rain scratching at the windowpanes. You must look only at the people who are here, inside the warm room. You must see clearly. Remove every impediment. Absorb the different voices of the large family. Summon your strength. Perhaps close your eyes. And try to give this the name of love (309).

The censure[15] grows out of the stance of the narrator and the fairy-tale suggestion that these central inhabitants of Metsudat Ram "live happily ever after." These matters, and several related ones, require our attention.

Since *Elsewhere, Perhaps* was Oz's first novel, it would have only been natural for him to experiment with the form the novel would take. One major purpose was to describe the kibbutz, and there were no doubt numerous occasions on which he observed visitors to his own kibbutz being shown around by a tour guide. The point here is that the narrator is not simply a tour guide. He is carefully crafted by Oz so that his dominant characteristic is gentle irony. In his ironical stance, he provides not only the appropriate aesthetic distance between the action and the reader but he also can and does make crucial distinctions between the idealism of the kibbutz philosophy, with its understructuring ethical aspirations, and the human weaknesses of the kibbutz inhabitants. He is wise, tolerant, forebearing, and optimistic, yet he is a realist at the same time; and he does not manipulate the lives of the people around him. He simultaneously encompasses the roles of "pater familias," impresario and master of ceremonies, a playwright and producer who, while he has a role himself, mediates between the characters onstage and the audience. He is reminiscent of both the narrator in Kafka's "In the Penal Colony" and Joel Gray's role in "Cabaret." In Kafka's story and in the musical comedy there is a sense of Brechtian foreboding, and that atmosphere is consistent with the concerns and fears of the kibbutzniks as they grapple with the internal and external forces challenging their survival. While the lives of the dwellers in Metsudat Ram change, the point of view and the attitude of the narrator remain consistent, providing the novel with a stabilizing center in which all the actions are held in focus without being compromised.

Because this stabilizing factor is present, the novel does not suffer from being cast in the merged forms of the fairy-tale and the morality play. (These two forms are complementary in that each posits a threat to the physical and/or spiritual well-being of the protagonist and, oftentimes by extension, to the whole society as well, and each contains closures where good triumphs over evil). At the outset, Oz makes it clear that the narrative will take the form of a fairy-tale in the epigraph: *"Do not imagine that Metsudat Ram is a reflection in miniature. It merely tries to reflect a faraway kingdom by a sea, perhaps elsewhere"* ([vi]). In fact, two "kingdoms" are reflected, Metsudat Ram and Germany. Noga, disgraced in the former and hoping to escape to the latter, consistently interprets the mishaps that have befallen her in fairy-tale fashion. She explains and justifies Eva's desertion thus:

> Uncle Isaac is Mother's cousin, and a match was arranged between them when they were children, as between kings and princesses in the Middle Ages. Then Daddy came and spoiled all the arrangements. The princess ran away with the minstrel. The kingdom was in a ferment. . . . At the end of the story the princess came back to the crown prince as the fairy grandmother had decreed. A young peasant lad had snatched her away, but she went back to the palace and lived happily ever after (157).

In similar fashion, Noga expresses her hope of escaping her predicament either by running away to Germany or by just going away with Ezra Berger, thereby punishing her father for his indiscretion and Ezra too for getting her with child:

I'm the queen's long-lost daughter [i.e. a princess]. I'm a little girl whose big sister took her to the desert and left her there and went back to the palace without her. But I'm going. I'm going to the palace. The murderers [the Germans] won't hurt me. I know a secret password. I'll go to the palace, and she'll scream with terror. She'll fall at my feet, and I'll spare her. Perhaps. Then I shall have a case to try. One man [Reuven] stole another man's wife, and I shall punish them both severely. The one who stole the poor man's lamb has sinned before me, and the other one [Ezra] will be punished because he didn't cry out and resist. Why did you give in, dear bear? ... A gypsy girl and a bear. Don't talk. A galloping horse is the most wonderful animal in the world. It will gallop into the distance, and we'll hear its hoofbeats like a clapper like a heartbeat like a drumbeat in the king's palace when the gypsies come and it suddenly turns out that the girl with the dancing bear is the princess is the clapper in the bell (158-159).

As the clapper of the bell, Noga is at the center of her universe, giving and withholding favors, exercising the power that in real life she lacks. But it is the fairytale context that counts. In this regard, Oz, in responding to Nitza Rosovsky's question in an interview elsewhere about his use of Europe as a setting, said, "aren't we all made up of lullabies, grandmothers' tales, family legends, and fairy tales? Of landscapes and adventures that we carry in our genes?"[16]

In the same interview, Oz went on to say that he writes out of his "guts," that "the genes start singing."[17] Whatever the location of his genius, Oz knows, as we all do, the tales of our childhood, and he reinforces his fairy tale by drawing upon that singular child's tale that applies to Noga's situation, the story of Little Red Riding Hood. When Noga is first introduced, the narrator emphasizes the "disturbing mixture" of her "girlish looks and womanly manner," adding that "An evil eye, a glazed, ravenous eye, is going to fasten on our enchanted little deer. There is a terrifying story about a little girl carrying a basket through a huge forest" (30). The wolf who will "fasten" on Noga is Siegfried who lives in a Germany, which has become "a nation of bloodthirsty wolves"(31). Noga is vulnerable because she paid no heed to the warning, implicit in the Grimm Brothers fairy-tale, that once she was given her "red riding hood" (i.e., reached puberty and began menstruating) she could no longer be carefree in the forest.[18] Earlier, Eva, too, had ignored the warning, and in a foreshadowing of what will happen to her, she says to Reuven while they are still together and happy, "I'm Little Red Ridinghood, I'm Little Red Ridinghood. But you're not the wolf, you're my lamb, my little pet lamb" (66). By connecting the fairy-tale to the children's rhyme about Mary and her little lamb, Oz allows Eva to keep her innocence until she relinquishes it to go to live with Isaac Hamburger in the "nation of bloodthirsty wolves." On another occasion Zechariah Siegfried Berger, tormenting Reuven as the latter is dying, offers hypocritically to comfort him with children's songs and stories. The story he mentions is about "An innocent, little girl meet[ing] a wolf" (305).

The chief danger with adapting the narrative and dramatic structures Oz uses to an Israeli kibbutz under siege and in turmoil is that fairy tales and morality plays are simple and static, but life is not. The characters in fairy-tales are usually restored at the end of their ordeals to the same innocence, and, frequently, to the same youth and optimism they possessed before their ordeals began. Oz avoids this static trap by keeping the reader aware constantly of the changes the principal characters undergo. If the dénouement seems to have been oversimplified through the removal by death of both Reuven and of Rimi's mother, Frumi, who would not have tolerated a marriage between her son and the fallen Noga, Oz redresses that simplicity by the narrator's emphasis upon the differences that events have made in the lives of everyone on the kibbutz. Oz preserves the fairy tale and morality play structure but the dénouement, and the book as a whole, are true to reality. Hence, reality and the fairy tale-morality play structure are not in conflict. Good does triumph over evil, and if in his closure Oz gives us a moment to reflect quietly on the power of good and the necessity of love, there is nothing unsophisticated or inconsistent in the ending. We know that life isn't static and that that moment is only a rare one among many other diverse and common ones, ones that confirm the impossibility of our living "happily ever after." Living "happily ever after" is the mark of innocence, and experience beyond innocence is our lot in life.

A more extreme experience beyond innocence was the lot of the German Jews and all those who perished in the Holocaust. That tragedy is ingrained in our consciousness, and those who remember the tragic event must forever see Germany in a different light from those who came afterward. It remains caught up in its past infamy, a "nation of bloodthirsty wolves." I would also argue that Germany, with its small handful of Jews is not the Diaspora, and that in its depiction of three "renegade" Jews who choose to live in Munich, *Elsewhere, Perhaps* is not Oz's indictment of Jews who remain in the larger Diaspora. Israel's quarrel over Diaspora is primarily with the Jews of America and with those dissident Russians Jews who first came to Israel and left for America. To attach significant symbolic political value to Isaac and Eva Hamburger and Zechariah Siegfried Berger is fruitless; they are simply the villains of the fairy tale-morality play, and in the conduct of their lives are sown the seeds of their punishment. Again, we have an example of how Oz, true to his creative principles, declines to use his fictions to achieve political ends. As Shakespeare put it in *Hamlet*, "the play's the thing."

Touch the Water Touch the Wind

In Oz's next book, *Touch the Water Touch the Wind*, translated by Nicholas de Lange in collaboration with the author and published in New

York by Harcourt Brace Jovanovich in 1974, following its appearance in Israel
the preceding year (published by Am Oved in Tel Aviv under the title *Laga'at
Bamayim Laga'at Baruach*), the play of the imagination continues to be the
thing. If Oz had allowed the imagination free rein in his earlier novels, in
Touch the Water Touch the Wind he outdid his previous efforts with so tre-
mendous a leap from the finite realities of the Holocaust and Israel's existential anguish into the infinite that he bewildered and confused critics and
readers alike. His story tells us about Elisha Pomeranz, a Jewish teacher of
mathematics and physics in the Polish town of M _____ (whose namelessness
reduces the dependence on a spatialized locale) in the winter of 1939.
Pomeranz devotes his spare time to theoretical research because "the secrets
of Nature aroused a powerful passion in him."[19] As the Germans approach, he
flees into the forests. His wife, the beautiful, proud, and irresistible Stefa,
minimally Jewish and maximally europeanized, a teacher of philosophy, who
corresponds with Martin Heidegger, remains behind, with her two Siamese
cats, Chopin and Schopenhauer. As conditions in the community deteriorate,
she brings to the apartment an aging friend, Professor Emanuel Zaicek, in
order to care for him. Pomeranz survives in the forests, living "there in a
state of pure spirit, lacking all physical needs," (3) playing his mouth organ
through whose music he levitates at will, on one occasion using his power to
defy gravity to escape from jail after his capture by a German patrol. Although
he finds his German captors coarse, repulsive and reeking of pork fat—pork
fat here symbolically replaces the image of the Germans in *Elsewhere, Perhaps*
as "a nation of bloodthirsty wolves"—he has no enmity toward his enemies
because from a metaphysical standpoint, "both he and they were part of the
same perpetual structure, and without either side the structure could never
materialize" (12). From a realistic standpoint it doesn't make any sense for a
Polish Jew on the run not to loathe the Germans, but realism is not the convention that informs Oz's novel.

Tiring of his primitive existence, Pomeranz plays his mouth organ might-
ily to end the war. We are not told whether it is the music or the military
might of the Allied armies that finally brings Germany to its knees, but for Oz
this negation of reality in rewriting history is rational. Still levitating, Pomeranz
makes his way to Israel in 1949, settling in Tiberias, earning a living as a
watchmaker. Both he and Professor Zaicek are the sons of watchmakers, and
both have learned to manipulate ordinary time because it is entirely subjective, "an affection of the mind" (9). Meanwhile, Stefa and Professor Zaicek are
taken into custody. Both are humiliated and Stefa subsequently sexually
abused in a metaphorical fantasy of rape that exceeds Hannah Gonen's nightmare abasements in *My Michael*, though here again the reality of the multiple attacks upon her by ancient Russian revolutionaries, slobbering and
toothless with rotting gums, is negated by our being told that her attackers
are "Cyrillic letters," the "lecherous fathers of the great Revolution [who are]

really no more than twilight shades of a period of change" (48). The presumption is that Stefa's Western, decadent intellectuality has been assaulted by rigorous subjection to Marxist ideology. It is mind-rape that has occurred, not physical assault.

Unlike Hannah, however, who goes into decline and madness, Stefa grows stronger; and because of her connections, her knowledge and her beauty, she gradually rises, after the Soviet occupation of Poland, to become the chief of Soviet intelligence, and a friend of Stalin. Without Pomeranz's knowledge, she locates him in Israel and has him shadowed by her agents who, in turn, are shadowed by the agents of Mosad. To escape these sinister nuisances, Pomeranz joins a kibbutz as a sheepherder. Though he never participates fully in the life of the kibbutz, he is tolerated because in addition to the faithful performance of his duties sheepherding, he repairs watches and tutors backward students at night in mathematics.

Continuing his researches, Pomeranz discovers the mathematical formula that solves the paradox of infinity and he becomes famous overnight. He does not allow his newly won fame to change his life. Subsequently, through the urging of another mysterious international agent, Stefa is prevailed upon to rejoin Pomeranz, arriving unannounced just as the kibbutz secretary, Ernst Cohen dies and the 1967 war begins. As the war drums beat, Emanuel Zaicek appears in many different places simultaneously, "knowing no rest, clad in a bear's skin, with his staff in his hand and his knapsack on his back" (172) to preach not against this war but against war in general, the authentic Wandering Jew (although this role has inappropriately been assigned by critics to Pomeranz as well). Reunited after a separation of nearly three decades, Pomeranz and Stefa both play their mouth organs as Syrian shells set the kibbutz assembly hall aflame. Amid the destruction the couple plays on, the earth beneath them opens in a welcoming vaginal cleft and, taking leave of their finite lives, they are swallowed into infinity forever.

Though this synopsis gives the impression that the narrative moves forward, despite its bizarre and sometimes incomprehensible actions, in a steadily progressive chronology, that is not actually the case. Marching to the tune of a very different drummer, the story is marked by unannounced shifts, abrupt stops, digressions and gaps, in apparent defiance of that other form of gravity, the seriousness with which an intelligent reader approaches a work of literary art in the expectation of gleaning from it some insights into human behavior, a defiance that is compensated for, however, by the intricate poetic beauty of Oz's prose. But that poetic beauty has, at best, only mildly assuaged his readers' frustrations over the choppiness of the action, the absence of adequate detail and what appears to be an arrogant negation of the basic truths of reality.

For example, Alan Friedman, while acknowledging that the book "offers a profusion of delightful passages couched in unfailing lovely language" says that it also "offers an elegant proof for the theorem that a novel as a whole can be less than the sum of its parts," because it is composed of "toys" from "the author's grab bag," its actions accomplished "by sleight-of-hand." Pomeranz, Friedman maintains, is "a nebulous trick-star-genius, insufficiently rendered."[20] Pearl K. Bell describes *Touch the Water Touch the Wind* as "dense and puzzling," reporting that "after several readings [she was] still maddeningly bewildered," convinced that Oz "abandoned the conventions of realism . . . for the purpose of a technical stunt," producing a work with an "air of meretricious contrivance" that "seems . . . a maze without an exit, a willful act of confusion."[21] John Thompson charges Oz with using the "most inept bits of foolish and obscure legerdemain," a usage that "seems oddly and frivolously cruel" in the light of his subject, the victims and survivors of the Holocaust.[22] Gila Ramras-Rauch writes that "Only by way of the absurd can one approach the secret of being, Oz seems to be saying," but that he does not "know how to resolve the problems" he sets for himself other than by employing "a variation of the *deus-ex-machina*" and in doing so, he "violate[s] the laws of aesthetics and probability."[23] It is curious to observe how frequently the terms "seems" or "seemingly" appear in the discussions of *Touch the Water Touch the Wind*, suggesting that the book is deceptive in the sense that it may have a hidden legitimacy that its readers can't quite grasp but one that experienced critics should know about but don't, so that the critics protect themselves by hedging.

Indeed, *Touch the Water Touch the Wind* does have a hidden legitimacy, the literary adaption of principles from relativity theory. As soon as Oz has introduced the principal characters, their situation and setting in *Touch the Water Touch the Wind* he establishes the relativity context, emphasizing the themes that his protagonist's view of the universe is totally subjective, that matter is nonexistent and that everything is composed of energy. There is no consistent relationship between cause and effect, and attempts at interpretation of actions or measurements are futile. Pomeranz's levitation is legitimated by music since music provides us with a spiritual, that is, an energized, escape from time, and since space and time are in a fourth-dimensional continuum, the escape from time is also an escape from space (gravity). The implications of Pomeranz's first real levitation in the forest are reported by Oz as follows:

> He rose and floated on the dark air, his body slack after the effort, borne high and silent over woods and meadows, churches, huts and fields.
> So he overcame all the obstacles in his way.
> He had once learned, perhaps from his wife, that time is subjective, an affection of the mind. And so he had a low opinion of it.
> Even material objects, if you plumb their depths, are no more than vague images. In brief: ideas cannot be perceived, and perceptible objects can never be grasped by thought.
> Ergo, nothing exists.

Germans, forests, huts, ghosts, wolves, dawn-stench of villages, haystacks, vampires, muddy streams, snowy expanses, all seemed to him a clumsy ephemeral convergence of abstract energies. Even his own body appeared to him to be a willful tide of transient energy (8-9).

As Pomeranz floats, Chagallesque, in the sky, we are told emphatically that subjectivity rather than objectivity is real, matter is nonexistent, and everything is composed of energy whose particles bond in a "clumsy ephemeral convergence." Though Oz continually broadens his use of relativity, he is sensitive to the difficulty human beings have in reconciling its principles with their perception of external reality. Pomeranz, too, has to struggle with the juxtaposition of relativity and reality. His fingers are frostbitten, but with them he can touch a star; his legs are frozen in the forest but in clasping them "he seemed to be struggling to reconcile two opposing ideas" (9). Though he can "soar high into the air, even discard his body," (9) he has to stuff sackcloth into his boots. Oz's gaze is neither contradictory nor confused; it is gently ironic but relentlessly uncompromising. It is understandable that readers and critics alike have been bewildered. The greatest bewilderment is registered over Pomeranz's levitation as a means of escaping his German captors. As we noted above, he holds no enmity for them since, we realize now, he and they are alike, composed of the same particles of energy, and he appreciates the interconnectedness of everything in the universe. Interconnectedness occurs randomly, however, and the chance collocation of atoms is used by Oz to refute the principle of casuality. The realistic fact that Pomeranz is in jail is no bar to his escape since the link between cause and effect is nonexistent. Through the application of this principle from relativity theory, his escape is not only certain but legitimated as well.

What is more, we are precluded by the Heisenberg principle from arguing that the escape cannot happen because objects, events and circumstances cannot be measured accurately. If Pomeranz's subjectivity wills his departure, it is as real to him as Jaromir Hladik's divine gift of a year in which to revise and complete his dramatic masterpiece in his mind, between 9:00 A.M. when the German firing squad raises its rifles to execute him and 9:02 A.M. when he falls dead, ripped by bullets, in Borges' short story "The Secret Miracle."[24] By the same token, all the disconcerting unannounced shifts, abrupt stops, digressions, and gaps in the narrative are legitimated by the concept of random, unpredictable movement of particles of energy and supported by our Heisenbergian incapacity to interpret them accurately.

Toward the close of *Touch the Water, Touch the Wind*, Oz sums up the propensities of music and mathematics to demonstrate the principles of this new metaphysics. Because the kibbutz secretary, Ernst Cohen, wants to understand Pomeranz's resolution of the paradox of infinity and also wants to discover whether or not he is a fraud, he engages Pomeranz in a series of discussions, during which he enters into his journal his impressions of Pomeranz's scientific discourse. The discourse centers upon the concepts of gravity, inertia, natural law, mass, energy, electricity, magnetic fields, time, space, motion, will and suffering, and the means whereby music and mathematics can elucidate these concepts. In the fifth observation he entered into his journal, he arrives at an understanding of the role relativity plays in Pomeranz's discovery: "The mathematical theorem which 'operates' great galaxies and tiny particles alike, as well as the elements of life, is a theorem which can be grasped and expressed in music. The paradox of mathematical infinity is not 'solved' but actually disappears: in the musical system it is no longer a paradox, it is no longer in conflict with the fundamental logical forms" (160). From the point of view of relativity, since no energy is ever lost in the universe, we are always immersed in infinity to the same extent we are immersed in our finite lives. Pomeranz's final proof of his discovery occurs when he and Stefa merge into that infinity as the earth gently opens up to take them in. They have returned to nature, that is, to the world according to the true natural law of the universe. Hence, Oz's closure, which appears to be absurd and unbelievable, is totally consistent with the scientific system that understructures the universe found in *Touch the Water Touch the Wind*. To argue that this closure is a bit of cleverness is to miss the point; it brilliantly confirms everything Oz puts into Pomeranz's view of his existence.

Oz invokes the principle of simultaneity when Pomeranz plays his mouth organ and the war ends and also when he and Stefa are playing music and slip into infinity, but his most explicit example is in Emanuel Zaicek's emergence in the role of the Wandering Jew. Oz tells us simply that he "appeared simultaneously in many different places" (172) to preach against war, justifying belief in the ancient myth through relativity that makes it possible to apprehend the concept of being in more than one place at the same time.

Oz's use of relativity is complex enough, but he appropriately combines and reinforces it, as Jorge Luis Borges, Lawrence Durrell, Malcolm Lowry, Thomas Pynchon and Cynthia Ozick also do, with Jewish Mysticism. Without going into a detailed discussion here, it may be observed that the "thermodynamics" of both relativity and Jewish Mysticism are closely akin. Each is concerned with heat and light, with disharmonies and harmonies (music) in the universe, with transcendence (levitation), with interconnectedness, and each rejects the principle of causality. Both function in and through infinity. Pomeranz's mouth organ is the equivalent of Ezekiel's chariot. The mouth organ and the chariot are vehicles of transcendance, and neither would work if the law of causality was irrevocable. Given the complementary "thermodynamics" of relativity and Kabbalah, an aura of Jewish Mysticism enhances the scientific discourse throughout the book. During the special radio program devoted to Pomeranz's discovery in which a panel of distinguished scholars, wryly carried aloft by the sense of their own importance, discuss infinity, Oz makes the connection between relativity and Jewish Mysticism explicit: "Rabbi Doctor Erich Vandenberg, for his part, took this opportunity to remind listeners that the mystical Jewish teachings of the Cabala mentioned several different kinds of infinity, such as the Enveloped Infinite, The Enveloping Infinite, and the supernal Infinite. Science itself had come, as it were—belatedly, as always—to make its peace with faith, and it was in this perhaps that the real importance of the discovery lay, as a first step toward Redemption" (104). That Oz has his tongue in cheek, allowing the panelists to preen and drone while basking in their super-serious fatuousness, is not, insofar as the relevance of Jewish Mysticism is concerned, reductionist. Its role is secondary but it is not insignificant.

Though it will not be obvious to many readers, Oz's use of relativity and Jewish Mysticism as the informing conventions of his novel are political, in Oz's usual subdued manner. While Pomeranz's feelings about the Germans is summed up in his frequent exclamations of "pork fat" and its offensive stench, Oz simultaneously treats his reader to a much more subtle interplay between the Nazis and the Jews in which the latter, like the soaring Pomeranz, are triumphant. The interplay is centered around the philosopher Martin Heidegger who disgraced himself in 1933-34 by collaborating with the Nazis, in return for which he was named Rector of the Unviersity of Freiburg. One of the rector's responsibilities was to purge the university of Jewish students and ideas. Among the ideas specifically named was relativity. In choosing to accept or reject certain concepts on the basis of racial prejudice, Heidegger demeaned himself as a philosopher and a scholar but his reputation, though tarnished, was and still is substantial. When an international convocation of scholars is convened to discuss Pomeranz's resolution of the paradox of infinity, Oz has Heidegger deliver the inaugural address. The irony of his role is immediately impressed upon us: the message, of course, is that Jewish philosophy and metaphysics has recovered its rightful place in the realm of higher ideas.

In his use of relativity theory and Jewish Mysticism, Oz has placed himself among the most sophisticated writers of serious fiction in the Western world, demonstrating that he can not only write what we call today "metafiction" but that he can artistically exploit its techniques in conjunction with the articulation of his ongoing concerns about the meaning of the kibbutz experiment, the siege mentality in Israel and its past and present relationship to the Diaspora. It is finally significant that *Touch the Water Touch the Wind* shares its particular combination of subjects: time-flight, space-flight, the Holocaust and World War II, with two other important novels that appeared at the same time in the early 1970s: Saul Bellow's *Mr. Sammler's Planet* and Thomas Pynchon's *Gravity's Rainbow*. Oz has earned the right to be in that company. Indeed, he has gone beyond both of them in his continuing preoccupations with these subjects.

Unto Death

In Israel, Oz's two novellas "Crusade" and "Late Love" were published by Sifriat Poalim in 1971 under the title *Ad Mavet* two years before the publication of *Touch the Water Touch the Wind* in 1973. In the United States, the two novellas, translated by Nicholas de Lange in collaboration with the author, were issued by Harcourt Brace Jovanovich under the title *Unto Death* two years later, in 1975. Whatever the minimal loss of reputation Oz suffered at the hands of American critics from the confusions and frustrations of *Touch the Water Touch the Wind* he recovered in the perspicuity and descriptive power of *Unto Death*. The two novellas, linked by the theme of misguided wanderers seeking the Kingdom of Heaven, one Christian, one Jewish, ironically mired in their earthly paranoias, primarily use linear reality and thus make only minor demands, in phantasmagoria and fantasies, on readers to realign temporal and spatial configurations. While both are allegorical quest narratives, they are firmly set into historical perspectives with which we are familiar: Europe in the time of the Crusades and Israel moving into its third decade, surrounded by enemies and increasingly transfixed by the attractions and repulsions of its required military might. Since the Arabs are not present in eleventh century France in "Crusade" and are regarded as only a secondary menace in "Late Love," it is Europe that emerges as the ultimate enemy of the Jews, an enemy whose destructiveness is so deeply ingrained that it requires a greater counter-destructiveness to defeat it. The result is a death-dealing totality from which no one escapes. The real cauldron for terror and havoc is human blood-lust. Oz seems to be arguing that the Europeans have exercised it all too often over the centuries at the expense of the Jews; the Jews, he implies, are wrong, if vengeance could be justified, even to fantasize about using it against the Europeans.[25]

Oz's attraction to Europe is a natural one. His forebears were long resident there, and his parents' memories were of their lives in Russia and Poland. That experience lies just under the surface of much of Oz's work and he has a fondness for recalling it in specific fictional allusions to the Klausner family, to Grodno, the district in Poland from which they went to Palestine, and in veiled references: Pomeranz's village in *Touch the Water Touch the Wind*, M_____, must surely derive from Mattersdorf, a centuries-old community where an early forebear settled. In the interview with Nitza Rosovsky mentioned above, Oz, speaking of the inheritances we carry in our genes, said, "Mine are European, and I am neither proud nor ashamed of it. This is my birth before birth. My parents used to speak with a mixture of longing and fear about the beautiful countries in which they grew up. They hoped that someday Jewish Jerusalem too would become a real city. It took me years to understand that by "real city" they meant a place with a cathedral, a river, and thick forests."[26] This latter phrase in various combinations appears frequently in Oz's narratives, and it always stands for Europe. So strong is Oz's sense of it in the first novella of *Unto Death* that his descriptions of the crusade route, though he had never traversed it, were so accurate that "French critics," he said in the same interview, "reacting to "Crusade," wrote in great astonishment of the clarity of the description of the landscape, from the Rhone lands to northern Italy."[27]

On the other hand, Oz had no delusions about the Jewish fixation with Europe. In a brief essay in *Time*, reflecting on Israel's thirtieth anniversary in 1978, he said, "For me, that long and sad love affair between Europe and ourselves, Christians and Jews, is over."[28] Freed from the fixation, Oz, again the virtuoso, employs a combination of Gothic laconicism and exotic realism to endow "Crusade" with a sharply vivid perspective of the twisted and tortured mindscape of Claude Crookback as he relates his trek across Europe under the command of his distant relative, Count Guillaume of Touron, from Avignon on their way to the Holy Land. Extracts from his journal become Oz's narrative. Their mission is not only to participate in the recovery of the Holy Land but "to expiate their sins through the hardship of the journey—for spiritual joy is achieved through suffering."[29] These crusaders, warriors, peasants, outlaws, and camp followers, few in number, leave the extermination of the Jewish ghettos to larger contingents of Christians, but they butcher every isolated Jew and every small band of Jews that they encounter. Even before the expedition begins, they burn a Jew at the stake. Subsequently, they rob a Jewish traveler and cut him down with arrows, root out a Jewish mother hiding in a haystack, dispatch her with one blow and then crush the head of her infant. Another Jew is tortured, blinded, driven through with a lance, beaten with an ax, and stabbed while his home is torched. These scenes are graphic and detailed, in order to heighten the sense of blood-lust and to convey the monumental hypocrisy of the crusaders who remain devout and worshipful as they move not so much toward the Holy Land as toward the Kingdom of Heaven. The irony is total and devastating, for they do not see the distinction between their protestations of Christian principle and the horrors they practice.

The horrors grow not only out of the butchering in which they indulge, but also from their increasing dread of having a secret Jew in their midst. They mistrust each other, suffer calamities on the road, the Count dies, and they are confronted with a severe winter that brings them to starvation. Still searching for the secret Jew, they are transfixed by their dread. In the end, only seven half-crazed, starving men are left, and their death is certain. Ironically, they have "expiated their sins through the hardships of the journey," but in their savage scapegoating they have effectively put the Kingdom of Heaven out of their reach. Their frantic hatred of the Jews, their blood-lust and their primitivism, make this story an allegory of the *human* capacity for destructiveness.

The theme with which *Unto Death* grapples is not the problem of Christian intolerance. That is ancillary. Oz's concern is with the universal destructiveness of hatred and the dangerous fanaticism it breeds. No one people or religion has a monopoly on it. In "Late Love", the second novella, Oz makes this point emphatically clear. The setting is switched from eleventh-century Europe to modern Israel, and the protagonist, Shraga Unger, is an elderly Jewish cultural worker, an old-fashioned Zionist, whose assignment is to give lectures at kibbutzim all over Israel. His ostensible subject is Russian Jewry, but he has become obsessed by what he believes to be the threat Russia poses to Israel's survival. Like the Count and Claude Crookback, he is paranoid and in dread. He seeks the destruction of the Russians as fervently as the crusaders seek the destruction of the Jews, and just as their fanaticism kills them, so his fanaticism heralds his end. Nothing mitigates his belief that there is a "Bolshevik plot to exterminate the Jewish people as a first step toward the dismemberment of the whole world" (98). Living alone, without the civilizing effect of a wife and family—the Count was also alone—he increasingly loses touch with reality, fantasizing more and more about a Jewish counterconspiracy to neutralize the Russians. Conflating time in his fantasy, he dreams of a massive preemptive strike led by the Israeli Army first against the Nazis and then against the present day Russians. In narrative prose that is dramatically rendered by Oz through an emphasis on strong, active verbs, Shraga invites his audience to revel in his demented vision:

> Imagine: not in Lower Galilee, not in the wilderness of Paran, but in the forests of Poland. Jewish armored columns suddenly start streaming furiously across the dark Polish forests. They shatter everything that stands in their way with bursts of savage fire: long Nazi convoys, trenches, bleak fortifications. ... Can you possibly share this grim fantasy with me: hundreds of furious Jewish tanks crossing the length and breadth of Poland, brutally trampling our murderers underfoot, inscribing a savage Hebrew message across the scorched earth with their tracks in letters of fire and smoke. ... Can the heart contain it? My thirst still rages unquenched. ... Then with lightning speed my tanks turn and thunder eastward. ... With furious wrath they hound all the bands of butchers of the Jews: Poles, Lithuanians, Ukrainians. ... The rage of the Jews all over the land. Defeated Red armies, fragments of shattered divisions. ... The whole of Russia is falling ... writhing in panic, writhing with the screams of desperate women ... The vengeance of the Jews is erupting. (154-157)

The idea of Jewish vengeance is totally repugnant to Oz and "Late Love" is the first of several works that consider the problem of fanaticism combined with the growing military prowess of Israel. Here it is an old man's delusion, an oddly twisted corruption of Zionist aspiration, seduced by the exigencies of living under siege for which the most pragmatic response is a fearlessly powerful military strike force. In *The Hill of Evil Counsel,* the collection of novellas that followed *Unto Death,* it is a child's delusion. Nowhere is it a viable response, for blood-lust can never be sanctioned, and at risk is the future of civilization. Because the Jews have suffered the most from blood-lust, it is the one option that can never be open to them. In presenting his readers with so much graphic horror, Oz may appear in *Unto Death* to be slipping away from his guiding principle of allowing the imagination free rein instead of making a political statement. But he is not. He is simply demonstrating once again his talent for exotic realism. The imaginative depiction of the graphic horror, along with character delineation, and the author's psychological insight into fantasy, delusion, and hypocrisy move far beyond a statement of political belief to the absolute need for human salvation. The imaginative presentation of this need is a primary function of literature. Oz's scope is cosmic and universal, and his work is directed to fulfilling that need. His sociopolitical message is certainly there, but as we have seen before, however compelling that message is, it remains subservient, even incidental to the creation of his artifact.[30]

The Hill of Evil Counsel

The Hill of Evil Counsel, consisting of three novellas, entitled *Har Ha'etza Ha'raah* and published by Am Oved in Israel in 1976, appeared in translation by Nicholas de Lange with Oz's collaboration, in 1978, issued by Harcourt Brace Jovanovich. In the three novellas, Oz returns to the Jerusalem of his youth in 1946-47, the last years of the British Mandate, a period of turbulence and uncertainty, leading up to the War of Independence. In 1946 Oz was seven years old, and the novellas are an evocation of his boyhood impressions in those stirring days. Central to each of the three stories is a boy Oz's age, perceptive, sensitive, highly imaginative, awkward, pudgy, tormented by the neighborhood children, just on the edge of curiosity about sex, fascinated by gadgets and ardent in his advocacy of Hebrew nationalism.

In the title story, "The Hill of Evil Counsel," (which appeared, prior to the book's publication, in the April, 1978 issue of *Commentary*)[31] the boy is called Hillel and is the son of Hans Kipnis, a stolid but uninspired government veterinarian married to Ruth, a beautiful Polish Jew, spoiled, slightly neurotic, and unhappy with her husband and her life in Palestine. In "Mr. Levi," the second novella, the boy is named Uriel and he is the son of a printer named Kolodny and his wife, not named, who is very similar to Ruth. In both of these novellas, the dominating point of view is that of the boy, and the women are frequently referred to simply as "Mother." This leads to some minor confusion[32] since two different boys are involved though they sound identical; and neither is an omniscient narrator though each is privy to information he is unlikely to possess. They all live in Tel Arza, a sparse suburb of Jerusalem within sight of the Schneller Barracks, the British military base. Among their neighbors is Dr. Emanuel Nussbaum, the protagonist of the third novella, "Longing". He is a Viennese chemist, growing old alone, suffering from the departure of his lover and from the onset of cancer. Uriel, or Uri, is his constant companion. A number of the same characters appear in the several stories. This third story conveys the boy's point of view through the medium of Dr. Nussbaum's unanswered letters (which constitute the entire narrative) to his lover.

All three novellas provide a marvelous insight into the mood of Jerusalem as British rule is coming to its end. Filtered through the boys' consciousness, there is a sense of wonder and expectation that is refreshing in light of the parents' ambivalence about Jewish prospects for the future: the fathers are wary but committed to taking the necessary risk to establish a Jewish state, knowing full well that a war is coming; the mothers disdain this fervor, remain uncommitted and seek to escape their boredom through music or through daydreams harking back to happier childhoods.

Hillel's mother actually escapes. After Dr. Kipnis attends a crusty, outspoken British dowager, who has fainted at the theater, he and Ruth are invited to the High Commissioner's grand ball at his palace, located on the Hill of Evil Counsel, the center of British government in Jerusalem at the time. At the ball, Ruth becomes enamored of a British admiral, the hero of the Battle of Malta and a notorious womanizer, with whom she "elopes." It is the crusty dowager who explains brutally to Dr. Kipnis that he has been abandoned, adding insult to injury by asking him how much his silence over the scandal will cost. In shock, Dr. Kipnis returns home from the ball at 4:00 A.M. sans his wife, while at the same time, Oz tells us

> the admiral, his lady friend, his driver, and his bodyguard crossed a sleeping Jericho with blazing headlights and with an armed jeep for escort, and turned off toward the Kaliah Hotel on the shore of the Dead Sea. A day or two later, the black-and-silver Rolls Royce set out eastward, racing deep into the desert across mountains and valleys, and onward, to Baghdad, Bombay and Calcutta. All along the way, Mother soulfully recited poems by Mickiewicz in Polish. The admiral, belching highspiritedly like a big, good-natured sheepdog, ripped open her blue dress and inserted a red, affectionate hand. She felt nothing, and never for an instant interrupted her gazelle song. Only her black eyes shone with joy and tears. And when the admiral forced his fingers between her knees, she turned to him and told him that slain cavalrymen never die, they become transparent and powerful as tears.[33]

Ruth identifies the admiral with Tadeusz, the non-Jewish son of a Polish nobleman to whom she was attracted when she was sixteen and living a pampered life in Warsaw. He is no different from this cavalryman of her fantasies and when he comes along she goes off with him, never to be heard of again. Her desertion of her husband for this renegade dream-lover is akin to Hannah Gonen's desertion in *My Michael*. This novella has other affinities to that work and, as it does, in turn, to *Madame Bovary*. In all three stories acute sexual debasement symbolizes the wife's need to destroy her husband—a provincial doctor, educated but dull—signifying the culmination of the power struggle between them. In the wake of the marital disaster, a child is rejected and left with the unromantic, prodding father. Hans Kipnis is a slightly older Michael Gonen. Though Ruth sees the admiral as Tadeusz, he is more like Rudolphe, Emma's lover in *Madame Bovary*. If these associations were not enough, Oz goes Flaubert one step better by permitting his Emma to realize her wildest dream, not merely in going to the grand ball but in being swept off her feet by a nobleman as important as the original Emma's Marquis at Vaubyessard, one of whose illustrious ancestors was an admiral.

While Ruth is dancing in wild abandon with her British war hero, setting into motion the motif of sexual debasement, the simultaneous debasement of Hillel acts as a parallel. Hillel has been sent to spend the night with two other neighbors, his Russian piano teacher and her grown daughter. When Hillel is sound asleep, they loosen his pajamas, fondle him and rub themselves against his erect penis. His first climax comes to him as a dream while he continues to sleep. Symbolically, his initiation into manhood coincides with the loss of his mother. This double shock is almost too much for him. Reluctant to give up his childhood innocence, he recklessly climbs to the topmost branch of the tree in the backyard, going so high as to invite a lethal fall that would stave off his forced entry into an uncertain and dangerous adult world.

Of the second and third novellas, little need be said here, other than to observe that they flesh out the impending danger of war and the discomforts of living under British rule. In "Mr. Levi" and in "Longing", various characters express their support of Jewish nationalism, their hatred of the British, and their dream of creating a super-weapon that would give the Jews either an equivalent to the atom bomb or a means of defying gravity by levitation to facilitate their escape from destruction. Uriel's impossible fantasies of Jewish military superiority, as we observed above, are no different from Shagra Unger's delusions.

The Hill of Evil Counsel was followed by the publication of *Soumchi*, a story for juveniles again involving a young boy in Jerusalem just after World War II. It appeared in America in 1980.[34] A year later, Oz's first book, a collection of short stories entitled *Where the Jackals Howl*, was published.[35] Two years afterward, Oz's *In The Land Of Israel* came out.[36] It consisted of a series of articles based on interviews with a cross section of Israel's inhabitants. In the interests of space and because my primary concern is with Oz's longer works of fiction, these three works are merely noted here in passing. Both *Where the Jackals Howl* and *In The Land Of Israel* are important and have been so recognized,[37] the former because of the quality of the stories that signified the arrival in Israel in 1965 of a new original talent, and the latter because it came to be widely read in the United States, making Oz's name a Jewish household word and creating for him the national audience that the novels and novellas, however remarkable, had not produced.

A Perfect Peace

The title story of *Where the Jackals Howl*, published nearly two decades earlier, and Oz's first novel *Elsewhere, Perhaps* were to provide Oz with fundamental plot formulas for his next novel *Menucha Nechona*, published by Am Oved in Tel Aviv in 1982, and by Harcourt Brace Jovanovich in the United States in 1985, with the title *A Perfect Peace*, translated into English by Hillel Halkin. "Where the Jackals Howl" deals with a question of paternity. In this short story, Galila, the sixteen-year-old daughter of Sashka and Tanya, is invited to the room of the older Matityahu Damkov, a bachelor who works in the smithy on the kibbutz where they reside. Ugly in face but lean and agile in body, one hand marred by the loss of several fingers, he is both repugnant and attractive to Galila. As Ezra Berger obtained yarn for Noga in *Elsewhere, Perhaps*, Damkov has ordered canvases and paints for Galila. During the course of her visit with Damkov, she learns that he is her natural father, her mother having been as wild in her youth as Galila herself is now. This startling revelation does not deter her from making love to Damkov, the beginning of an incestuous relationship. It was Damkov's intention to seduce her with the gift of artist's supplies and with the revelation. In a directly related concurrent metaphor, a young jackal has been caught in a steel trap on the edge of the kibbutz, and as it writhes in pain, it licks the metal holding it.

Not one but two cases of questioned paternity influence the relationships of the major characters in *A Perfect Peace*, and the protagonist, Yonatan Lifshitz, one of the two cases, is moreover, like the young jackal and Galila, held in a different kind of kibbutz trap: he is locked into a sexually dysfunctional marriage and a routinized existence in which he stands perpetually in the shadow of his hated "father," Yolek, the kibbutz secretary who earlier in his life was a minister in Ben Gurion's cabinet, and is now one of the famous old men in Israel's gallery of heroes, presently troubled with poor health and grave doubts as to the validity and meaning of his Tolstoyan and socialist principles and accomplishments.

In *A Perfect Peace*, the problems of disputed paternity and entrapment are merged with the fairy tale format Oz employed in *Elsewhere, Perhaps*. Like Noga at Metsudat Ram, Yonatan at Kibbutz Granot dreams of going to "A faraway place where anything is possible—love, danger, arcane encounters, sudden conquests."[38] Noga doesn't escape, but Yonatan, for a time does, and he experiences love and danger, an arcane encounter and a conquest. The opening doesn't start with the "once upon a time" beginning of *Elsewhere, Perhaps* but it does end with problems resolved and the turmoil of the family dissipated into a generalized possibility of living "happily ever after" although Yonatan belies this possibility in one of his first conversations in the novel when he says to his friend, Udi:

> I was thinking of a dirty little book I once read in English about what the seven dwarfs really did to Snow White while she was sleeping off the poisoned apple. It was all a fraud, Udi. That, and Hansel and Gretel, and Little Red Riding Hood, and The Emperor's New Clothes, and all those sweet stories where everybody lived happily ever after. It was all a fraud. (11)

Oz nonetheless plays out the formula of the young hero's facing threats to his physical and spiritual well being, coming through them successfully to find if not "a perfect peace," at least one imbued with a potential for happiness. Although Oz does not include the fairy tale of "Sleeping Beauty" in Yonatan's list above, it will be that story that substructures his narrative and legitimizes the otherwise difficult to understand *ménage à trois* that Yonatan encourages, including himself, his wife Rimona, and a newcomer to the kibbutz, Azariah Gitlin. Rimona is the sleeping beauty.

Rimona, like a number of Oz's other young women, is flawed. Though she is beautiful she is simpleminded and believed by many of her fellow kibbutzniks to be slightly retarded. But her simplemindedness is not stupidity. It is in reality the virtue of innocence, veiled and carried to an extreme. And while she is charged with being indifferent to everything going on around her, she actually possesses an open child-like receptivity to everything in the universe, making her naturally maternal responses applicable to all her relationships. But by failing to assign special values to anyone, particularly Yonatan, Rimona earns his contempt. Though she is sweet-natured, good, passive and infinitely patient, he rails at her continuously. Her only real passion appears to be an anthropological one: she is fascinated by the customs and lives of various African tribes.

Corresponding to Rimona's seeming indifference is her frigidity. Since he experienced it three years before, Yonatan has considered their love dead and he looks upon Rimona as a "cold, exquisite slab of marble . . . a corpse" (60). He feels cheated and is continually infuriated with her. When she becomes pregnant Yonatan insists on an abortion. Because of the abortion a second child is stillborn, a girl they planned to name Efrat, and this misfortune reduces Rimona's worth even more. Yonatan is not so insensitive that he doesn't recognize the damage his fury is doing, nor insensitive enough to escape the guilt inherent in his role in manipulating Rimona's life. The guilt becomes one more impossible burden for him to carry. Yonatan's resolution of these problems is simply to walk away from his marriage.

Yonatan has other problems, also. His father, Yolek, is harsh and over-bearing, and despite Yonatan's twenty-six years, he treats him like a child, even ordering him to get a haircut. The generational rift is deep and abusive on both sides. It reflects another deep-seated animosity, that between Yolek and his wife Hava, that began more than two decades before when Yolek forced Benya Trotsky, who may very well be Yonatan's biological father, to leave the kibbutz because he discovered that Hava was involved in a passionate affair with that emotional Russian Jew whom everyone believed to be crazy. Trotsky has settled in Miami and become a hotel magnate. No evil Zechariah Berger, he nonetheless attempts to use his power to recover Yonatan, who he is con-vinced is his son, and he even sends Hava a ticket to fly to America.

Trotsky has become a legend on the kibbutz because of his tragicomic actions at the time when the affair was broken. On guard one night with the kibbutz's only weapon, an antiquated pistol, he went beserk, firing the pistol wildly at Yolek and Hava, then at the kibbutz's bull only three feet away from him, and finally at himself. He missed every shot and subsequently is remem-bered by the old timers as "That joker . . . from three feet away he managed to miss a bull. And a bull, mind you, isn't a matchbox" (56). But his affair with Hava and her resentment at Yolek for sending him away has wrecked their marriage. Yolek becomes hardened, Hava bitter. Between the two of them, Yonatan is crushed. Their stormy marriage and his failed one are ample rea-sons for just turning his back on the kibbutz and on his wife, and leaving.

Into their midst comes Azariah Gitlin, another Russian, always quoting Spinoza, a wanderer, recently discharged from the army, looking to settle into a ready-made communal family. Yolek allows him to stay because the kibbutz needs a tractor repair man. Soon afterward, Yonatan comes to regard the strange young man as his replacement. He can make the tractor run smoothly when Yonatan cannot, and on an outing he is the only one capable of lighting a fire. He will be the only one to light the sexual fire in Rimona, which is to say that he awakens the sleeping beauty. Yonatan invites him to move in with him and Rimona. Soon she is pregnant, presumably with Azariah's child. After postponing his departure for some months, Yonatan disappears one night, putting the kibbutz into an uproar. He has gone in search of his perfect peace.

The perfect peace Yonatan believes he wants is death. He heads for the Negev, determined to slip across the border into the fabled, long-abandoned rose-tinted city of Petra. He knows all too well that marauding Arabs living in the desert wastes will track and capture him once he has crossed into Trans-Jordan. On his way to his death in this faraway land he experiences love, danger, an arcane encounter, and a sudden conquest. He spends one night making passionate love to Michal, a woman soldier, then he falls asleep out-side the army encampment. He is awakened by a strange old man who describes himself as a "Certified surveyor, desert rat, devil of a fellow, geolo-gist, lover and lush," who looks after him for a few hours, alternately berating him and quietly persuading him in this arcane encounter against trying to get to Petra. Although Yonatan has told this bushranger nothing, he has realized that Yonatan is running away from his family and seeking punishment for his guilt, and he warns him what to expect at the hands of the marauding Arabs. It will not be pleasant:

> Ten, twenty, thirty Atallah, all with their pricks up your ass. And then down your throat. How does that grab you, *malchik*? And when they've fucked you fair and square, they'll kill you. But not all at once. They'll kill you piece by piece. First, they'll slice off your ears. Then they'll slit open your belly. Then they'll chop off your cock. And maybe then they'll get around at last to cutting your throat. (330)

Despite the old bushranger's warning, Yonatan goes across the border after dark. Borders are always menacing in Oz's fiction and this one is particularly so. Usually borders are merely seen from a distance and their dangers are a matter for comment. Here Oz's protagonist must cross the border because it symbolizes a ritual passage: either into life with Yonatan's problems and weaknesses confronted and solved, or death as the punishment for his trespasses against others. Walking eastward, his automatic rifle loaded, he reflects on the ecstasy of his total freedom and reminisces about his life with Rimona. This brings him to a confrontation with the cause for his guilt and he asks himself

> Why did I kill them all? Why am I killing them now? What did they do to me? What did I ever want that I didn't get? Who am I looking for out here in this wild? I must be stark raving mad. That old man in Ein-Husub called me a wretch. My mother is a wretch. And my father. For I killed Efrat, and that other baby before her, and turned Rimona into a corpse. And now I'm killing their son. (339)

He is looking for the devil, the madman within himself, and he must either exorcise it or provide it with an executioner. He fires his automatic rifle wildly at this devil in the dark and at the moon, making himself physically sick. Like Benya Trotsky, he doesn't hit anything. Having alerted the Arabs to his presence, he runs, lurching and sobbing, for his life. That is to say he chooses life, exorcising the devil within him. It is a sudden conquest. He gets back alive to Ein Husab where the old man looks after him until he is ready to go home and pick up his life again. He returns to Kibbutz Granot, the *ménage à trois* continues, Rimona gives birth to a little girl, and for a brief moment, we see the family together, their difficulties resolved. The novel's closure parallels the end of *Elsewhere, Perhaps*. The fairy tale ends.

Nowhere has Oz written more brilliantly of the desert and its role in fomenting (and illustrating) the insanities that inhabit the Israeli psyche.

The desert and that insanity meld together here. It is exotic realism at its finest, providing the reader with a thoroughgoing and profound gaze into the Israeli consciousness. Yet for all the descriptions of the desert and its dread, of kibbutz life—ranging from the emphasis upon the old socialist idealism of the past to the disenchantments of the Israeli present and onward to questions about Israel's options and directions in the future—*A Perfect Peace* is grounded in the Western literary tradition. The fairy tale format is as European as Oz's own origins. At the narrative's climax, Oz draws, I believe, on two other modern masters, Malcolm Lowry and Joseph Conrad in portraying Yonatan's recovery of selfhood. Two steps are essential: he must achieve again a sense of himself as a normal, decent human being and turn his negative feelings about Rimona into an affirmative and compassionate acceptance, and he must understand how far he has traveled into the destructive reaches of his own unconscious to find and defeat the devil within himself before he can be restored.

The first step he takes through his passionate night of lovemaking to Michal. We are led to view this as a final fling before death, but it is more generative than frivolous. It parallels Geoffrey Firmin's sexual encounter with the whore Maria in the cantina Farolito, just before he is shot to death by the Mexican fascist police at the end of Lowry's *Under the Volcano*. Earlier that morning Yvonne, Firmin's estranged wife, had returned to Quauhanhuac to effect a reconciliation with the alcohol-saturated ex-British Consul. The attempt to reconsummate their marriage fails when Firmin is impotent with Yvonne. Though his marital situation is hopeless, Firmin recovers something of his essence as a man through his sexual encounter with Maria. Lowry says of Firmin that immediately afterward, "All solutions [to their marital woes] now came up against their great Chinese wall [the impossibility of reconciliation], forgiveness among them. He laughed once more, feeling a strange release, almost a sense of attainment. His mind was clear. Physically he seemed better too. It was as if, out of an ultimate contamination he had derived strength. He felt free to devour what remained of his life in peace."[39] Yonatan's reaction is identical to Firmin's, with the difference that for the former the sexual act is a renewal whereas for the latter it signifies resignation because he has capitulated completely to his death wish.

Oz gives us three clues to his use of Lowry's work. They are minor but given their proximity to each other in the text, it hardly seems possible that the association with Lowry is accidental. One clue is in Oz's only use in the novel of the word "canteen" when Yonatan is taking water with him into the desert. It relates to Lowry's "cantina." The second clue is that Michal is a redhead as was Yvonne. And the third clue is that Michal's roommate is named Yvonne. When Yonatan and Michal come into Michal's quarters, they send Yvonne away, a symbolic equivalent to Firmin's intention when he makes love to Maria.

So versatile is Oz's multilayering strategy in the climax to *A Perfect Peace* that he invokes Joseph Conrad in addition to Lowry. He prepares us for his parallel usage of Conrad just in advance of the climax when Yolek's old friend and colleague, former premier Levi Eshkol, comes to stay with Yolek for a few days after Yonatan's disappearance. In one of a series of heated political discussions, Azariah, haranguing Eshkol, tells him that the "bottomless pits of [internal] hatred" (288) in Israel are destroying the nation, a hatred so full of rancor that "It's the heart of darkness" (289). Israel, he says, "is a snake pit, not a country. A jungle, not a commune. Death, not Zionism" (289). At the same time Azariah is talking, Yonatan is traveling into the interior of the desert, as Marlow in the *Heart of Darkness*, goes up the Congo River deep in the jungle. Yonatan's journey and Marlow's are identical: both are symbolic trips into the primitive, bestial wilds of their unconscious to confront raw evil. Marlow seeks Kurtz, the devil of his own soul, Yonatan, the Arabs, who symbolize the bestial, destructive impulses in himself. Both Yonatan and Marlow manage to escape with their lives, returning to civilization as chastened somber men who know how close they came to the edge of insanity and to death. Conrad's achievement in mapping the human unconscious came about largely through his ability to convey the mood of the jungle. By the same token, Oz's narrative succeeds in his ability to map the human unconscious through the mood of the desert.

One additional parallel with Conrad's *The Heart of Darkness* is also noteworthy. Eight miles below Kurtz's station in the upper reaches of the Congo, Marlow comes upon a deserted shack, a stack of wood for his river steamer's fuel, and scrawled in front of the cabin a warning to approach cautiously. Soon thereafter, the river steamer is attacked by natives hiding in the jungle along the shoreline. Marlow's helmsman is killed. Proceeding on, he comes to Kurtz's station where he is greeted by a man who looks like a harlequin. In a long conversation, the harlequin informs Marlow that he was the one who urged caution. Conrad's harlequin, it seems to me, is transformed into Oz's bushranger whose sole function is also to urge caution and whose life is a colorful collage of emotional crazy quilt patches, that is to say, he is harlequinesque.

Ultimately any pilgrimage into the heart of darkness, whether it is the protagonist's journey into the jungle or into the desert, is a trip into madness. Madness in *A Perfect Peace* appears in Benya Trotsky's lunatic love for Hava, Hava's bitterness and contempt for Yolek, Yolek's fanaticism over Zionist aspirations and his cruelty to Yonatan, Yonatan's hatred of his father and his willingness to destroy his marriage with Rimona by inviting Azariah into his home, and Azariah's fanaticism in seeking to escape his overwhelming loneliness and his frustration over the absence of compassion and order in the lives of these kibbutzniks. The madness begins with Trotsky's beserk firing of the antique revolver and ends with Yonatan's beserk firing of his automatic rifle. It is also conveyed in the two triangles that bring turmoil to the kibbutz. The narrative is so shot through with insanity that Leon I. Yudkin asks if *A Perfect Peace* is "the novel of the system's demise,"[40] the swan song of the kibbutz experiment. On the basis of Oz's statement quoted above that the kibbutz system is the "least bad" of all places, one is constrained to answer that Oz intends to demonstrate in *A Perfect Peace* the need for change if the kibbutz system is to survive. But as he has done so many times before, his sociopolitical belief is secondary to his artistic insistence on giving his imagination free rein. Through the emphasis on madness he confronts the reality of the system's internal weaknesses: it is simply another imperfect human institution. Through the freeplay of the imagination, he defines and elaborates that weakness through exoticism. The result is exotic realism.

Black Box

The consideration of madness and fanaticism, and the motifs of desertion, triangular attachment and uncertain paternity are carried full-blown into Oz's most recent novel *Kufsa Shechora*, published by Am Oved in Israel in 1987, and in the United States under the title *Black Box* by Harcourt Brace Jovanovich in 1988, translated by Nicholas de Lange with Oz's assistance. The book itself is the "black box," the flight recorder of an airplane, that gives us an account of the flight or journey of the passengers in this narrative, providing explanations for their "crashed" lives.

Oz's exotic realism is even more explicit in *Black Box* than it was in *A Perfect Peace*. The principal characters possess none of the attributes we associate with romanticism: they are not idealists, there is nothing glamorous or transcendent in their lives, and they do not seek the infinite. They are earthbound pragmatists. Though they are intensely emotional, they are presented to us with cool detachment. Yet they are transformed into exotics, made into giants by the enlarging of their fierce egos set against the miniaturization of their landscapes. Like Gulliver in the land of the Lilliputians—the exotic realism here is nothing if it is not Swiftian—they loom larger than life but are held captive by their own pettiness, living lives of shrieking desperation, defiant in defeat, unyielding even when hope is gone. Their exoticism is defined by various extravagances of self-indulgence, exploitation and, principally, fanaticism. These extravagances, when combined, alchemize into an exquisitely torturous litany of victimization. Written entirely in epistolary form, except for a smattering of cablegrams and notes, it is Oz's most powerful book.

Oz sets the tone for *Black Box* with an epigraph of three stanzas from Nathan Alterman's poem "Weeping." Victimization, rejection, grief and irretrievable loss are the tragic lot of the poem's lovers:

> But you, you knew the night is still and silent,
> And I alone remain alert and brood.
> I am the only victim of your weeping:
> The beast has fixed his eye on me to be his only food.

At times I shudder suddenly and tremble,
I wander, lost, and panic drives me wild:
I hear you calling me from all directions,
I feel like a blind man being tormented by a child.

But you, you hid your face. You did not stop me,
With pigeon's blood and darkness in your tears,
Entangled in the dark, remotely sobbing,
Where memory or sense or understanding disappears.[41]

The "I" of the novel is the protagonist, Ilana, once married to and subsequently divorced by Alexander A. Gideon, Alec, the "you" of the poem, an Israeli political scientist, a former war hero, internationally renowned for his book *The Desperate Violence: A Study in Comparative Fanaticism* (which might very well have served for a subtitle to *Black Box*), now teaching at a midwestern American university. Theirs was a marriage made not in heaven but forged on Mt. Olympus, for they disport themselves like gods, trading mainly in caprice and treachery. All the elements of Greek tragedy, especially its fatalism, are present here.

After nine years of marriage and the birth of a son, Boaz, whose paternity Alec denies, the marriage comes apart, following six years of Ilana's frequent cuckholding of Alec with his colleagues and friends, with strangers, the electrician and the plumber, its purpose to reduce Alec's superhuman ego to shreds. Subsequently, Ilana marries Michel Sommo, another tyrant, equally ruthless, a Sephardic Jew from Algeria via Paris, a right wing Orthodox zealot. They have a young daughter, Yifat, whom they idolize. Though he appears meek, unsophisticated and pious, Michel is cunning and hard as nails, the epitome of religious fanaticism, a worthy match for both Ilana and Alec who though their marriage has been sundered, are forever locked into a love-hate relationship, a "fusing of fire and ice" (41). In an early letter to Alec, after describing Michel as her father, her child and her brother, Ilana confirms their eternal intertwined dependency on one another:

But you were and remain my husband. My lord and master. Forever. And in the life after life Michel will hold my arm and lead me to the bridal canopy to my marriage ceremony with you. You are the lord of my hatred and my longing. The master of my dreams at night. Ruler of my hair and my throat and the soles of my feet. Sovereign of my breasts my belly my private parts my womb. (42-43)

It is a dependency into which they are both locked, one nurtured by the memory of past infidelity and fueled by present cruelty.

When their son Boaz enters adolescence, he matures rapidly in a wild, undisciplined way. He leaves school, loses jobs, gets into scrapes and is picked up by the police. Ilana writes to Alec for help. Inordinately rich, he begins to shower all of them with money despite the raging near-comic objections of Manfred Zakheim, his attorney—Zakheim is one of Oz's most brilliantly drawn minor portraits—who has devoted a substantial portion of his professional career to protecting and enlarging the fortune Alec's now senile father, Volodya Gudonski had acquired. With both devotion and exasperation, Michel provides Boaz with paternal advice, but it is through Alec's gift that Boaz finds a direction, occupying himself by restoring the abandoned family estate at Zikhron, creating there a personalized mini-kibbutz. He turns it into a hippie commune, based not on drug-related exploitative escapism but on humane principles. It is Tolstoyan without being socialist. He eases the hard lives of those who come under his care through decency, hard work and a love of all living things. If Oz ever intended to send a sociopolitical message about the direction in which Israel's disillusioned, uninspired and aimless kibbutz and city bred youth might go, it is here. Boaz is his first young character to escape both the destructive damage inflicted on children by the marital disorders of their parents and their own rebellious disinclination to move their lives forward in positive ways.

Alec's lavish gifts of large sums of money are motivated by vengeance against Ilana in an attempt to destroy her second marriage by co-opting Michel. But Michel is wily enough to co-opt Alec instead, obtaining even larger sums of money from him to use in the building of a Greater Israel. An orthodox fanatic, Michel is no different and no better than Alec. One would wrest total control of the occupied territories by irresistible real estate offers, the other by taking the land with a gun. While both of them appear to be essentially political, it is not their politics but their fanaticism that occupies Oz's attention. They have that in common.

Alec and Michel also have in common the love of a woman whose spirit neither can tame, and whom few men could even understand. In one of his epistolary tirades against her, Alec writes to Ilana, "With you, anything is possible. Everything, Ilana, except for one thing: for me to know who you really are. I would give all I have to know" (65). The reason Alec is so willing to part with his money is that he will soon have no use for it: he is dying of cancer. As the disease overtakes him, he comes back to Zikhron to die. Ilana takes Yifat and goes there to nurse him through his last days. Michel, convinced the couple has resumed conjugal relations, an impossibility, removes Yifat and institutes divorce proceedings. Ilana explains the situation fully to Michel, but he is unmoved. Begging mercy, she appeals to him to take her back when Alec dies. His cryptic response, in a letter that closes the novel, consists of a quotation of Psalm 103, praising God's mercy. The brutal message of the letter is that while God might forgive her, Michel never will.

The exotic realism of the novel is expressed in two ways. One is the immense verbal power invested lyrically in Ilana's role and dynamically in the roles of Alec and Michel. In their fanaticism these characters are, as I have suggested, gods and giants bestriding the earth—the Gideon family all have large physiques and powerful features—and Oz's language mirrors, enlivens and enlarges their perpetually overloaded and overcharged circuitry. Nowhere has Oz written more cogently than in the exchanges of letters among these figures, and the ones exchanged by Ilana and Alec particularly are filled with dazzling similes and metaphors, with soaring prose poems of great beauty, detailing on the one hand the anguish of the human heart in Ilana's remarks, and, on the other hand, the cruelty of a proud and powerful man's extended wrath following years of sexual humiliation. It is comparable to the anger of Cuchulain when he has been tricked into slaying his own son in W. B. Yeats's powerful poetic dramas about the Irish legendary hero. In the end, as Alec is dying, he and Ilana finally begin to understand one another and each responds with some softening, some reluctant tenderness.

Power-laden as Oz's language is, the most graphic manifestation of exotic realism is in Ilana's characterization as a goddess. She carries out all of the functions of the fructifying female spirit. Not hemmed in by patriarchal dominance, she has freely bestowed her favors (like Molly Bloom?) on scores of men so that the whole earth may be enriched. Like the women in ancient times who are said to have given themselves to strangers on the temple steps, she expects to find a god in these men, and it is to that god she pays her respects, not the mere mortals she services. She gives birth to a boy and a girl, lives close to the earth, celebrating its seasons, its turns and returns; she waits for renewal, nurturing with her maternal strength all who come within her sway. And, traditionally, she fulfills the woman's role in readying the male for his burial by tending to Alec's needs as he is dying, washing and dressing him, feeding him, cleaning him when he can no longer control his functions.

She is the positive, fructifying mother in that aspect of the goddess configuration. But she is no less the destroying goddess in the other aspect of the configuration, negative, deceptive, raging, and treacherous. She is not unlike Justine in Durrell's *The Alexandria Quartet*, in the sense that she is "a tiresome old sexual turnstile through which," Pursewarden wearily and wryly observes, "presumably we must all pass—a somewhat vulpine Alexandrian Venus."[42] Even so, she is neither a "born harlot," (41) as she sarcastically describes herself in a letter to Alec, nor the nymphomaniac that both she and Justine are often taken for. Mary Gordon criticizes Oz for his nymphomaniacal portrayal of Ilana, observing that she "seems to have appeared out of a libidinous fog" and charges Oz with attempting to "render the inner life of a woman who spends her days lurching from swoon to swoon."[43] What Gordon fails to perceive is that Oz intends to give us a modern incarnation of an ancient Mediterranean earth-goddess in all of her principal manifestations. She is primal, archetypal, universal.

It is through the dynamic characterization of Ilana that we may assess the true worth of *Black Box*. By bringing all of his imaginative power to bear on her creation, and by consistently sustaining the intensity of the language by which Ilana and the other fanatics assert themselves, Oz has created a narrative in which the whole is greater than the sum of its parts. One base of support for such high praise is in the diversity of interpretation to which the book lends itself. In an article based on an interview with Oz when he came to America to promote the novel, Andrew Silow Carroll wrote that critics both in Israel and in America declared that Oz intended *Black Box* to be either "an anatomy of attitudes that gave Menachem Begin's Likud Party its political base; [or] a metaphor for the struggle between Ashkenazic and Sephardic traditions; [or] a symbolic clash between secular Israelis."[44] It is all of these and none of them (and a lot more besides), for the sociopolitical commentary is, as we know, always present in Oz's work and always subservient to his creative intention. In the interview with Carroll (as in the interview here), Oz admitted the presence of political matter in his novels, but he went on to tell Carroll that this material puts "a burden on the Israeli writer. 'It is the same way with a writer from Latin America, South Africa, Eastern Europe. . . . Whatever you write about is immediately interpreted as an allegorical statement about the state of your nation.' "[45]

With the passing of time, it has become increasingly difficult for Oz to convince critics and readers that any political message is in fact secondary to his art. It is unfortunate but understandable that his public should resist this interpretation. But Oz has himself provided the corrective in the part of his interview here that discusses the writing coming out of Israel, Eastern Europe, South Africa, and Latin America. With respect to the Latin American writers, particularly Gabriel Garcia Marquez and Manuel Puig, Oz observes

> . . .those Latin American writers have a way of integrating political materials into meta-political writing which is very attractive to me. It is not unlike what I have been trying to do in some of my works, to use political materials, not in order to promote a political cause or make a political statement disguised as literature, but as a way of observing the deeper and more mysterious dimensions of human existence and human experience. I think the political dimensions, the political sphere for, say, Garcia Marquez is a tremendously wonderful vehicle into spheres which go far beyond politics. I'm thinking about *The Autumn of the Patriarch*, for example. On the surface, one would say it is a novel about a ruler, about a tyrant. But this tyrant is a metaphor for God Almighty. Here is a way of using political reality which is thoroughly familiar to anyone who has even a faint idea of what Latin American life and Latin American dictatorships are like. The political reality provides the springboard to writing a metaphysical or symbolic novel about God.

If we are to appreciate Oz's fiction properly and enrich our own reading and understanding of his literary canon, we are obliged to accept at face value this explanation of his use of politics in art. His accomplishment, like that of

Garcia Marquez, is in his bypassing polemicism to move upward to a substantially higher plateau of metapolitical writing, from which he can launch and set his imaginative constructs, like satellites in orbit, into an ultimate mythopoetic realm. Oz is nothing less than a modern mythmaker who has been highly successful in taking the exoticism of Israel's location in the desert and on the Mediterranean Sea, a country already saturated with a biblical, mystical, apocalyptic and miraculous history, and combining it with the myriad realities of contemporary life in that fabled nation. Exotic realism and mythopoetic vision are Oz's winged steeds on his trip to literary fame.

Reflecting on Oz's achievement, his adaptation of western models, Melville, Flaubert, Lowry and Conrad to the Israeli setting, his expertise in utilizing the relativity theory, his penetration into the human psyche, and his development and use of exotic realism, all bespeak a versatility of major dimensions. His lyrical prose and his soaring imaginative powers bespeak a talent of uncommon proportions. His disciplined control of the socio-political issues underlying his work reflects a mature capacity to address vital issues without sacrificing art to politics. And his ability to raise his work to a mythopoetic level and sustain it there mark him as a major literary figure in our time.

Interview 5   Amos Oz

November 21, 1986

JC: Tell me about your European origins.

AO: Well, my great uncle was a quite well known literary figure, a literary and a political figure. His name, I'm sure you already know, Professor Joseph Klausner. I was born as Amos Klausner, originally. I changed my name when I was fifteen and was rebelling against my father's world. Anyway, the paternal part of my family originates from a small, not very small place, in Austria. My father has traced the origin of the family to a 15th century rabbi who lived in Mattersdorf, Austria, called Mattersberg now. This rabbi, Abraham Klausner by name, wrote a book which advocated a very strict code of behavior in everyday life. It was not a very significant work of the imagination, rather it was a legalistic work. An interesting one though. He presumably got himself a rabbinical position in Vienna. Then at some point in time which we haven't quite managed to figure out, one of his offspring went to Lithuania. We don't know why. It was not the usual direction of Jewish migration at the time. Presumably, it was a matter of his finding a Chair. We assume this relative was offered a Chair in a small town in Lithuania called Oulkeniki, and settled there. And the family lived there for several hundred years until my great grandfather moved down to Odessa, making it back to civilization so to speak, for Odessa had become a center of Jewish education and culture. So my father was born in Odessa. When he was ten or so, two or three years after the Bolshevik Revolution, the family went to Vilna and lived there. My father went to school and graduated from Vilna University in comparative literature. He was in command of a number of languages. Part of the family subsequently left Vilna to live in Palestine, my grandfather, my grandmother and my father. My uncle, who was my father's elder brother, had a teaching position originally at Vilna University, and he decided to stay right there. He was a devoted European. One of those! Tragically enough, he happened to be a European in a time when no one else in Europe was a European. Everyone was a pan-Slavonic, or a pan-Germanic, or a Communist or just a Bulgarian patriot. The Europeans in Europe at that time were Jews like my family. So he and his family were murdered by the Nazis. I never knew them, my uncle David and his wife, and a cousin, who was about my age, by the name of Daniel, after whom my young son is called.

JC: What about your maternal origins?

AO: My mother came from a very small town in the Ukraine, from a family of businessmen. My grandfather had a grain mill there. He was a miller. Though they were business people, they had an interesting tradition of writing poetry privately in that family for at least three generations. No one ever published anything. Most of the stuff is lost. It was usually the women who were the writers. It was impossible, of course,in the traditional Jewish family in a small town in the Ukraine for a woman to publish her work, nonetheless, they were in this business of writing poetry. They read poetry in Russian and Polish and wrote poetry in Yiddish.

JC: When did your mother's family go to Palestine?

AO: They came to Palestine also in the early thirties. And my parents actually met in Jerusalem at the Hebrew University where my father was working on his master's degree, and my mother was studying for her bachelor's degree. It was very sad for my father, of course, because he aspired all of his life to become a professor of comparative literature. He was well qualified. The tragedy was that in his day, there were probably more professors of comparative literature in Jerusalem than students. And they, being refugees from Germany's Austria, had a better command of German than he did, so he had no chance. He spent most of his life as a librarian at the Hebrew University, and he wrote a few scholarly books in comparative literature. Very late in his life he discovered an unknown manuscript by Peretz. And even though the tradition of the family was a *Mithnagdic* tradition, my parents were very inclined toward Hasidism, and my father, in his last years, got very interested in it and even in mysticism. His last unfinished book was a study on Peretz's Hasidic origins and on the mystical traditions in Peretz's works which inspired him.

JC: Now that we've talked about your background, I want to ask you what your impressions are about literary trends in Israel. How would you describe the Israeli literature written over the past twenty-five years?

AO: Well, I would say that the first years of Independence—it is also true for the last years before Independence—were somewhat shallow and less interesting compared to what had happened in modern Hebrew letters before then and what has happened since then. There was a short period of literary as well as national euphoria, a kind of interlude. The literature of that period was imbued with heroism. It was macho, perhaps, with a touch of Hemingway, if you will. But since the 1960s, luckily, I think we have experienced the return of a set of sensibilities which used to be typical of the great generation of Hebrew letters, Bialik, Brenner, Agnon and Berdyczewski. Mainly these sensibilities were concerned with soul-searching and a secret fascination with theology.

JC: With theology?

AO: With theology. Even the atheist writers were as obsessed by the absence of God as religious writers were obsessed by the presence of God. The short episode of Soviet inspired social realism is gone. It lasted from the mid-forties to the mid-fifties. It was replaced by what I would describe as a combination of social, ideological concerns on the surface with a theological quest underneath.

JC: Do you think this theological quest is a major motif that runs through most all of Israeli writing? Is it a kind of obsession with God that could be described as being natural for the Jewish people?

AO: I think it is very Jewish. Whether it is specifically Jewish or not, I am not sure, but it is very Jewish, and I think it probably conveys a certain uneasiness with the heavy political, ideological focus of letters in the early years of statehood. And it is possibly a quest for something that goes beyond the boundaries of politics and ideology.

JC: How would you describe the literary situation in Israel today?

AO: Well, it is a volcano in action. To me, contemporary Israeli literature is operating within a language that right now is in the Elizabethan age. Bubbling and simmering. One can potentially take wild liberties with Hebrew, and some people do. They legislate into the language, so to speak. By saying that the language is in an Elizabethan phase, I'm not suggesting that everyone of us is a William Shakespeare. We hardly have half a dozen of those in Tel Aviv nowadays. But the production is there, and it is very fascinating how the language is being formed by literature, and vice versa. By and large, I'd say that the literature of the last few years, the very last three or four years, is taking more of the direction of using colloquial Hebrew. Hebrew writers were traditionally very reluctant to rely on colloquial Hebrew, partly because there were no colloquialisms used and partly because whatever colloquialisms existed were very artificial, having been invented by the writers rather than coming from the depths of the people.

JC: In what direction do you think Israeli literature will move?

AO: Well, it is very hard to speak of a single trend or direction of literature where you have an Aharon Appelfeld, who to me is a distinguished heir of a central European Jewish community and a central European writer all the way. Even when his books are set in Israel, he still is a central European novelist with the same fascination for the middle class that used to be typical of the central European writers, Jewish and non-Jewish. And you have A. B. Yehoshua, who reflects a strange combination of influences, nineteenth-century Russian writers and William Faulkner. He is the offspring of an unlikely marriage between Faulkner and Dostoevsky.

JC: I, myself, explored the Faulknerian connection, particularly in *A Late Divorce*. I see what you mean about defining trends where there is so much diversity. How would you describe the influences on your work? Who are your mentors, your idols?

AO: My direct ones were Hebrew ones, obviously because in my formative years I read them in the original. I would say Berdyczewski, Brenner, and Agnon in that order. Outside the immediate tradition of modern Hebrew, I would name the great nineteenth-century Russians, Tolstoy, Chekhov, and Dostoevsky, in that order. The one who is most intriguing to me in American literature is Herman Melville.

JC: Tell me about your interest in Melville and the way in which Melville is an influence?

AO: Well, Melville dawned on me when I was 16 or 17 years old with *Moby Dick*, which was as big and as colorful as any novel in the world can be. It enabled me to realize that the place I was living in, my time and my place, had certain biblical qualities about them, and that beyond ideology, religion, and politics, there were people oceans away whose lives were of compelling literary interest. I hadn't realized that before reading *Moby Dick*. At the same time, I can point to another very different American influence, Sherwood Anderson, who unlike Melville, was a provincial rather than a global storyteller. I am thinking of *Winesburg, Ohio*.

To a young kibbutzik like myself, living in a very small village with an overall population of four hundred, the fact that one could find a microcosm everywhere was a remarkable discovery. To some extent the idea of my first collection of short stories, *Where the Jackals Howl*, came from Sherwood Anderson. I used his idea of creating a body of interrelated stories where major characters from one story may reappear as minor characters in the next.

JC: Anderson had a substantial vogue several decades ago but it seems to have paled now. His providing a direction for you I find fascinating, especially given the distance of the experience he wrote about in his *Winesburg, Ohio* and your experience in a kibbutz. How did you discover Anderson's book?

AO: I bumped into *Winesburg, Ohio* by sheer chance. I just picked it up in the kibbutz library. It was, on the surface, as far away from Kibbutz Hulda as one can get. And yet this notion of discovering the whole world in a microcosm, in a drop of water, a whole world of ordinary people just lying there on the surface with their lives described colloquially, even trivially, was very impressive. Anderson's influence on me was similar to Chekhov's influence. The two writers were not very different in this respect. From them, and Melville, I learned that anyone's life or situation could be used for fiction. Their novels helped me a great deal to see the value of my own locale, to realize it was important enough to use.

JC: Do you read the more recent modern American writers, Jewish or non-Jewish? Are there any contemporary ones to whom you can relate?

AO: I have a sense of kinship with some of the American Jewish writers. Henry Roth's *Call It Sleep* touched me very deeply, though I'm not sure that it influenced me. And I'm very fond of some of the works of Saul Bellow, not the latest ones though. I like the earlier ones. I find a sense of kinship with Bellow in his combining intellectual "dash" with emotional and moral sensibilities that is not so different from the approach taken earlier by the great generation of Hebrew writers. *Mr. Sammler's Planet* is a novel that despite its differences could have been written by Brenner. Cynthia Ozick is intriguing to me, too. And, yet, I have to plead partial ignorance. I'm not a systematic reader of contemporary American literature, Jewish or non-Jewish. I have to admit, moreover, that I am more at home with a second-rate Hebrew novel than with a first-rate English novel.

JC: You've been telling me how you realized a long time ago that the kibbutz could be a microcosm, and obviously the kibbutz is the setting for much of your work. Will it continue to be the setting? Or have you done everything with it that you can do?

AO: I don't think I have exhausted the subject because I am still fascinated by
what is happening on the kibbutz. What's happening on my own kibbutz.
You know, in having lived there for more than thirty years now, I have
seen genetics at work. I have had a chance to get a very intimate acquaintance with three or four hundred quite different people, not just intellectuals and other writers, which probably would have been the case if I had
lived in a literary community or in a big city. I don't think if I lived in
New Orleans or in Tel Aviv I'd ever get to know that well four hundred
different people. Of course, the price I am made to pay for living on the
kibbutz is that those people know a hell of a lot about me, more than I
would like them to know. But that is only fair. Whether I shall write
another kibbutz novel immediately or in the long run is not for me to say
because I never enjoyed the freedom to choose a subject. It never works
like this, you know, that I wake up in the morning and scratch my head
and ask myself what is it that I'm going to write about next. Normally, a
story or a novel for me begins with voices, with characters, not with global
or local settings. Characters eventually bring with them the location, the
settings and the time. What they do to each other is the plot. So I don't
really have a choice. In one or two cases, I strongly resisted the characters and didn't want to write their story. In the end, I had to write about
them in order to get them out of my system. If the characters don't take
over after awhile, then I know it is going to be a miscarriage or an abortion rather than a birth-giving.

JC: Are your characters in your various stories based upon actual people
whom you know; are they stereotypes, or are they a mixture of real people and stereotypes?

AO: They are a mixture of real people and stereotypes, but even that description of my characters is not totally accurate. I have never used a real life
model all the way. But of course, gestures, composites really are bound
to be there. If I would have used real live models, they would have kicked
me out of the kibbutz a long time ago. Even now, I do have a next door
neighbor in Kibbutz Hulda who is in the habit anytime he crosses in
front of my little office of stopping for awhile and combing his hair so
that in case he gets into a novel he'll get there with his hair combed.
That is not the way that I operate.

JC: Have you been accused of using actual living characters?

AO: No. Not even once. My fellow kibbutzniks are very open with me. I get a very
gutsy immediate reviewing in Kibbutz Hulda. They will tell me straight
away whether they like a book or don't like it, or if it's boring, or if they
stopped reading it in the middle. They don't have any inhibitions about
telling me how they feel, which I take as a sign of confidence and friend-

ship, and which is very important to me. But not even once have I been accused of actually exploiting a real life character for literary purposes.

JC: The reason I have pursued this question is obvious, that in living in a microcosm like Kibbutz Hulda there could be a strong temptation to use live models. The variety of types you encounter and the closeness associated with the encounters nonetheless presents you with an unusual opportunity not unlike, say, Faulkner's experience in his creation of Yoknapatawpha County. Oxford, Mississippi is a small town. Everybody there knew everything about everybody else. Faulkner found himself with an excellent milieu in which to work. Isn't the same thing true for you?

AO: No, it's not the same for me. You see, Joseph, the name of the game or the rule of the game is sometimes to do obscene things. For example, I look at a person, a woman, and then I look at another person, a man unrelated to the woman. Presume that those two marry and have a child. Knowing that couple well, knowing their parents and families, knowing the genetic potential involved, I am moved to wonder what this child will be like, and in my writings an entirely new human being emerges. This is a stretching of the imagination indirectly relying on real life, but relying on real life in a way that is never a photographic way.

JC: You are working on a new novel, I understand. Does it have a kibbutz setting? What, if I may ask, is it about?

AO: It's set in Jerusalem in 1976. In a sense it is very much like an English eighteenth-century novel because it is epistolaric all the way. It consists entirely of an exchange of letters between five different characters, letters, a few cables, and a couple of legal documents, no narrator. There is not even a narrator's introduction. It moves right into the action. It is a family tale. There is a woman in the center of this novel and she is exchanging letters with her former husband, and with her son who lives far away. Eventually, as circumstances change, she exchanges letters with her present husband. There is a solicitor, a shrewd solicitor somewhere on the fringe of the story. This is the cast of characters, along with the woman's sister.

JC: Are you particularly fond of the epistolary structure?

AO: I have used epistolaric components in previous works such as A *Perfect Peace*. I wrote a novella in 1975 that consisted entirely of a series of letters from one person to a woman who had deserted him many years earlier. It was no two way exchange. There was only the man's voice, because the woman never answered him. The novella was called "Longing." I find the epistolary approach attractive from the standpoint of language. I think when a novel attempts simply to imitate colloquial speech, it may often get very shallow. The voice of the narrator in a language such as Hebrew can easily get very high flown, whereas the epistolaric language structure is somewhere in between. The approach also gives me a variety of perspectives simply because people write differently when they write to different people. They adopt different voices, and use different tools. In terms of language, using the letter, for me, is fascinating. For this new novel I feel this is the right form even though I have never been too devoted to any particular literary structure. I hope never to become a servant to a specific form.

JC: I don't think that will happen. In *A Perfect Peace*, you use a variety of devices. You switch back and forth between letters and documents. Incidentally, in *A Perfect Peace* Yonatan appears to be deserting his wife, and in *Elsewhere, Perhaps* there is a desertion when the poet's wife leaves him. "Longing" deals also with desertion, and your description of your new novel suggests there will be still further use of the theme of desertion. Desertion seems to run through much of your work. If it is a theme, why is it so important to you?

AO: I'm not sure, Joseph, if I can really answer that question, why any theme or motif is really important to me, but it is a fact that it is important to me. There must be a certain biographical background to it. Yet, I have always thought that the biographical background is kind of shallow. Just as I haven't used living models, I haven't drawn directly on my biographical background. But let me stress the point that both *Elsewhere, Perhaps* and *A Perfect Peace* are not only novels about desertion but they are also novels leading to some kind of a mystical merger between certain, different people. Both novels end with the formation of an unlikely extended family, a *ménage à trois* in *A Perfect Peace*, a kind of comprehensive family of potential enemies in *Elsewhere, Perhaps*. To some extent this mystical merger between decent human beings is a lot more exciting to me than the desertion theme.

JC: The desertion may simply appear to be a realization that you have to go away first in order to come back home again. And it is the homecoming that is significant.

AO: That is a fair description.

JC: In *Elsewhere, Perhaps* you give us some of the poet's poems. Have you written poetry? Is that a genre that you're interested in professionally? Those poems, while they are not great, are competently executed. Were they meant to stand on their own, or were they there for window dressing?

AO: It has been a very long time since I looked at *Elsewhere Perhaps* really. I don't think I would be proud to sign my name to those verses. I did publish a couple of poems when I was frightfully young, poems that I would rather forget. I have been writing poetry all these years but I hardly ever publish one of them. I don't feel the urge to publish them.

JC: You mentioned earlier that this was a tradition in your mother's family. But as it was kept private in previous generations, you're doing much the same. Don't you think the world might be interested in seeing some of the poetry that you've composed?

AO: The world might be interested or not interested, but I am not interested in sharing it with the world; at least, not at this point in time.

JC: We've talked about Hebrew, Russian, and American writers whose works have been important to you. What about European influences?

AO: I think first of three short tales by Herbert Musil. He's not very well-known in America. Those stories became a powerful presence to me. I read them in the Hebrew translation. The collection itself is called *Three Women*.

JC: Did Musil's *The Man Without Qualities* impress you?

AO: I'm less familiar with it than the short stories. I read it in a superficial way, and I was not particularly moved by it. Thomas Mann always intrigued me and fascinated me from a distance. I can't claim any immediate kinship to English poets, to Eliot, for example. I know the kinship is there with Yehuda Amichai and many others. I would not regard myself as in any sort of way related to Eliot. I find Ezra Pound more exciting, much as I get angry with myself about this sometimes. But he excites me a lot more than T. S. Eliot.

JC: Pound poses a problem for any Jew in modern times who has a sensitivity about literature either as a writer or a critic or whatever. Your response is different from what one normally hears. What is it in Pound's work that attracts you?

AO: A certain gutsy shameless passion, which is very rare in recent literature. By and large, gutsy shameless passion is becoming more and more rare in contemporary Western European writings.

JC: Are you saying that there is kind of anemia in Western writing?

AO: A sort of bloodlessness. Yes, anemia. That is a good word for it. I think that the stuff coming nowadays out of Latin America, and, to some extent South Africa, Eastern Europe, is a lot more shameless and gutsy than the stuff coming out of France and England.

JC: You have an attraction to Latin American writers.

AO: Oh yes!

JC: Would you elaborate on that for me?

AO: I can relate to the mythopoetic approach they use. It is a quality that is not found in Western European writing nowadays. And I like the integration of folk materials into sophisticated and sometimes mystical forms. The Latin American writers are very good at it.

JC: The kind of primitivism there tends to the mystical.

AO: That's a fair rendering.

JC: Which Latin American writers do you like particularly?

AO: Garcia Marquez and, to some extent, the Argentinian Manuel Puig.

JC: His *Kiss of the Spider Woman* has made him a cult figure in America.

AO: Oh yes! That is a novel that I admired very much. Now the thing is that some of those Latin American writers have a way of integrating political materials into metapolitical writing which is very attractive to me. It is not unlike what I have been trying to do in some of my works, to use political materials, not in order to promote a political cause or to make a political statement disguised as literature, but as a way of observing the deeper and more mysterious dimensions of human existence and human experience. I think the political dimensions, the political sphere for, say, Garcia Marquez is a tremendously wonderful vehicle into spheres that go far beyond politics. I'm thinking about *The Autumn of the Patriarch*, for example. On the surface, one would say it is a novel about a ruler, about a tyrant. But this tyrant is a metaphor for God Almighty. Here is a way of using political reality that is thoroughly familiar to anyone who has even a faint idea of what Latin American life and Latin American dictatorships are like. The political reality provides the springboard to writing a metaphysical or symbolic novel about God.

JC: Would you say it moves from being just a consideration of the extension of power and its uses and abuses into a kind of mythos?

AO: Absolutely. It is a myth of creation, a theological myth.

JC: As your books, increasingly, are being translated, I am curious about how comfortable you are with the translation of your stories into English. You told me earlier that reading a translation was like making love through a blanket.

AO: Translating Hebrew into any European language, and certainly into English is a very long trip. English is a different musical instrument. It has a different system of tenses, and consequently, a different concept of time and possibly a different notion of reality. That makes it pretty much of an effort to play a violin concerto on the piano. This can be done as long as you don't try to make the piano produce the sounds of the violin. That is grotesque. It refuses to be philosophical about certain concessions and compromises that ought to be done in the process of translating.

JC: Do you have a favorite translator in this country for your work?

AO: My works have been translated mainly by Nicholas de Lange, who was away but is back on board now, and working on my new novel. I think he is an excellent translator. This is not to say that he and I don't fight sometimes like a pair of best enemies. But I think he and I share the same philosophy that translation should avoid any attempt to neutralize the characters. There is no point in making a Sephardic Jew speak like a black person from the South of the United States even though the temptation is there, or vice versa. A Faulknerian black should never speak in the Hebrew version of a Faulkner novel like a North African Jew. Time and again, I have had disagreements with my translators about issues such as "a cup of tea" or "a glass of tea." They normally tend, as an immediate response, to translate "a glass of tea with milk" into the obvious English term, "a cup of tea," which is officially correct for the British. Otherwise, it is lemon tea. I therefore normally insist that the translation, at the cost of sounding peculiar, odd or even outlandish sometimes, or clumsy, that where the circumstances require, it ought to remain "a glass of tea with milk" rather than "a cup of tea." That is what I mean by avoiding the temptation to neutralize the characters.

JC: Translators do have a tendency to localize everything. I can remember several years ago, I saw *Amadeus* on the stage in London and there were a lot of "loveys" and "blimeys" in it. It was totally absurd for the character playing Mozart and the others to be using those colloquialisms.

AO: I think this is a wrong attitude to translation. Anna Karenina is Anna Karenina, not Mrs. Karenina.

JC: It reminds me of Dannie Abse's poem "No More Mozart." In it there is a short stanza which reads,

> The German streets tonight
> are soaped in moonlight.
> The streets of Germany are clean
> like the hands of Lady MacBeth."[1]

When the poem was translated into German, the last line was rendered "the hands of Mrs. MacBeth." That change destroyed everything.

AO: That is precisely what I am talking about. There is a character in *A Perfect Peace* who refers to another character as having gone years before to live in Miami in East America. Now the translator changed this to read "Miami, Florida." I vetoed this. I said for this particular Israeli old time pioneer it is not "Miami, Florida," it is "Miami, East America" and that is the way it should read in the English translation. We do have to avoid neutralization of the characters. They are not to become Americans, they are not to be converted.

JC: I'm especially interested in this point because it is widely known that when *A Perfect Peace* was published, your translator, Hillel Halkin, was extremely upset by changes that had been made in the text that modified his rendering.

AO: It is true that Hillel was not happy with the final version of the translation, and I can see why. He has his point, his approach, and his attitude about translations. I think that he is a good translator, but it may be that he and I are philosophically divided over the art of translation.

JC: A little while ago, we were talking about the way in which Latin American writers have been using political subject matter in an effort to establish new myths. Has your creative writing been affected by your own political activity in behalf of the Peace Now movement? For example, did the death of Emil Gruenzweig have an impact on you in terms of what you do in a strictly literary way? Or do you keep these matters separate?

AO: That is a complicated one. These matters are not separate, and, yet, I have never written a story or a novel in order to make a political point, even though many of my works are full of politics. Let me put it this way, whenever I am in total agreement with myself over anything, I don't write a novel or a story. I write an angry article telling my government what to do, sometimes, telling it where to go altogether. It's normally when I'm in a slight disagreement with myself that I hear more than just one voice in me, that I sometimes sense the embryo of a story or a novel. It may or may not be developed actually into a *work of prose*. I'm not using the English term "fiction" here because I am unhappy with that term. I've never felt comfortable with the English term "fiction." We don't even have a Hebrew word for it except for a new scholarly term which is intended as a Hebrew equivalent for the word "fiction." I like to think of myself as a writer of prose, not as a writer of fiction. Narrative prose. But back to that point about politics. Many of my characters have their personal politics. Some of them have political stances that are very different from my politics. I do introduce the political stances in order to describe a character, but I never introduce a character in order to make a political point.

JC: When you were in the United States year before last, you were widely quoted to the effect that American Jews, and Jews in the Diaspora, lead a museum existence. That is to say that the Disapora, and American Jewry, in particular, is encased as it were in a museum. It has a past but no future. Do you still feel that way about American Jewry?

AO: The point I made was slightly more complex than your summation of it. What I said was that even though a lot of remarkable, individual creation was evident in the American Jewish scene, I couldn't detect the presence of "collective creation." I'm worried about this because I have always believed that "collective creation" lays the groundwork for future individual "creation." And in terms of individual creation, many of the significant American Jewish writers lean heavily on the collective creations of Eastern European Jewry. But this bank account is going to be depleted eventually. And if this happens, you will have in the future, creators of Jewish extraction, American creators of Jewish extraction, but not American Jewish creators, in literature and the other arts. I don't see any collective creation. I see remarkable collective institutions and I see remarkable individual "creations," but no collective creations in religion, in education, in American Jewish life; whereas the Israelis have revived the Hebrew language, developed methods of collective settlements, built Jerusalem, and I mean the new city of Jerusalem, not the old one. All those creations are problematic, and endangered, and vulnerable but that is the name of the game for live drama. It can never happen in a well preserved museum. I'm worried that the next generation of American Jews, or the generation after, may not be terribly attracted to the role of museum curators for life, polishing the glass cases and inviting guests to enjoy the riches of the inheritance. In other words, I think part time Judaism is a futile concept. But let me add, this is an argument that I would love to lose. I don't want to win the argument, I want to win the American Jewish community. I want to see it alive and kicking and creative.

JC: I see. I think that is a good note on which to close our conversation, and I thank you for sharing your thoughts with me.

Conclusion

I have argued in this study that the five writers I have interviewed, whose works have been analyzed here, are the literary voices of Israel. They are not the only voices, of course, but for this crucial period in Israel's history they are the dominant ones. It is through their works that the outside world can best understand the Israeli psyche and come to grips with the existential *angst* of the Israeli people. Because the inhabitants of this Jewish state have never been secure within their borders, have fought four wars, and face an uncertain future, they have developed a siege mentality that has made serious inroads into every aspect of their existence. That existence, its interpretation, and the meaning of its multifarious ramifications provide these writers with an all-encompassing, highly diverse subject matter. Since they are intensely involved and committed to Israel and its survival, the views expressed in their poems and novels are of primary significance to all those who are interested in the Jewish experience of the twentieth century.

However important the role politics plays in the lives and works of these poets and novelists, it is secondary to the quality of their literary inventiveness, the range and fluidity of their imagination, their mastery of figurative language, the profundity of their thought, and the inspiration of their vision. As accomplished writers they are the equal of their contemporaries anywhere in the Western world, and their genius is most ably demonstrated in their capacity to explore the nature of the Israeli experience in the context of modern Western literary tradition, drawing upon its themes and motifs, its imagery and its techniques. Each of them has acknowledged the influence of Western writers and thinkers in the interviews; and the analyses of their works are filled with the points of contact in thought and in expression with the most accomplished writers and thinkers in the Western world. Among the Western techniques at which the Israelis have become especially adept is their adaptation of relativity principles to their temporal and spatial designs, a technique still so new that its use has largely confounded their otherwise sympathetic and frequently enthusiastic critics.

They have lived in a time when their native language, particularly in its prose usage, has undergone a startling transformation from a medieval tongue into a modern, flexible vehicle responsive to the sophisticated linguistic complexities of contemporary life. They have had the opportunity and the privilege of participating in this revitalization, and each of them, poet and novelist alike, has joined in the experimentation by which Hebrew has been immeasurably enriched. Making Hebrew adaptable to the soaring of their talents has linked them to the reality of the daily social intercourse of their nation whether it manifests itself in formal utterances, informal conversation, colloquialisms or slang, whatever its rhythms and cadences.

They are linked to reality in other ways as well. In the interview with Amichai he said, "Life in Israel is absorbed in reality." The reality reflected in the New Wave literature is one suffused with social and political commitment. From the time these writers achieved their maturity, following the birth of the nation, they realized that the Zionist idealism and the socialist exhortations of the Palmah generation were outmoded. Generally supportive of the political Left, their writing (with the sometime exception of Carmi's poetry, the interests of which tend to be more universal than localized), is marked by social and political commitment. Yehoshua openly uses his fiction to achieve political goals, Oz and Amichai are equally political but less polemical, the political stances they take are always subservient to the creative intention. In Oz's most recent novels, however, the space of demarcation between political statement and creative intention seems to be narrowing. Appelfeld largely resorts to irony to convey his social and political beliefs.

The beliefs of these writers are largely shared. Together they seek a just settlement with the Arabs, security for Israel and the opportunity for its people to fulfill in humane, nonmilitary ways the nation's aspirations. By dramatizing the damaging effect of the prolonged siege mentality in terms of its toll on marriage and family life, they seek to restore tranquility to domestic relations, now awash in malaise and mental instability, afflicted by turmoil, infidelity, desertion and divorce. This inner sickness finds its external manifestations in the landscape, frequently depicted as hostile and threatening. There are borders and limits everywhere; to go beyond them is to affirm the ever present inner irrationality. Frequently, they address the despair of the young, the meaninglessness of their lives, their restlessness and disillusion with the burdens they have inherited, and they give us warnings in their adaptations of the *Akedah* that for whatever reasons, theological, territorial, or punitive, the older generation has no right to sacrifice the younger one. Somehow, they plead, war must be abolished from the face of the earth, and they deplore with all the fervor of the prophets of old the increasing militarism in their country.

With abiding respect for the historic Jewish experience, they maintain that modern day Jews cannot live on their ancient heritage. Primarily secularists, they express their Jewishness not in prayer, piety or participation in institutional religious practices but in their insistence on social justice and on peace, on accepting the principle that we are our brothers' keepers, and on the redemptive power of love. They abhor the hypocrisy and willingness to do violence on the part of the extreme right wing Orthodox zealots, objecting strenuously to fanaticism whatever form it takes.

If they do not believe in Zionism, they are steadfast in their view that the only future for the world's Jews is in the continued development of the Jewish state. Their views about Diaspora are forthright and unequivocal: Amichai and Appelfeld point to the absolute futility of trying to go home again to central Europe. Yehoshua and Oz, perhaps idiosyncratically in the eyes of most American Jews, insist that the voluntary exile of the Jews must end speedily for their own good and for the preservation of the Jewish state. There is no viable alternative; there is only the return to Eretz Israel. To think that the world's animosity toward the Jews will abate is to live in the same kind of fool's paradise that was Badenheim in 1939.

Beyond polemics, beyond political beliefs couched in various literary guises, these writers express what good and great writers have always articulated: a concern not just for the people from whom they spring but for the well-being of all humanity. "I'm not concerned at all about the Jewishness, the Israeliness, the Hebrewness of my poetry," Amichai says in the interview, because it is his life and by extension all humankind that is his subject, it is there to be explored and to be explained. Carmi writes of the interconnectedness of all things in the universe, exalting life and love and primordial energizing forces in nature that fuel our lives and endow them with mystical meaning. Joyce Carol Oates speaks of Appelfeld's "stern and moral vision" that has "opened windows of universal significance on the human condition in some of its darkest hours." The fictions of both Yehoshua and Oz cry out in universal terms on behalf of human salvation. Again I am reminded of the comparison Oz made between the contemporary literary situation in Israel and Elizabethan England. The British dramatists in that most fruitful of eras captured humanity's essence in their comedies and tragedies which, though localized, were universal. The likelihood of a contemporary Israeli parallel, it seems to me, is growing stronger with each new book these writers publish. Of course, it will be a long time before we can know just how truly significant their contribution is. Their time too will pass, and a new generation of writers will spring up to take their places. But I am satisfied that on the basis of their artistry and the dignity, humanness and profundity of their beliefs their contribution to world literature must be a memorable and lasting one.

Notes

Introduction

1. See Leon I. Yudkin, *Escape Into Siege* (New York : Oxford University Press, 1974), pp. 111, 115, 118.

2. Nurith Gertz, "Israeli Novelists," *The Jerusalem Quarterly* no. 17 (Fall 1980), p. 67. This article (pp. 66-77) contains the best short analysis of the motivations behind New Wave writing. For fuller surveys in English of the development of modern Hebrew literature in Israel, see the following: Leon I. Yudkin, *1948 and After: Aspects of Israeli Fiction* (Manchester: University of Manchester Press, 1984); and Gershon Shaked, *The Shadows Within: Essays on Modern Jewish Writers* (Philadelphia: Jewish Publication Society, 1987).

3. Gertz, "Israeli Novelists," p. 67.

4. *Ibid*, p. 67.

5. *Ibid*, p. 67.

6. *Ibid*, p. 67.

7. The term refers originally to the defense forces of the *Haganah*. Its policies were socialistic and closely tied to the kibbutz movement. The kibbutzniks who composed its membership were given military training.

8. Gertz, "Israeli Novelists," p. 71.

9. Shaked, *The Shadows Within:* . . . p. 148.

10. Ibid, p. 153.

11. Ibid, p. 157.

12. One of Yizhar's key stories, which is believed to have accelerated the advent of realism in Israeli fiction, is entitled "Hirbet Hiz'ah." It is discussed in some detail by Nurith Gertz. Another influential work in this same regard is Amos Kenan's novel *Holocaust II*. Kenan was one of the original satirists who helped to undermine the romanticism of the Palmah generation.

13. Both Gertz and Shaked, (and, I am sure, others writing Hebrew literary criticism not translated into English), have affirmed the connections between Western writing and New Wave writing. However, neither of them has made a detailed analysis of those connections, and they do not discuss the fundamentals of time-space usage to which a substantial portion of my analysis is devoted.

14. This discussion of the literary usage of the relativity theory is taken in the main from my article " 'Shots': A Case History of the Conflict Between Relativity Theory and the Newtonian Absolutes," in *Studies in American Jewish Literature: The World of Cynthia Ozick*, vol. 6 (Fall 1987), pp. 94-104, which analyzes Ozick's metaphysics in her short story "Shots" from *Levitation: Five Fictions* (New York: Knopf, 1982), pp. 39-57.

15. See Lawrence Durrell's early seminal statement on the use of relativity in literature, "Space Time and Poetry," in *A Key To Modern British Poetry* (Norman Okla.: The University of Oklahoma Press, 1970), pp. 24-48 and Robert Nadeau's *Readings From The New Book On Nature.* (Amherst: The University of Massachusetts Press), 1981.

Chapter 1   Yehuda Amichai

1. These works include *Poems* (1968) trans. Assia Gutmann; *Songs of Jerusalem and Myself* (1973) trans. Harold Schimmel; *Amen* (1977) trans. Yehuda Amichai in collaboration with Ted Hughes; *Time* (1979) trans. by various people; *Love Poems A Bilingual Edition* (1981) trans. by various people; *Great Tranquillity: Questions And Answers (1983) trans. Glenda Abramson and Tudor Parfitt; Selected Poetry of Yehuda Amichai* (1986) trans. Chana Bloch and Stephen Mitchell; and *Poems of Jerusalem A Bilingual Edition* (1988) trans. by various people, and all published by Harper & Row in New York. Another translation of "Travels of the Last Benjamin of Tudela" by Ruth Nevo, entitled *Travels A Bilingual Edition* (1986) was published by The Sheep Meadow Press in New York. For commentaries on certain of these works, see the following: *Songs of Jerusalem and Myself*: Leon Wieseltier, "A Hebrew Poet," *Commentary*, vol. 57, no. 5 (May 1974), pp. 68, 70; *Amen*: Ted Hughes, "Introduction" [to *Amen*] pp. 9-18; M. L. Rosenthal, "Hebrew, Arabic and Death," *The New York Times Book Review* (July 3, 1977), pp. 6, 16; *Time*: Gila Ramras-Rauch, "Near East: Time," *World Literature Today*, vol. 54, no. 2 (Spring, 1980), pp. 330-331; *Love Poems: A Bilingual Edition*: Moshe Ron, "Love Poems by Yehuda Amichai," *The New Republic*, vol. 189, no. 9 (March 3, 1982), pp. 39-40; Grace Schulman, "In My Time, In My Place," *The Nation*, vol. 234, no. 21 (May 29, 1982), pp. 662-664; *Great Tranquillity: Questions and Answers*: Robert Pinsky, "Memory and the Immediate," *The New York Times Book Review* (November 13, 1983), p. 27; *The Selected Poetry of Yehuda Amichai*: Gabriel Josipovici, "Translating the World," *The Times Literary Supplement, no. 4,359 (October 17,1986), p. 1158 (reviewed together with Amichai's Travels: A Bilingual Edition,* trans. Ruth Nevo); Mark Rudman, "Car, Bomb, God' ", *The Nation*, vol. 243, no. 19 (December 6, 1986), pp. 646-648. See also Warren Bargad, "Children and Lovers: On Yehuda Amichai's Poetic Works, *Midstream* vol. 21, no. 8 (October 1975), pp. 50-57; Howard Schwartz, "On Amichai's Poetry," *The American Poetry Review*, vol. 8, no. 3 (May-June 1979), p. 42; Anthony Rudolf, "Mediterranean East: an Interview with Yehuda Amichai," *London*

Magazine, vol. 19, no. 11 (February 1980), pp. 68-77; "Yehuda Amichai," *World Authors 1970-1975,* ed. John Wakeman (New York: H. W. Wilson, 1980), pp. 20-22; Naomi B. Sokoloff, "On Amichai's *El male rahamim,*" *Prooftexts A Journal Of Jewish Literary History,* vol. 4, no. 2 (May 1984), pp. 127-140; Nili Scharf Gold, "Images in Transformation in the Recent Poetry of Yehuda Amichai," *Prooftexts A Journal Of Jewish Literary History,* vol. 4 no. 2 (May 1984), pp. 141-152; Robert Alter, "Israel's Master Poet," *The New York Times Magazine* (June 8, 1986), pp. 40-46, 50, 54, 57.

2. Amichai, *Selected Poetry* . . . , p. xii. All further quotations of Amichai's poetry, unless otherwise indicated, are from this compilation and are noted in the text.

3. Shapiro, *Poems of a Jew,* (New York: Random House, 1958) pp. ix-x.

4. C. Day Lewis ed., *The Collected Poems of Wilfred Owen* (New York: New Directions, 1964); "The Show," pp. 50-51; "Greater Love," p. 41.

5. C. Day Lewis ed., *The Collected Poems of Wilfred Owen,* p. 31.

6. Edward Hirsch, "In a Language Torn From Sleep," *The New York Times Book Review* (August 3, 1986), p. 14.

7. Glenda Abramson, "Amichai's God," *Prooftexts A Journal Of Jewish Literary History,* vol. 4, no. 2 (May 1984), p. 115. I am indebted to Abramson's fine essay, which I read for the first time in the process of revising this chapter. It goes into considerably more depth than I have felt the need to do in this part of my discussion, and it is particularly valuable not only in its comparison of attitudes toward God by Amichai's contemporaries, particularly Natan Zach, but in also relating Amichai's feelings about God to the feelings he had for his father. Abramson does not consider the poems written about God by Amichai after 1968, (except for a brief reference to *Great Tranquillity*) and, as I do, the overlapping between her discussion and the one here is minimal. While her discussion of these matters, happily, is extended still further in her book *The Writing of Yehuda Amichai* (Albany: State University of New York Press, 1989), that appeared in print when this one was already in production, a perusal of the chapter entitled "The Father and God" pp. 50-70, indicates only minimal overlapping.

8. C. Day Lewis ed., *The Collected Poems of Wilfred Owen,* p. 58.

9. *Justine.* New York: E.P. Dutton, 1961, p. 168.

10. David Montenegro, "Yehuda Amichai: An Interview By David Montenegro," *The American Poetry Review,* vol. 16, no. 6 (November/December 1987), p. 20.

11. *The Poems of Stanley Kunitz 1928-1978* (Boston: Little, Brown, 1979), pp. 157-158.

12. Abramson, "Amichai's God," p. 118.

13. Abramson, "Amichai's God," p. 118.

14. Abramson, "Amichai's God," p. 119.

15. Abramson, "Amichai's God," p. 120.

16. On Amichai's metaphorical versatility, see also Robert Alter, "Hebrew To English," *The New York Times Book Review* (April 15, 1979), pp. 11, 18-19; and Paul Breslin, "Four Poets Collected and Selected," *Poetry*, vol. 150, no. 5 (August 1987), pp. 286-298. In his review of *The Selected Poetry of Yehuda Amichai*, Breslin writes, "In Amichai, metaphorical invention seems paramount, that virtue which Aristotle thought the surest mark of genius, the least attainable by craft" (295).

17. Although my analysis of "The Visit of the Queen of Sheba" is concerned primarily with the abundant metaphorical content of the poem, it should not be overlooked as an outstanding example of Amichai's early love poetry. The most detailed analysis of Amichai as a love poet is Glenda Abramson's "The Love Poetry of Yehuda Amichai," *AJS Review The Journal of the Association for Jewish Studies*, vol. 11, no. 2 (Fall 1986), pp. 221-247, reprinted in her book *The Writing of Yehuda Amichai* (Albany: State University of New York Press, 1989), pp. 91-123.

18. Montenegro, "Yehuda Amichai: An Interview," p. 16.

19. Montenegro, "Yehuda Amichai: An Interview," p. 16.

20. See, for example, Paul Breslin, "Four Poets Collected and Selected," *Poetry* vol. 150, no. 5, (August 1987), p. 295.

21. Yehuda Amichai, *Not of This Time, Not of This Place* (New York: Harper & Row, 1968), pp. 210-211. Further references to *Not of This Time, Not of This Place* will be included in the text.

22. Robert Alter, *After the Tradition: Essays on Modern Jewish Writing* (New York: E.P. Dutton, 1969), p. 165; and "Home and Away," no. 3,744 (December 7, 1973), p. 1512. For another commentary on the novel, see Amos Elon, "Israeli and Jewish," *The New York Times Book Review* (August 4, 1968), pp. 4, 22.

23. Robert Alter, *After the Tradition*, p. 165.

24. Vernon Young, "It Makes You Wonder," *New York Review of Books*, vol. 26, no. 18 (January 15, 1979), pp. 39-41. Vernon adds that in 1963 he spent two weeks in Wurzburg, which had been "one of the rococo showcases of Central Europe," without having "encountered anyone who had been living there in 1945." The fate of Amichai's home city lends an additional dimension of signficance to his novel's title.

25. Robert Alter, *After the Tradition*, p. 165.

26. e.e. cummings, *The Enormous Room* (New York: Liveright, 1978).

Interview 1   Yehuda Amichai

1. Chana Block, Stephen Mitchell ed., and trans., *The Selected Poetry of Yehuda Amichai* (New York: Harper & Row, 1986), p. 107. All further quotations of Amichai's poetry are from this volume and will be included in the text.

2. Yehudit Kirschen, "Reflections on Love, War and Tradition," *Jewish Press* (February 15, 1983), Omaha, Neb. p. 13.

3. Cynthia Ozick's view of Philip Roth seems to have softened substantially in recent years, and she appears today to be more accepting of him as a Jewish writer. It is interesting to note that she dedicated her novel, *The Messiah of Stockholm*, to him in 1987.

4. Joseph Cohen ed., "Conversations With Dannie Abse," *The Poetry of Dannie Abse* (London: Robson Books, 1983), p. 163.

Chapter 2   A. B. Yehoshua

1. A. B. Yehoshua, in *Three Days And a Child*, trans. Miriam Arad (New York: Doubleday, 1970). For convenience and expediency, references, where a work has been translated into English, will be to the English language translation, which are examined in the order of their appearance in the United States.

2. Yehoshua, *Three Days And A Child*, p. 103.

3. A. B. Yehoshua, *Early In The Summer Of 1970*, trans. Miriam Arad (New York: Doubleday, 1970).

4. Yehoshua, *Early In The Summer Of 1970*, p. 148.

5. A. B. Yehoshua, *The Lover*, trans. Philip Simpson (New York: Doubleday, 1977; reprint E. P. Dutton, 1985).

6. A. B. Yehoshua, *A Late Divorce*, trans. Hillel Halkin (New York: Doubleday, 1984).

7. A. B. Yehoshua, *Five Seasons*, trans. Hillel Halkin (New York: Doubleday, 1989).

8. For a fuller discussion of the stories in this collection, see Nili Wachtel, "A. B. Yehoshua: Between the Dream and the Reality," *Midstream* vol. 25, no. 7 (Aug-Sept, 1979), pp. 48-49; and Esther Fuchs, *Israeli Mythogynies* (Albany: State University of New York Press, 1987), *passim*.

9. Vineta Colby ed., "A. B. Yehoshua," *World Authors 1975-1980 (New York: H. W. Wilson Co., 1985), p. 814.*

10. Colby, *"A. B. Yehoshua," p. 814.*

11. For an English language review of this volume, see Yosef Oren, "Facing The Forests," *Hebrew Book Review,* no. 6 (Fall 1968), pp. 18-21.

12. See Hugh Nissenson, "Evil, Muted but Omnipresent," *The New York Times Book Review* (Oct 25, 1970), p. 56; and Jerome Greenfield, *"Three Days And A Child," Jewish Frontier,* vol. 37, no. 10 (Dec, 1970), pp. 27-28. For a detailed analysis, see Gilead Morahg's "A Symbolic Psyche: The Structure of Meaning in A. B. Yehoshua's 'Flood Tide,'" *Hebrew Studies,* vol. 29 (1988), pp. 81-100. Writing in a semniotic context, which emphasizes the narrative's extensive use of metaphorical signification, Morahg maintains that "Flood Tide" is an eloquent statement of Yehoshua's rejection of an "existential code that attempts to confront the often absurd, and ultimately tragic, exigencies of human existence through repression and misdirection of human emotions" (100).

13. For a discussion of Yehoshua's "opening signals" in this story, see Naomi Sokoloff, "Contrast, Continuity And Contradiction: Opening Signals In A. B. Yehoshua's 'A Poet's Continuing Silence' ", *Hebrew Annual Review,* vol. 5 (1981), pp. 115-136. See also Gilead Morahg, "Outraged Humanism: The Fiction of A. B. Yehoshua," *Hebrew Annual Review,* vol. 3 (1979), pp. 141-155. In this study, Morahg discusses Yehoshua's early stories leading up to and including *The Lover.*

14. Nili Wachtel, "A. B. Yehoshua: Between the Dream and the Reality," *Midstream,* vol. 23, no. 7 (August-September 1979): p. 49.

15. A. B. Yehoshua, *Two Plays: A Night In May and Last Treatment* (New York: Schocken, 1974).

16. For a counter view of women in Yehoshua's work as marginal, passive and often silent, see Esther Fuchs's chapter on Yehoshua in *Israeli Mythogynies* (Albany: State University of New York Press, 1987), pp. 47-56. Her analysis is rich and incisive but lacking balance and objectivity in its total feminist approach. Fuchs sees Yehoshua's portrayal of women as a continuation of the Palmah tradition, with its insistence on traditional male hegemony, a view that is open to question by virtue of the fact that Yehoshua's males are frequently powerless, and rendered so by their women. His stance is closer, it seems to me, to the way in which writers in contemporary Western literature treat men and women. The men are Prufrockian or are ineffectual husbands dominated by strong-willed women, as in Philip Roth's *Goodbye Columbus,* Saul Bellow's *Herzog,* Ernest Hemingway's *The Sun Also Rises,* and F. Scott Fitzgerald's *Tender Is The Night.*

17. For commentary on various of the three novellas, see Nili Wachtel, "A. B. Yehoshua: Between the Dream and the Reality," pp. 51-52; Esther Fuchs, *Israeli Mythogynies,* p. 43, 49-50; Anatole Broyard, "Books of The Times," *The New York Times* (February 4, 1977), p. C21; Robert Alter, *Defenses of the Imagination* (Philadelphia: Jewish Publication Society, 1977), pp. 229-230; Warren Bargad, "War, Allegory and Psyche," *Midstream* vol. 24, no. 8 (Oct 1978), pp. 76-78; and Alan Mintz, "New Israeli Writing," *Commentary* vol. 65, no. 1 (January 1978), pp. 64-67.

18. Mintz, "New Israeli Writing," p. 66; Wachtel, "A. B. Yehoshua: Between the Dream . . ." p. 52.

19. Warren Bargad, "Private Testimonies, Public Issues," *Midstream* vol. 25, no. 7 (Aug-Sept 1979), p. 56. See also Elliot King's interview with Yehoshua, "I Want to go Deeper into Reality," *Jewish Frontier,* vol. 46, no. 7 (August-September 1979), pp. 5-9.

20. See Durrell's seminal statement on the use of relativity in literature "Space, Time and Poetry," *A Key To Modern British Poetry* (Norman: University of Oklahoma Press), pp. 24-49; and Robert Nadeau, *Readings From The New Book On Nature* (Amherst: University of Mass. Press, 1981).

21. For other critiques of *A Late Divorce* see Harold Bloom, "Domestic Derangements," *New York Times Book Review* (Feb 19. 1984) pp. 1, 31; Leon Wieseltier, "The Fall of a Family," *The New Republic* vol 190, no. 10 (Mar 12, 1984), pp. 38-40; Robert Alter, "A World Awry," *Times Literary Supplement,* no. 4, 283 (May 3, 1985), p. 498; Gabriele Annan, "Breaking Up in Haifa," *The New York Review of Books,* vol. 31, no. 10

(June 14, 1984), pp. 11-13; and Leah Hadomi, "The Family Novel As A Reflection Of History: Billiards At Half Past Nine (H. Boll) And A Late Divorce (A. B. Yehoshua)," *Hebrew Annual Review*, vol. 11 (1987), pp. 105-127.

22. For further commentary on *Five Seasons* see Shmnel Huppert, "A. B. Yehoshua's Novel 'Molcho' ", *The Jewish Spectator*, vol. 52, no. 2 (Summer 1987), pp. 48-51, reprinted in a slightly different version as "One Has To Fall In Love," *Modern Hebrew Literature*, vol. 13, nos. 1-2 (Fall-Winter 1987), pp. 7-11; and Lore Segal, "Post-Mortem Possibilities," *The New York Times Book Review* (January 29, 1989), pp. 1, 36.

Chapter 3   T. Carmi

1. See, for example, the selections in Ruth F. Mintz, ed. and trans. *Modern Hebrew Poetry A Bilingual Anthology* (Berkeley: University of California Press, 1966), pp. 328-339; and Howard Schwartz and Anthony Rudolf eds. *Voices Within The Ark The Modern Jewish Poets* (New York: Avon Books, 1980), pp. 63-68.

2. The introduction appeared first as "Israeli Poetry—Carmi and Pagis," *The Nation*, vol. 216, no. 14 (April 2, 1973), pp. 436-438.

3. T. Carmi, *The Brass Serpent*, trans. Dom Moraes and T. Carmi (Athens: Ohio University Press, 1964) p. 9. Further references to *The Brass Serpent* will be included in the text.

4. D. H. Lawrence. *Birds, Beasts And Flowers* (New York: Haskell House Publishers, 1974), p. 11.

5. Lawrence, *Birds, Beasts . . .* p. 11.

6. Lawrence, *Birds, Beasts . . .* p. 115.

7. Lawrence, *Birds, Beasts . . .* p. 116.

8. *The Zohar* (The Book of Splendor) is the central work of Jewish mysticism. It is attributed to a thirteenth-century Spanish Jewish Kabbalist, Moses de Leon, living in Guadalajara, and according to J. Abelson, it "purports to be a record of discourses carried on between Rabbi Simeon ben Yohai, who lived in the second century of the common era, and certain contemporary Jewish mystical exegetes" (*The Zohar*, trans. by Harry Sperling and Maurice Simon [London: The Soncino Press, 1933], pp. ix-x).

9. *The Collected Poems Of Dylan Thomas* (New York: New Directions,1953), p. 10.

10. Lawrence, Birds, Beasts . . . p. 116.

11. T. Carmi, trans. Grace Schulman *At the Stone of Losses* (Philadelphia: Jewish Publication Society, 1983), p. 21. Further references to *At The Stone Of Losses* will be included in the text.

12. Mintz, *Modern Hebrew Poetry . . .*, p. 328.

13. Mintz, *Modern Hebrew Poetry . . .*, p. 356. The quotation is from Marx And Engels, *Literature and Art* (New York International Publishers), p. 60.

14. Mintz, *Modern Hebrew Poetry* ... p. 356.

15. Mintz, *Modern Hebrew Poetry* ... p. 356.

16. Schulman, *At The Stone of Losses,* p. xii. Given the paucity of critical writing about Carmi in America, Schulman's introduction to *At The Stone of Losses,* although brief, provides an excellent overview of his life and themes. Other critical dicta in English include the following: (unidentified reviewer) "Broken Silences," *The Times Literary Supplement,* no. 3,273 (November 19, 1964), p. 1040; Anne Stevenson, "Across the Language Lines," *The Times Literary Supplement,* no. 3,894 (October 29, 1976), p. 1370; "T. Carmi," *World Authors 1970-1975,* John Wakeman ed. (New York: The H. W. Wilson Co., 1980), pp. 148-150 (largely biographical); Jon Silkin, "Domestic Discontinuities," *The Times Literary Supplement,* no. 4,248 (August 31, 1984), p. 962, and Rebecca Toueg, "Half My Desire," *Modern Hebrew Literature,* vol. 11, nos. 1-2 (Fall-Winter 1985), pp. 44-45. Probably Carmi's best known book is *The Penguin Book of Hebrew Verse* (New York: Penguin Books, 1981), which he edited and whose selections he translated in this bilingual compilation. It contains a long and useful introduction recounting the history of Hebrew poetry through the ages. It is a pity he did not include any of his own poems. Another shorter survey of Hebrew poetry by him, entitled "The Heritage of Hebrew Poetry" appeared in *The Times Literary Supplement,* no. 3,894 (October 29, 1976), p. 1,355.

17. This is an allusion to the midrashic notion that during the time the fetus is in the womb, God reveals to it all the knowledge of the universe and the story of its earthly life to come. At birth, this "wisdom" is forgotten.

Interview 3   T. Carmi

1. T. Carmi, *At The Stone Of Losses* (Philadelphia: Jewish Publication Society of America/Berkeley: The University of California Press 1983), p. 5. Further quotations from *The Stone Of Losses* will be included in the text.

2. Abraham Abulafia, a native of Sargossa, Spain, was born in 1240 and died in 1300. He authored many kabbalistic texts; few have survived.

3. The *Sefer Yetsirah* (Book of Creation) is the earliest surviving work of Jewish Mysticism. Its author (or authors) is unknown. It appears to have been transcribed by the ninth century of the common era but was probably in circulation much earlier.

4. Carmi's translation in *The Penguin Book of Hebrew Verse.* (New York: Penguin Books, 1981), p. 48.

5. Carmi's translation in *The Penguin Book of Hebrew Verse,* p. 560.

6. Lewis ed., *The Collected Poems Of Wilfred Owen,* p.42.

Chapter 4   Aharon Appelfeld

1. Chaim Grade, *My Mother's Sabbath Days A Memoir.* (New York: Alfred A. Knopf, 1986).

2. Primo Levi, *Survival In Auschwitz and The Reawakening, Moments of Reprieve, The Drowned And The Saved* (New York: Summit Books, 1986, 1988).

3. Larence Durrell, *Justine* (New York: E. P. Dutton, 1961), p. 17.

4. Irving Howe maintains that Appelfeld, as "a spiritual descendant of European modernism" was chiefly influenced by Kafka and Mann who "also made vacation resorts into homes of disease. . . ." "Novels of Other Times and Places," *The New York Times Book Review* (November 23, 1980), p. 40.

5. Gershon Shaked, *The Shadows Within* (Philadelphia: The Jewish Publication Society, 1987). Shaked also sees in Kafka, (p. 18) and to a lesser extent, Agnon, the source for Appelfeld's use of "the cyclic plot, the paranoia of the antihero, and [certain unspecified] allegorical hints."

6. Shaked, *The Shadows Within*, p. 18.

7. Aharon Appelfeld, *Badenheim 1939*, trans. Dalya Bilu (Boston: David R. Godine, 1980), p. 147. Further references to *Badenheim 1939* will be included in the text.

8. Gabriele Annan, "Before the Deluge," *The New York Review of Books*, vol. 28, no. 1 (February 5, 1981), p. 3.

9. Sander Gilman, *Jewish Self-Hatred* (Baltimore: The Johns Hopkins University Press, 1986) *passim.*

10. Christopher Lehmann-Haupt "Badenheim 1939," *The New York Times*, sec 3 (December 9, 1980), p. 86. For other commentaries on *Badenheim 1939* see Thomas Flanagan, "We Have Not Far To Go," *The Nation*, vol. 232, no. 4 (January 31, 1981), p. 122; Lesley Hazleton, "Badenheim 1939," *New Republic*, vol. 184, no. 7 (February 14, 1981), p. 40; David Evanier, "A Summer Resort," *National Review*, vol. 33, no. 11 (June 12, 1981), pp. 674, 676-677; Robert Fyne, "Not Far To Go," *The Christian Century*, vol. 98, no. 22 (July 1-8, 1981), pp. 712-713; Idris Parry, "The Voices of Sickness" *Times Literary Supplement*, no. 4,103 (November 20, 1981), p. 1,374; Ruth R. Wisse, "Aharon Appelfeld, Survivor," *Commentary*, vol. 76, no. 2 (August, 1983), p. 73-76.

11. Aharon Appelfeld, *The Age of Wonders* trans. Dalya Bilu (Boston: David R. Godine, 1981), p. 6. Further references to *The Age of Wonders* will be included in the text.

12. Gabriel Josipovici, "Silently Mending," *The Times Literary Supplement*, no. 4,155. (November 19, 1982), p. 1,269.

13. Virginia Woolf, "Time Passes," *To The Lighthouse*, (New York: Harcourt, Brace & World, 1955), pp. 189-214.

14. See, for example, Dov Vardi, "Israel: *Tor hapelaot*," *World Literature Today*, vol. 53, no. 2 (Spring 1979), p. 342-343; P. S. Prescott, "The Jewish Virus," *Newsweek*, vol. 98, no. 24 (December 14, 1981), pp. 106, 109; Joel Agee, "The Calm Before the Storm, *The New York Times Book Review* (December 27, 1981), pp. 1, 20; A. Alvarez "Enemies Within," *The New York Review of Books*, vol. 29, no. 1 (February 4, 1982), pp. 33-34; Deborah Kops, "Austrian Jews in a Crumbling World," *Christian Science*

Monitor, vol. 74, no. 92 (April 7, 1982), p. 17; Mark Levene, "Oblique Histories," *Canadian Forum,* vol. 62, no. 719 (June-July 1982), p. 27; and also Wisse, "Aharon Appelfeld Survivor," cited above, pp. 74-75.

15. Josipovici, "Silently Mending," p. 1,269.

16. Aharon Appelfeld, *Tzili The Story of a Life* (New York: E. P. Dutton, 1983), p. 1. Further references to *Tzili The Story of a Life* will be included in the text.

17. The significance of the relationship between Tzili and Mark in terms of the connection between Jewishness and humanity is explored further by Blair T. Birmelin in "A Folk Tale of the Holocaust," *The Nation,* vol. 236, no. 15 (April 16, 1983), pp. 486-488.

18. Rochelle Furstenberg, "The Shirt and the Stripes," *Modern Hebrew Literature,* vol. 9, nos. 1-2 (Fall-Winter 1983), p. 79.

19. Furstenberg, "The Shirt and the Stripes," p. 80.

20. Furstenberg, "The Shirt and the Stripes," pp. 80-81.

21. Patricia Blake, "Exact Fit," *Time,* vol. 121, no. 15 (April 11, 1983), p. 97.

22. Blake, "Exact Fit," p. 97.

23. Joyce Carol Oates, "A Fable of Innocence and Survival," *The New York Times Book Review* (February 27, 1983), p. 9. For other views of *Tzili The Story of a Life* see Thomas LeClair, "Passage Through the Inferno," "Book World," *The Washington Post* (April 3, 1983), pp. 3, 6; Robert M. Adams, "Double Exposure," *The New York Review of Books,* vol. 30, no. 10 (June 16, 1983), pp. 34-36; and also Wisse, "Aharon Appelfeld, Survivor," cited above, pp. 75-76.

24. Michael F. Harper, "Assimilation, Humiliation, Human Being, Being Human," *Los Angeles Times Book Review* (July 8, 1984), p. 2.

25. Aharon Appelfeld, *The Retreat* (New York: E. P. Dutton, 1984), p. 103. Further references to *The Retreat* will be included in the text.

26. Walter Goodman, "The Retreat," *The New York Times,* sec C (April 3, 1984), p. 17. For another mixed response, see Robert Alter, "A World Awry," *The Times Literary Supplement,* no. 4,283 (May 3, 1985), p. 498.

27. Vivian Gornick, "End of the Holocaust Myth," *The Village Voice,* vol. 29, no. 17 (June 5, 1984), p. 51.

28. Michael F. Harper, "Assimilation, Humiliation, Human Being, Being Human," p. 2.

29. Jakov Lind, "Despair on a Lonely Hill," *The New York Times Book Review* (May 20, 1984), p. 38. For another positive impression of *The Retreat* see also John Skow, "Magic Mountain," *Time,* vol. 123, no. 22 (May 28, 1984), p. 86.

30. Robert Alter, "Mother and Son, Lost in a Continent," *The New York Times Book Review* (November 2, 1987), pp. 1, 34-35.

31. Patrick Parrinder, "Charmed Lives," *London Review of Books*, vol. 9, no. 8 (April 23, 1987), p. 16. For other views of *To The Land Of The Cattails* see Merle Rubin, "Novel Evokes Dreamlike Stillness Before Holocaust Nightmare," *The Christian Science Monitor* (November 12, 1986), p. 38; D.J. Enright, "Bridges & Boundaries," *New York Review of Books*, vol. 33, no. 21 (January 15, 1987), pp. 40-41; and Gabriel Josipovici, "Time on the Palms of Their Hands," *The Times Literary Supplement*, no. 4,378 (February 27, 1987), p. 207.

32. Aharon Appelfeld, *The Immortal Bartfuss*, trans. Jeffrey M. Green (New York: Weidenfeld & Nicholson, 1988), p. 62. Further references to *The Immortal Bartfuss* will be included in the text.

33. Philip Roth, "A Talk With Aharon Appelfeld," *The New York Times Book Review* (February 29, 1988), p. 31. This entire exchange (pp. 1, 28-31) between Roth and Appelfeld greatly complements the one in this book since Roth's questions focus directly on all six of Appelfeld's translated novels whereas my inquiries were intended to elicit from Appelfeld statements about his life and Israeli and Western literature in general. This same issue of *The New York Times Book Review* also contains Leonard Michaels' review of *The Immortal Bartfuss*, pp. 1, 26-27. A third interview with Appelfeld in English was originally published by Esther Fuchs in *Genesis 2* (June 1978), and subsequently reprinted in her *Encounters With Israeli Authors* (Marblehead, Mass.: Micah Publications, 1982), pp. 52-63. See also Matthew Nesvisky, "Aharon Appelfeld: A Profile," *Present Tense*, vol. 12, no. 2 (Winter 1985), pp. 58-60.

34. Philip Roth, "A Talk With Aharon Appelfeld," p. 31.

Chapter 5   Amos Oz

1. See *Be'or hatkhelet ha'aza* (*Under This Blazing Sun*) (Tel Aviv: Sifriat Poalim, 1979), p. 213. This volume of critical essays has not been translated and published in English. The English translation cited here is from Esther Fuch's *Israeli Mythogynies* (Albany: State University of New York Press), 1987, pp. 75-76. Fuchs describes the statement by Oz as an "endearingly playful expansion of the romantic idea that the artist is the slave of his creation," arguing that "Oz is playfully justifying not only his use of a female protagonist-narrator, but also the novel's omissions, repetitions, and excesses (p. 76). Fuchs's feminist purpose is to discredit Oz by rejecting his view of his personal creative process. However, when Oz desribed it for me in the interview in this book, he was earnestly serious about it, and I am satisfied to take him at his word. After all, his process is no different from that of many poets who also consider themselves to be the mediums for the poems that they record. The truth is that we don't know enough about the nature of the creative process to disallow a distinguished writer's insight into the way he functions creatively.

2. Amos Oz, *My Michael* (New York: Alfred A., Knopf, 1972), pp. 6-7. Further references to *My Michael* will be included in the text. The film and scattered techical explanations of Michael's geological interests and research were very likely motivated by Oz's interest in Melville's *Moby Dick*, which contains technical descriptions of whaling. Allu-

sions to *Moby Dick* are conspicuous throughout *My Michael* confirming the importance Oz attaches to it in the interview.

3. Nehama Aschkenasy, "Women and the Double in Modern Hebrew Literature: Berdichewsky/Agnon, Oz/Yehoshua, *Prooftexts A Journal Of Literary History*, vol. 8, no. 1 (January, 1988), p. 121.

4. Walker Percy, *The Moviegoer* (New York: Avon Books, 1982), p. 16.

5. For a fuller discussion of Oz's use of the technique of "doubling" in *My Michael* see Nehama Aschkenasy's "Women and the Double in Modern Hebrew Literature," pp. 121-125.

6. Milton Rugoff, "My Michael," *Saturday Review*, vol. 55, no. 26 (June 24, 1972), p. 60.

7. See Fuchs, *Israeli Mythogynies*, p. 76; and Yosef Oren, "My Michael," *Hebrew Book Review*, no. Six (Fall 1968), pp. 22-24. Oren maintains that *My Michael* is both an intellectual and artistic failure totally, citing the self-pity of the protagonist along with a lack of honesty and courage on the author's part in confronting the problems of contemporary existence. He cites superficiality, incomplete formulation and repetitiveness as grounds for dismissing the book.

8. Esther Fuchs describes *My Michael* as "Oz's version of Madame Bovary" in *Israeli Mythogynies*, p. 76; and Nehama Aschkenasy sees the elderly charcoal seller in *My Michael* as "one of several terrifying old men recalling the similar figures of doom in *Anna Karenina* and *Madame Bovary*" in "Women and the Double in Modern Hebrew Literature," p. 122. Robert Alter observes that Hannah clings to Michael's body "in fear and desperation, as Emma Bovary grasped at Rudolphe and Leon," in *Defenses of the Imagination* (Philadelphia: Jewish Publication Society 1977), p. 223. However, Pearl K. Bell, in quoting an unidentified American reviewer's remark that *My Michael* is a modern Israeli *Madame Bovary* contends that calling on Flaubert is "a wild [reach] into left field" not "relevant" to the work, "Lost In The Land Of Oz," *The New Leader*, vol. 58, no. 1 (January 6, 1976), p. 16.

9. Hana Wirth-Nesher, "The Modern Jewish Novel and the City: Franz Kafka, Henry Roth and Amos Oz," *Modern Fiction Studies*, vol. 24, no. 1 (Spring 1978), p. 100.

10. Wirth-Nesher, "The Modern Jewish Novel . . ." p. 102.

11. Wirth-Nesher, "The Modern Jewish Novel . . ." p. 103. On this point, see also Robert Alter, "My Michael," *The New York Review of Books* (May 21, 1972), p. 5.

12. David Stern, "Morality Tale," *Commentary*, vol. 58, no. 1 (July, 1974), p. 100.

13. Amos Oz, "The Quality of Equality," Center for Kibbutz Studies, Overseas Department of the United Kibbutz Movement, for distribution in the Diaspora. Published variously, the essay was printed in the *Greater Phoenix Jewish Times*, Phoenix, Arizona (September 17, 1986), p. 15.

14. Amos Oz, *Elsewhere, Perhaps* (New York: Harcourt Brace Jovanovich, 1973), p. 17. Further references to *Elsewhere, Perhaps* will be included in the text.

15. Michael Wood, "Victims of Survival," *The New York Review of Books* (February 7, 1974), p. 12.

16. Nitza Rosovsky, "The Novelists: Amos Oz," *The New Republic,* vol. 179, no. 16 (October 14, 1978), p. 26.

17. Rosovsky, "The Novelists: . . .," p. 26.

18. The real danger to Noga's welfare is from Zechariah Siegfried Berger who is depicted as a dog that has turned into the dog's close cousin, the wolf. He rather than Ezra is the culprit. Ezra is a bear, in Noga's eyes a "cuddly" bear and no mortal threat to her. Oz associates Zechariah Siegfried with dogs in two respects: as a lascivous animal always ready to commit fornication, and as pariahs to be exterminated.

19. Amos Oz, *Touch The Water Touch the Wind* (New York: Harcourt Brace Jovanovich, 1974), p. 1. Further references to *Touch the Water Touch the Wind* will be included in the text.

20. Alan Friedman, "The Magical and the Mundane," *The New York Times Book Review* (November 24, 1974), p. 7.

21. Pearl K. Bell, "Lost In The Land Of Oz," p. 16.

22. John Thompson, "At Least One Way," *The New York Review of Books* (January 23, 1975), p. 40.

23. Gila Ramras-Rauch, "The Re-Emergence Of The Jew In The Israeli Fiction Of The 1970's," *Hebrew Annual Review,* vol. 2 (1978), pp. 139-140.

24. Jorge Luis Borges, *Labyrinths* (New York: New Directions, 1964), pp. 88-94.

25. For other interpretations of *Unto Death,* see Ivan Sanders, "Unto Death," *The New Republic,* vol. 173, no. 22 (November 29, 1975), pp. 36-37; Warren Bargad, "Amos Oz and the Art of Fictional Response," *Midstream,* vol. 22, no. 9 (November, 1976), pp. 61-64; Zephyra Porat, "The Golem from Zion," *Ariel,* no. 47 (1978), pp. 74-75; and Gershon Shaked, "Challenges And Question Marks," *Modern Hebrew Literature,* vol. 10, nos. 3-4 (Spring-Summer 1985), p. 21.

26. Rosovsky, "The Novelists: . . . ," p. 26.

27. Rosovsky, "The Novelists: . . . ," p. 26.

28. Amos Oz, "Reflections on an Anniversary," *Time,* vol. 111, (May 15, 1978), p. 61.

29. Amos Oz, *Unto Death* (New York: Harcourt Brace Jovanovich, 1975), p. 4. Further references to *Unto Death* will be included in the text.

30. The most succinct non-fictional prose corollary to the imaginatively presented anti-fanaticism in *Unto Death* is in Oz's "Reflections on an Anniversary," cited above. A reading of this short statement will readily demonstrate two things: (1)How closely Oz's ideas are paralleled in his political prose and his fiction; and (2) how much richer the fiction is in his application of exotic realism to his subject.

31. Amos Oz, "The Hill of Evil Counsel," *Commentary,* vol. 65, no. 4, pp. 72-87.

32. Lis Harris in "O Pioneers," *The New Yorker*, vol. 54, no. 25 (August 7, 1978), pp. 79-81, incorrectly assumes that the Kipnis and Kolodny families are one and the same, observing that it is disconcerting "to see the mother calmly setting the family tea cart and passing bowls of oranges when just a few pages earlier we have witnessed her" [desertion]. Far from being confused, Oz's parallel representations, I believe, are intentional, given the similarity of these neighbors' lives. Though relativity does not provide the framework for these novellas, the absence/presence of the mother would both be legitimated by it.

33. Amos Oz, *The Hill of Evil Counsel* (New York: Harcourt Brace Jovanovich, 1978), pp. 57-58. Further references to *The Hill of Evil Counsel* will be included in the text.

34. *Soumchi* first published by Am Oved in Israel in 1978; translated by Penelope Farmer and published in the United States by Harper and Row.

35. *Where the Jackals Howl* first published by Massada in Israel in 1965, containing nine short stories; translated by Nicholas de Lange and Philip Simpson and published in the United States by Harcourt Brace Jovanovich with one story deleted.

36. *In the Land of Israel* first published by Am Oved in Israel in 1983; translated by Maurie Goldberg-Bartura and published in the United States by Harcourt Brace Jovanovich.

37. See for example, *Where the Jackals Howl:* A. G. Mojtabai, "Perpetual Stranger in the Promised Land," *The New York Times Book Review* (April 26, 1981), pp. 3, 35; Lesley Hazleton, "Tales from Israel," *The New Republic*, vol. 184, no. 26 (June 27, 1981), pp. 39-40; Judith Chernaik, "The Story-Teller in the Kibbutz," *The Times Literary Supplement*, no. 4,095 (September 25, 1981) p. 1092; Daniel P. Deneau, [untitled review] *Studies in Short Fiction*, vol. 19, no. 1 (Winter, 1982), pp. 82-84; Nehama Aschkenasy, "On Jackals, Nomads, and the Human Condition," *Midstream*, vol. 29, no. 1 (January, 1983), pp. 58-60; Esther Fuchs, "The Beast Within: Women In Amos Oz's Early Fiction," *Modern Judaism*, vol. 4, no. 3 (October 1984), pp. 311-320; and Leon I. Yudkin, "The Jackal and the Other Place: the Stories of Amos Oz," *1948 And After: Aspects Of Israeli Fiction* (Manchester: University of Manchester, 1984), pp. 135-140. *In The Land Of Israel:* Clive Sinclair, "Israelis Versus Jews," *The Sunday Times* (November 6, 1983), p. 43; Irving Howe, "Journey To Other Sites," *Atlantic*, vol. 252, no. 6 (December 1983), pp. 106-108; Eliahu Matz, "Oz's Odyssey," *Midstream*, vol. 30, no. 3 (March 1984), pp. 62-63 ; Robert Alter, "The Writers and the War," *The New York Times Book Review* (March 27, 1983), pp. 11, 34-35; Roger Rosenblatt, "From the Battlefield of Beliefs," *The New York Times Book Review* (November 6, 1983), pp. 1, 46-47; Grace Schulman, "Israeli Visions of Israel," "Book World," *The Washington Post* (November 13, 1983) pp. 4, 14; Steven G. Kellman, [untitled review] *The Village Voice*, vol. 29, no. 7 (February 14, 1984), pp. 57-59; and Ruth R. Wisse, "Matters of Life & Death," *Commentary*, vol. 77, no. 4 (April 1984), pp. 68, 70-71.

38. Amos Oz, *A Perfect Peace* (New York: Harcourt Brace Jovanovich, 1985), p. 6. Further references to *A Perfect Peace* will be included in the text.

39. Malcolm Lowry, *Under The Volcano* (Philadelphia: J. B. Lippincott Co., 1965), p. 354.

40. Yudkin, "The Jackal . . ." p. 170.

41. Nathan Alterman, "Weeping." In Amos Oz, *Black Box,* trans. Nicholas de Lange and Amos Oz (New York: Harcourt Brace Jovanovich 1988) [p. 7]. Further references to *Black Box* will be included in the text.

42. Lawrence Durrell, *Balthazar* (New York: E. P. Dutton, 1961), p. 115. Another parallel characterization seems to exist between Oz's Volodya Gudonski, Alec's father, and Capodistria, Justine's uncle who raped her when she was a child.

43. Mary Gordon, "Abasement Was Irresistible," *The New York Times Book Review* (April 24, 1988), p. 7.

44. Andrew Silow Carroll, "Amos Oz Writes Political, Not Partisan, Novels," *The Jewish Journal,* Los Angeles, Ca (August 12, 1988), p. 20. This article was printed in many American Jewish newpapers.

45. Carroll, "Amos Oz Writes . . ." p. 20.

Interview 5   Amos Oz

1. Dannie Abse, "No More Mozart" *Collected Poems* (Pittsburgh: University of Pittsburgh Press, 1977), p. 156.

Selected Bibliography

Israeli Authors' Works Translated Into English

Yehuda Amichai

Poems. Translated by Assia Gutmann. New York: Harper & Row, 1968.

Not of This Time, Not of This Place. Translated by Shlomo Katz. New York: Harper & Row, 1968.

Song of Jerusalem and Myself. Translated by Harold Schimmel. New York: Harper & Row, 1973.

Amen. Translated by Yehuda Amichai and Ted Hughes. New York: Harper & Row, 1977.

Time. Various translators. New York: Harper & Row, 1979.

Love Poems A Bilingual Edition. Various translators. New York: Harper & Row, 1981.

Great Tranquillity: Questions And Answers. Translated by Glenda Abramson and Tudor Parfitt. New York: Harper & Row, 1983.

The World Is A Room and other stories. Various translators. Philadelphia: Jewish Publication Society, 1984.

Selected Poetry of Yehuda Amichai. Translated by Chana Bloch and Stephen Mitchell. New York: Harper & Row, 1986.

Travels A Bilingual Edition. Translated by Ruth Nevo. New York: Sheep Meadow Press, 1986.

Poems Of Jerusalem A Bilingual Edition. Various translators. New York: Harper & Row, 1988.

Aharon Appelfeld

Badenheim 1939. Translated by Dalya Bilu. Boston: David R. Godine, 1980.

The Age of Wonders. Translated by Dalya Bilu. Boston: David R. Godine, 1981.

Tzili The Story of a Life. Translated by Dalya Bilu. New York: E.P. Dutton, 1983.

The Retreat. Translated by Dalya Bilu. New York: E.P. Dutton, 1984.

To The Land Of The Cattails. Translated by Jeffrey M. Green. New York: Weidenfeld & Nicolson, 1986.

The Immortal Bartfuss. Translated by Jeffrey M. Green. New York: Weidenfeld & Nicolson, 1988.

T. Carmi

The Brass Serpent. Translated by Dom Moraes and T. Carmi. Athens: Ohio University Press, 1964.

The Modern Hebrew Poem Itself. Edited by Stanley Burnshaw, T. Carmi and E. Spicehandler. New York: Holt, Rinehart & Winston, 1965; reprinted by Schocken Books, 1966.

Somebody Like You. Translated by Stephen Mitchell. London: Andre Deutsch, 1971.

T. Carmi and Dan Pagis, Selected Poems. Translated by Stephen Mitchell. London: Penguin Books, 1976.

The Penguin Book of Hebrew Verse. Edited and translated by T. Carmi. New York: Penguin Books, 1981.

At The Stone Of Losses. Translated by Grace Schulman. Philadelphia: Jewish Publication Society/University of California Press, 1983.

Amos Oz

My Michael. Translated by Nicholas de Lange and Amos Oz. New York: Alfred A. Knopf, 1972.

Elsewhere, Perhaps. Translated by Nicholas de Lange and Amos Oz. New York: Harcourt Brace Jovanovich, 1973.

Touch the Water Touch the Wind. Translated by Nicholas de Lange and Amos Oz. New York: Harcourt Brace Jovanovich, 1974.

Unto Death. Translated by Nicholas de Lange and Amos Oz. New York: Harcourt Brace Jovanovich, 1975.

The Hill of Evil Counsel. Translated by Nicholas de Lange. New York: Harcourt Brace Jovanovich, 1978.

Where the Jackals Howl and other stories. Translated by Nicholas de Lange and Philip Simpson. New York: Harcourt Brace Jovanovich, 1981.

In The Land Of Israel. Translated by Maurie Goldberg-Bartura. New York: Harcourt Brace Jovanovich, 1983.

A Perfect Peace. Translated by Hillel Halkin. New York: Harcourt Brace Jovanovich, 1985.

Black Box. Translated by Nicholas de Lange and Amos Oz. New York: Harcourt Brace Jovanovich, 1988.

A.B. Yehoshua

Three Days And A Child. Translated by Miriam Arad. New York: Doubleday, 1970.

Early In The Summer of 1970. Translated by Miriam Arad, Pauline Shrier. New York: Doubleday, 1970.

Two Plays: A Night In May and Last Treatment. New York: Schocken, 1974.

The Lover. Translated by Philip Simpson. New York: Doubleday, 1977, reprinted by E.P. Dutton, 1985.

Between Right And Right. Translated by Arnold Schwartz. New York: Doubleday, 1981.

A Late Divorce. Translated by Hillel Halkin. New York: Doubleday, 1984.

Five Seasons. Translated by Hillel Halkin. New York: Doubleday, 1989.

Selected Criticism

Abramson Glenda. *The Writing of Yehuda Amichai.* Albany: State University of New York Press, 1989.

Alter, Robert. *After the Tradition: Essays on Modern Jewish Writing.* New York: E. P. Dutton, 1969.

_____. *Defenses of the Imagination.* Philadelphia: Jewish Publication Society, 1977.

Durrell, Lawrence. *A Key To Modern British Poetry.* Norman: University of Oklahoma Press, 1970.

Fuchs, Esther. *Encounters With Israeli Authors.* Marblehead, Ma.: Micah Publications, 1982.

_____. *Israeli Mythogynies.* Albany: State University of New York Press, 1987.

Gilman, Sander. *Jewish Self-Hatred.* Baltimore: The Johns Hopkins University Press, 1986.

Mintz, Alan. *Responses To Catastrophe In Hebrew Literature.* New York: Columbia University Press, 1984.

Nadeau, Robert. *Readings From The New Book On Nature.* Amherst: The University of Massachusetts Press, 1981.

Shaked, Gershon. *The Shadows Within.* Philadelphia: Jewish Publication Society, 1987.

Yudkin, Leon I. *Escape Into Siege.* New York: Oxford University Press, 1974.

_____. *Jewish Writing and Identity in the Twentieth Century.* London: Croom Helm, 1982.

_____. *1948 And After: Aspects Of Israeli Fiction.* Manchester: University of Manchester, 1984.

Articles and Interviews

Abramson, Glenda. "Amichai's God." *Prooftexts* 4. 2 (May 1984): 111-126.

_____. "The Love Poetry of Yehuda Amichai." *AJS Review* 11. 2 (Fall 1986): 221-247.

Aschkenasy, Nehama. "Women and the Double in Modern Hebrew Literature: Berdichewsky/Agnon, Oz/Yehoshua." *Prooftexts* 8. 1 (January 1988): 113-128.

Bargad, Warren. "Children and Lovers: On Yehuda Amichai's Poetic Works." *Midstream* 21. 8 (October 1975): 50-57.

_____. "Amos Oz and the Art of Fictional Response." *Midstream* 22. 9 (November 1976): 61-64.

_____. "War, Allegory and Psyche." *Midstream* 24. 8 (October 1978): 76-78.

Cohen, Joseph. " 'Shots': A Case History of the Conflict Between Relativity Theory and the Newtonian Absolutes." *Studies in American Jewish Literature* 6 (Fall 1987): 94-104.

Gertz, Nurith. "Israeli Novelists." *The Jerusalem Quarterly* 17 (Fall 1980): 66-77.

Gold, Nili Scharf. "Images in Transformation in the Recent Poetry of Yehuda Amichai." *Prooftexts* 4. 2 (May 1984): 141-152.

Hadomi, Leah. "The Family Novel As A Reflection Of History: At Half Past Nine (H. Boll) And A Late Divorce (A.B. Yehoshua)." *Hebrew Annual Review* 11 (1987): 105-127.

Huppert, Shmnel. "Molcho." *The Jewish Spectator* 52. 2 (Summer 1987): 48-51.

King, Elliot. "I Want to go Deeper into Reality." *Jewish Frontier* 46. 7 (August/September 1979): 5-9. [Interview with A.B. Yehoshua]

Morahg, Gilead. "Outraged Humanism: The Fiction of A.B. Yehoshua." *Hebrew Annual Review* 3 (1979): 141-155.

_____. "A Symbolic Psyche: The Structure of Meaning in A.B. Yehoshua's 'Flood Tide.' " *Hebrew Studies* 29 (1988): 81-100.

_____. "Facing the Wilderness: God and Country in the Fiction of A. B. Yehoshua." *Prooftexts*, 8.3 (September 1988): 311-331.

Montenegro, David. "Yehuda Amichai: An Interview." *The American Poetry Review* 16, 6 (November/December 1987): 15-20.

Porat, Zephyra. "The Golem from Zion." *Ariel* 47 (1978): 71-79.

Ramas-Rauch, Gila. "The Re-Emergence Of The Jew In The Israeli Fiction Of The 1970's." *Hebrew Annual Review* 2 (1978): 131-144.

Rosovsky, Nitza. "The Novelists: Amos Oz." *The New Republic* 179.16 (October 14, 1978): 25-27. [Interview]

Roth, Philip. "A Talk With Aharon Appelfeld." *The New York Times Book Review* (February 29, 1988): 1, 28-31. [Interview]

Rudolf, Anthony. "Mediterranean East: an Interview with Yehuda Amichai." *London Magazine* 19. 11 (February 1980): 68-77.

Shaked, Gershon. "A Great Madness Hides Behind All This." *Modern Hebrew Literature* 8. 1-2 (Fall/Winter 1982/3): 14-26.

Sokoloff, Naomi B. "Contrast, Continuity And Contradiction: Opening Signals In A.B. Yehoshua's 'A Poet's Continuing Silence.'" *Hebrew Annual Review* 5 (1981): 115-136.

_____. "On Amichai's *El male rahamim*." *Prooftexts* 4. 2 (May 1984): 127-140.

Wachtel, Nili. "A.B. Yehoshua: Between the Dream and the Reality." *Midstream* 25. 7 (August-September 1979): 48-54.

Wirth-Nesher, Hana. "The Modern Jewish Novel and the City: Franz Kafka, Henry Roth and Amos Oz." *Modern Fiction Studies* 24. 1 (Spring 1978): 91-109.

Index

Abelson, J., 203n.8

Abramson, Glenda, 12, 19-20, "Amichai's God," 199n.7

Absalom, Absalom (Faulkner), 75

Abse, Dannie, 42-43, "No More Mozart," 189

Abulafia, Abraham, 99, 204n.2

Ad Mavet (Oz), 162

Age of Wonders, The (Appelfeld), 114-115, 118-120, 122-123, 125, 128

Agnon, S. Y., xiv, 3, 37, 45, 55, 73, 133, 142, 181-182

Ahat, Hi Li (All One To Me) (Carmi), 105

Akedah, 17-18, 55, 103, 194

Akhsahav u-ve-yamin Aherim (Now and in Other Days) (Amichai), 9

Alexandria Quartet, The (Durrell), 6, 8, 17, 71-72, 109, 131, 147, 177

Aliyah, failure of, 63, 68; hope for, 137

All One To Me (Carmi), 105

Alter, Robert, 26, 29, 127; *Defenses of the Imagination*, 208n.8

Alterman, Nathan, 4, 97. Translation: *Othello* (William Shakespeare) 101; 102; "Weeping," 174-175

American Jewish novelists, 39-40, 76, 139, 183, and individual authors

American Jewish Press, 35, 79

American literature, 138, 182, and individual authors

American poetry, nature of contemporary, 35

"Amichai's God" (Abramson), 199n.7

Amichai, Yehuda, 73, 78, 102-103, 105, 110, 135, 138, 187, 194-195; arguments with God, 9-20, 29; Auden, indebtedness to, 11; background, 1, 9, 32; break with orthodoxy, 36; career of, 9; Carmi, compared to, 94-95;

causality, breakdown of, 25-26, 31, 39; e. e. cummings, compared to, 29-30; desert in, 41; explicitness of poetic imagery, 40-41; family, 31; father and fatherhood, poems about, 36; father as God, view of, 19-20; father's orthodoxy, 35-36; guilt in, 20; on Hebrew poetry, 37; Holocaust, treatment of, 25-29, 31, 37-38; irony in, 11, 15; on Israeli fiction, 37; on Jewish Mysticism, 41, 89; love poetry, 21-23; love, views on, 33-34, 95; metaphor and simile in, 19, 21-26, 30-31; Montenegro, David, interview with, 19, 24; mother, 36; on pain, 11-12, 16; poetic techniques in, 20-21; Orthodox Judaism, rejection of, 19; relativity theory, use of, 6, 25-27, 29, 31, 39; similarities with Philip Roth, 27; symbolism in, 21, 24; visit to New Orleans, xiv, xvi; war poetry, 11, 13-14, 33-34. Works: *Akhsahav u-ve-yamin Ahreim* (Now And In Other Days), 9; "And That Is Your Glory," 12; *Ba-ruah ha-norá ah ha-zot* (The World Is A Room And Other Stories), 9; "God's Hand in the World," 12; "God Has Pity on Kindergarten Children," 10-11; "A Great Tranquillity: Questions and Answers," 14-15; *Hotel in the Wilderness*, 29; "I Am A Live Man," 36; "Ibn Gabirol," 11-12; *Lo Me-Akhshav, Lo Mi-Kan* (Not Of This Time, Not Of This Place), 9; "Look: Thoughts and Dreams," 12-13; "My Father," 36; "My Father in a White Space Suit," 36; *Not Of This Time, Not Of This Place*, xvi, 6, 20, 25-29, 147; "Poems for a Woman," 17; "The Real Hero," 17-18, 55; "Relativity," 39; *Selected Poetry of Yehuda Amichai*, 9-10; "Songs of Zion the Beautiful,"

219

14-15, 17, 32-33; "A Sort of Apocalypse," 103; "The Times My Father Died," 36; "Travels of the Last Benjamin of Tudela," 13-17, 20; "The Visit of the Queen of Sheba," 21-24, 28; *The World Is A Room And Other Stories,* 6, 29-31, 39

"And That Is Your Glory" (Amichai), 12

Anderson, Sherwood, 142; *Winesburg, Ohio,* 182-183

Animals, in Yehoshua's fiction, 50-51, in Oz's fiction, 141, (jackals), 168, 209n.18

Annan, Gabriele, 112-113

Anti-hero, the, in Appelfeld's fiction, 110; in Yehoshua's fiction, 48

Anti-Semitism, 113, 118, 125

Appelfeld, Aharon, 3, 6, 29, 37, 68, 73-74, 76-77, 182, 194-195; anti-hero in, 110; assimilation in, 107-108, 110, 112, 123, 127, 132-133, 140; background, 2, 108, 131-133, 136; bizarre in, 127, causality, breakdown of, 110-111; central European Jewry, reconstruction of, 107, 109, 111, 119, 126-127, and self-delusion of, 108, 110-111, 116, 118, 125; desert on, 135; detachment in, 109, 114, 120; generational conflict in, 134; Great Moment in, 111-112, 114, 116-117; Holocaust in, 74, 107-109, 112, 114, 116-120, 126-136, 139-140; irony in, 107-108, 110-114, 117, 120, 126-128, 134-135; Jewish Mysticism in, 123, 137; Jewish self-hate in, 110, 114, 118, 123; marital discord in, 117, 129; mood evocation in, 110, 114, 120; nature in, 110, 123; pan-Germanism, use of, 107, 110, 115, 123; relativity theory, use of, 6, 110, 127; subjectivity in, 109-111; symbolism in, 110, 114-116; trains, train stations and transports in, 111, 116-118, 127-128; visit to New Orleans, xiv, xvii, 127. Works: *The Age of Wonders,* 114-115, 118-120, 122-123, 125, 128; *Badenhaym Ir Nofesh* (Badenheim, Holiday Resort), 111; *Badenheim 1939,* 6, 110-116, 119-120, 123-126; *Essays in the First Person,* 107; *The Immortal Bartfuss,* 128-131; *The Retreat,* 123-127, 132; *Shanim vesha'ot* (Years and Hours), 111; *To The Land Of The Cattails,* 6, 94, 127-128, 134-135; *To the Land of the Reeds,* 128; *Tzili The Story of a Life,* 94, 120-123, 126, 128, 134-135

Arab-Israeli conflict, the, 149

Arabs, birthrate of, 79, 137; hostility of, 3, 31, 49, 69, 141, 148, 151-152, 170-171, 173; just settlement with, 194

Arad, Miriam, 47, 54

Arrtzot Hatan (Where the Jackals Howl) (Oz), 142

As I Lay Dying (Faulkner), 59

Aschkenasy, Nehama, 144, 208nn.5, 8

Assimilation, in Appelfeld's fiction, 107-108, 110, 112, 123, 127; 132-133, 140

Assistant, The (Malamud), 139

At The Stone Of Losses (Carmi), 81, 88, 92-93, 98

Auden, W. H., 11

Austria, 110, 113, 119, 125; Nazi Anschluss in, 127; 131

"Author's Apology" (Carmi), 93-94, 99

Autumn of the Patriarch, The (Garcia-Marquez), 178, 188

"Awakening" (Carmi), 91-92

Badenhaym Ir Nofesh (Badenheim, Holiday Resort) (Appelfeld), 111.

Badenheim 1939 (Appelfeld), 6, 110-116, 119-120, 123-126

Balthazar (Durrell), 58, 211n.42. *See also The Alexandria Quartet*

Ba-rauh ha-norá ah ha-zot (The World Is A Room And Other Stories) (Amichai), 9

Bargad, Warren, criticism of Yehoshua's fiction, 58

Barth, John, 7

Bartov, Hanoch, 4

Bauer, Yehuda, xiv

Beaux Stratagem, The (Farquhar), 100

Beckett, Samuel, 98

Begin, Menachem, 178

Bell, Pearl K., 158, 208n.8

Bellow, Saul, xv, 40; *The Dean's December,* 63; *Henderson the Rain King,* 65; *Herzog,* 20, 74, 139; *Humboldt's Gift,* 74; *Mr. Sammler's Planet,* 74, 161, 183; 75

Ben Gurion, David, 168

Be'or hatkhelet ha'aza (Under This Blazing Sun) (Oz), 207n.1

Berdycewski, M. J., xiv, 3, 141, 181-182

Between Right and Right (Yehoshua), 50, 79

Bialik, H. N., 3, 97, 102, 181

Bible, see Hebrew Bible; New Testament

Bilu, Dalya, 111, 114, 120, 123

Birds, Beasts And Flowers (Lawrence), 82

Birmelin, Blair T., "A Folk Tale of the Holocaust," 206n.17

Bitzaron Quarterly, 96

Bizarre, use of the, in Appelfeld, 127; in Yehoshua, 46-47, 57, 62-63

Black Box (Oz), 174-178, 185

Blake, Patricia, 123

Bloch, Chana, 9-10

Blum, Yehuda, xiv

Bohr, Niels, 26

Borges, Jorge Luis, 7, *Labyrinths,* 6; 31; "The Secret Miracle," 159; 160

"Brass Serpent, The" (Carmi), 82-86, 88

Brass Serpent, The (Nehash Hanehoshet) (Carmi), 81-82, 91

Brecht, Bertolt, 153

Brenner, Y. H., xiv, 3, 133, 141, 181-183

Breslin, Paul, "Four Poets Collected and Selected," 200n.16

British Mandate, 165

Brod, Max, 132-133

Brothers, The (Rubens), 70

Browning, Robert, 46

Buber, Martin, 112, 132

Cabala, 161. *See also* Kabbalah

"Cabaret," 153

Cahan, Abraham, *The Rise of David Levinsky,* 151

Call It Sleep (Roth, H.), 122-123, 183

Camus, Albert, 6, 68, 75

Cancer, 52-53, 62-63, 176

Canetti, Elias, 133

Carmi, T. (Carmi Charny), Amichai, compared to, 94-95; background, 2, 96; Hebrew poetry, objectives in, 81, 97-98; Holocaust in, 89-91; Kabbalah, use of, 82, 85-86, 88-91, 95, 99-100; D. H. Lawrence, compared to, 82-83, 85-86; love in, 82, 88-89, 91-92, 95, 105; metaphorical imagery in, 82-83; nature in, 82, 84; Paris, in, 96-97; symbolism in, 86; translation, on, 100-101; visit to New Orleans, xiv, xvi-xvii; war in, 18, 55, 92-94; *Zohar* and Zoharic references in, 84-85, 87, 89, 91, 99. Works: *At The Stone Of Losses,* 81, 88, 92-93, 98; *Ahat Hi Li* (All One To Me), 105; "Author's Apology," 93-94, 99; "Awakening," 91-92; "The Brass Serpent," 82-86, 88; *The Brass Serpent* (Nehash Hanehoshet), 81-82, 91; *T. Carmi and Dan Pagis, Selected Poems,* Mitchell, S., ed., 82;

Davar Aher (Another Version, Selected Poems and Translations, 1951-1969), 81; "Diary Entry," 92; *Eyn Prahim Shehorim* (There Are No Black Flowers), 89; "From This Day On," 99-100; *Hayam ha'Aharon* (The Last Sea), 81; "I Said A Familiar Name," 86-88; "I Say Love," 88-89, 91, 99; "An Israeli Abroad," 99; *Leyad even Hato'im* (At The Stone Of Losses), 81; "Military Funeral at High Noon," 94; *Mum Vahalom* (Blemish and Dream), 81; *The Penguin Book of Hebrew Verse,* ed., 204n.16; "Platform No. 8," 95; "René's Songs," 89-91; "The Song of Thanks," 99; "Story," 98; "To A Pomegranate Tree," 82-83. Translations: *The Beaux' Stratagem* (George Farquhar), 100; *Cyrano de Bergerac* (Edmond Rostand), 100-101, 105; *A Midsummer Night's Dream* (William Shakespeare), 101; *Rosenkrantz and Guildenstern Are Dead,* (Tom Stoppard), 100

T. Carmi and Dan Pagis, Selected Poems (Mitchell, ed.), 82

Carroll, Andrew Silow, 178

Catch-22 (Heller), 113

Catholicism, 10, 35, Mediterranean Catholics, 40

Causality, breakdown of, 6-7, in Amichai's fiction, 25-26, 31, 39; in Appelfeld's fiction, 110-111; in Oz's fiction, 142, 158-160; in Yehoshua's fiction, 58

Cave, The (Warren), p. 18

Central European Jewry, reconstruction of, 107, 109-111, 119, 126-127; self-delusion of, 108, 110-111, 116, 118, 125; 132-133

Charny, Carmi. See T. Carmi

Chazen, Naomi, xiv

Chekhov, Anton, 4, 72, 142, 182-183

Child-women, in Yehoshua's fiction, 52, 57, 63, 67

Christ, Jesus, crucifixion of, 10, 117

Christians, in Oz's fiction, 163-164

Closures, in fiction, 7, in Oz's fiction, 155, 160, 171

Cohen, Joseph, "'Shots': A Case History of the Conflict Between Relativity Theory and the Newtonian Absolutes," 198n.14

Coleridge, S. T. "The Rime of the Ancient Mariner," 85

Connectedness. See Interconnectedness

Conrad, Joseph, 6, 172 , *Heart of Darkness,* 173; 179

Counterlife, The (Roth, P.), 27
Covenant, 10, 16
Creative process, in Oz, 143
Crime and Punishment (Dostoevsky), 75
"*Crusade" (Oz),* 162-163
Crusades, the, in Oz's fiction, 162-163; in
  Yehoshua's fiction, 48-49
Cuchulain, 177
cummings, e. e., *The Enormous Room,* 29-30;
  romantic individualism, 30
Cyrano de Bergerac (Rostand), 100, 105

Daver Aher (Another Version, Selected Poems
  and Translations, 1951-1969) (Carmi), 81
Days of Tiklag (Yizhar), 5, 78
Dean's December, The (Bellow), 63
Death camps, 108, 114, 116, 120, 129
"Death of an Old Man, The" (Yehoshua), 46
Defenses of the Imagination (Alter), 208n.8
de Lange, Nicholas, 142, 155, 162, 165, 189
de, Leon, Moses, 203n.8
Delillo, Don, 7
Desert, pervasiveness of, xv; Amichai on, 41;
  Appelfeld on, 135; Oz on, 141, 171-173, 179
Desertion, in Oz's fiction, 150, 153, 166-167,
  169, 186; 194
Detachment, in Appelfeld's fiction, 109, 114, 120
Devotions Upon Emergent Occasions
  (Donne), 7
"Diary Entry" (Carmi), 92
Diaspora, the, 56, 72, 77, 79-80, 102, 149, 155,
  161, 190-191, 195
Don Giovanni (Mozart), 66
Donne, John, *Devotions Upon Emergent
  Occasions,* 7
Dostoevsky, Fedor, 4-5, 68, 72; *Crime And
  Punishment,* 75; 142, 182
Dreams (and nightmares), 6, in Oz's fiction,
  144-145, 147-149, 151, 156, 164, 166-167;
  temporal and spatial configurations of, 127,
  142; in Yehoshua's fiction, 45, 51, 55-56, 58
Duino Elegies (Rilke), 34
Durrell, Lawrence, 8, 31, *The Alexandria
  Quartet,* 6-8, 17, 71-72, 109, 131, 147, 177;
  Balthazar, 58, 211n.42; *Justine,* 58; 95, 160

"Early In The Summer Of 1970" (Yehoshua), 6,
  46, 54-56
Early In The Summer Of 1970 (Yehoshua), 54
Earth-goddess (earth-mother) characterization,
  31; in Oz's fiction, 177

East European Jewry, 109, 131, 191
Eban, Abba, xiv
Ecclesiastes, 33-34
Egypt and Egyptians, 32, 71, 137, 147
Einstein, Albert, 6, 26, 39, 110
Eliot, T. S., 4, 6, 35, 81-82, 97; "The Hollow
  Men," 128; *The Wasteland,* 98; 138, 187
Elizabethan drama, Israeli literature compared
  to, 1, 181, 195
Elsewhere, Perhaps (Oz), 147, 149-156,
  168-169, 171, 186
Energy, in relativity theory, 7, 25-26, 158-160
Enormous Room, The (cummings), 29-30
Erlich, Haggai, xiv
Eshkol, Levi, 173
Essays in the First Person (Appelfeld), 107
"Evening Journey of Yatir, The" (Yehoshua), 47
Exile, Jewish, 79, 195. *See also* Golah
Existential despair, in Yehoshua's fiction,
  45, 47
Existentialists, Christian, 6; French, 5-6
Exotic realism, in Oz, 142, 145, 163, 165, 172,
  174, 176-177, 179
Eyesight, impaired or defective, in Yehoshua's
  fiction, 48-49, 51, 53
Eyn Prahim Shehorim (There Are No Black
  Flowers) (Carmi), 89

"Facing the Forests" (Yehoshua), 46-51
Fairy tale, the, 149, 152-155, 168-169, 172
Fanaticism, in Oz's fiction, 164, 173-178; 195;
  in Yehoshua's fiction, 48
Farquhar, George, *The Beaux' Stratagem,* 100
Fatalism, Greek, 175
"Father and Son" (Kunitz), 19
Faulkner, William, 4-6, 37, *Absalom, Absalom,*
  75; *As I Lay Dying,* 59; *Light in August,* 74;
  The Sound and the Fury, 59-61, 75; stream-
  of-consciousness in 45, 56; 47, 55, 58, 62-
  63, 68, 73-76, 145, 182, 185, 189
First World War, 29, 46
First World War literature, 33, 46. *See also*
  World War I poets and individual authors
Five Seasons (Yehoshua), 46, 62-68
Flaubert, Gustave, 4-5, 142-143; *Madame
  Bovary,* 146-147, 167, 208n.8; 179
"Flood Tide" (Yehoshua), 47, 54
"Folk Tale of the Holocaust, A" (Birmelin),
  206n.17
"Force That Through the Green Fuse Drives
  the Flower, The" (Thomas, D.), 84

"Four Poets Collected and Selected" (Breslin), 200n.16

Fowles, John, 7

Freud, Sigmund, 6

Friedman, Alan, 157-158

"From This Day On" (Carmi), 99-100

Fuchs, Esther, 202n.16, 208n.8

Furstenberg, Rochelle, 122

"Futility" Owen), 13

Garcia Marquez, Gabriel, *The Autumn of the Patriarch*, 178, 188; 179

Generational conflict, in Appelfeld's fiction, 134; in Oz's fiction, 151, 170; in Yehoshua's fiction, 46, 48-49, 54, 62-63

Germany, 1, 27-28, 31-32; Weimar Republic, 38; 64, 110, 132, 147, 149, 151, 154-156

Gertz, Nurith, 3-5, 197nn.2, 12, 198n.13

Gilboa, Amir, "Isaac," 18, 55, 103-104; 97, 103

Gilman, Sander, *Jewish Self-Hatred*, 113

"Gimpel the Fool" (Singer), 121

Ginsberg, Allen, 35

Gluck, Christoph, *Orpheus and Eurydice*, 66

God, and Amichai's father, 19-20; negative traits in Amichai's view: 9-16, 18; positive traits in Amichai's view: 9-10, 15, 17; 35, 90, 94-95, 178, 181, 188

"God Has Pity on Kindergarten Children" (Amichai), 10-11

God's Grace (Malamud), 18

"God's Hand in the World" (Amichai), 12

Golah (Exile), the, 56, 62, 68

Goodbye Columbus (Roth, P.), 76, 139

Goodman, Walter, 126

Gordon, Mary, 177

Gornick, Vivian, 126

Gothic laconicism, 163

Gothic novel, the, 60

Gouri, Chaim, xvii, 102, 105

Grade, Chaim, 108

Graves, Robert, 100

Gravity's Rainbow (Pynchon), 6, 161

Gray, Joel, 153

Great Moment, the, in Appelfeld's fiction, 111-112, 114, 116-117

"Great Tranquillity: Questions and Answers, A" (Amichai), 14-15

"Greater Love" (Owen), 11

Green, Jeffrey M., 127-128

Gruenzweig, Emil, 190

Grumet, Elinor, 29

Gulliver's Travels (Swift), 174

Hadoar, 96

Haganah, 32, 197n.7

Halkin, Hillel, 29, 62, 78, 168, 190

Halkin, Simon, 97

Hameirit-Sarell, Ada, 29

Hamlet (Shakespeare), 101, 155

Har Ha'etza Ha'raah (The Hill of Evil Counsel) (Oz), 165

Harlow, Jules, 29

Harper, Michael F., 124, 126-127

Harris, Lis, 210n.32

Hartman, David, xiv

Hasidism, 180-181

Hayam ha'Aharon (The Last Sea) (Carmi), 81

Heart of Darkness (Conrad), 173

Hebrew Bible, 10, 12, 37, 42, 85; passages cited from: Ezek. 1:90, 99; Hosea. 19: 90; Micah. 4: 103; Num. 21:8: 83-84; Psalm 103: 176; Sec. Kings. 2: 90.

Hebrew language, xiv, 32, 37, 72, Ashkenazi pronunciation of, 96, 102; iambic pentameter in, 100; rate of obsolescence in theater, 101; Sephardic pronunciation of, 96, 102; 98, 132-133, 182, 194

Hebrew literature, 76, 96, 142, 182, and individual authors

Hebrew poetry, Amichai on, 37; Carmi on, 81, 97-98; 102, 105; rhythms of speech in, 101

Heidegger, Martin, 156, 161

Heisenberg, Werner, 6, 26. *See also* Indeterminacy theory

Heller, Joseph, *Catch-22*, 113

Hemingway, Ernest, 4, 123, 181

Henderson the Rain King (Bellow), 65

Herzl, Theodore, 112

Herzog (Bellow), 20, 74, 139

Hesse, Herman, 112

"Hill of Evil Counsel, The" (Oz), 165-167

Hill of Evil Counsel, The (Oz), 93-94, 165-167

"Hirbet Hiz'ah" (Yizhar), 197n.12

Hirsch, Edward, 11

Hollander, John, 105

"Hollow Men, The" (Eliot), 128

Holocaust, the, xiv, in Amichai, 25-29, 31, 37-38; in Appelfeld, 74, 107-109, 112, 114, 116-120, 126-136, 139-140; in Carmi, 89-91; 77, 79, 81; in Oz, 142, 156, 158

Holocaust II (Kenan), 197n.12

Hotel in the Wilderness (Amichai), 29
Howe, Irving, 205n.4
Hughes, Ted, 42
Humboldt's Gift (Bellow), 74

"I Am A Live Man" (Amichai), 36
"Ibn Gabirol" (Amichai), 11-12
Imagination, in Oz, 142, 156, 165, 174, 177, 179, 185; 193
Immortal Bartfuss, The (Appelfeld), 128-131
Indeterminacy theory (measurement inaccuracy, unpredictability), 6-7, 25-26, 31, 39, 58, 110-111, 158-159
Infidelity, in Oz's fiction, 150-151, 166-167, 170, 175-176; 194.
Infinite, the (infinity), 135, 156-157, 159-161
Insanity (madness), in Oz's fiction, 143, 146, 162-163, 170-174
Insomnia and insomniacs, in Yehoshua's fiction, 52-53, 57-58
Interconnectedness, in human affairs, 30; in Kabbalah, 85, 160; in relativity theory, 7; in the universe, 159, 195
Interviews, format of, xiv-xv
In The Land Of Israel, (Oz), xvii, 167-168
"In the Penal Colony" (Kafka), 47, 54, 153
Irony, in Amichai, 11, 15; in Appelfeld, 107-108, 110-114, 117, 120, 126-128, 134-135; in Owen, 11; in Oz's fiction, 144, 146, 153, 159, 161-163; in Palmah fiction, 4
"Isaac" (Gilboa), 18, 55, 103-104
"I Said A Familiar Name" (Carmi), 86-88
"I Say Love" (Carmi), 88-89, 91, 99
Israel, State of: austerity, 149; cross-cultural influences, 2; existential *angst* of, 193; impact on Appelfeld, 136; incendiary nature of, 2; internal dissension in, 173; language transformation, 2, 101; literary situation in, 1-6, 36-37, 72-73, 101-105, 181-182, 195; madness (mental sickness) in daily life of, 2, 45, 47; 62, 171-174, 194; middle class in, 2, 45, 49, 63; militancy 55, 58, 164-165, 194; publishing in, 105, 139; orthodox extremism in, 40, 57-58, 62, 63, 195; role of the writer in, 3-4, 39; survival of, 46, 50, 79-80, 104, 137, 149, 174, 191, 193.
"Israeli Abroad, An" (Carmi), 99
Israeli fiction, Amichai on, 37
Israeli literature, creativity in, 138; irony in, 4; nationalism in, 72, 138; 1950's group in, 35; 181; political content of, 3;

psychological studies in, 3; satire in, 4; terror, emphasis on, 3
Israeli poetry, Amichai on, 36; Carmi on, 102-104
Israeli writing, direction of, 72, 138; ethnic concerns of, 72-73
"It Makes You Wonder" (Young), 200n.24

James, Henry, 37, 76
Jerusalem, xiii, 27-28, 32, 60, 63, 69, 137, 141, 146-149, 162, 165-166, 180
Jew, definition of, 10
Jewish experience, the, 136
Jewish Mysticism, xv, Amichai on, 41-42, 89; in Appelfeld, 123, 137; in Carmi, 82, 85-91, 95, 99-100; in Oz, 160-161, 181. *See also* Kabbalah
Jewish self-hate, in Appelfeld's fiction, 110, 113-115, 118, 123-125
Jewish Self-Hatred (Gilman), 113
Jewish Studies, Tulane University program, xiii-xiv; 106
Jews, American, 80, 155, 191
Jews, German, in Oz's fiction, 150-151; in Yehoshua's fiction, 63-64; 155
Jews, Russian, 150-151, 155. *See also* East European Jewry
Job, the biblical, 14, 16
Josipovici, Gabriel, 118-120
Joyce, James, 4-6, 35, 45, 47, 55, *Portrait of the Artist as a Young Man,* 61; *Ulysses,* 56, 78; 58, 63, 139-140, 143
Judaism (Jewishness), 38-39, 133, 194-195
Jung, Carl, 6, 138
Justine (Durrell), 58. *See also The Alexandria Quartet*

Kabbalah, Amichai on, 41-42; Carmi's use of, 82, 85-86, 88-91, 95, 99-100; 160. *See also The Zohar* and zoharic passages
Kafka, Franz, 4-5, existential despair of, 45, 55; "In the Penal Colony," 47, 54, 153; 110, 115, 119, 126, 132-133
Kahana-Carmon, Amalia, xvii, 77
Katz, Shlomo, 25
Kefsa Shechora (Oz), 174
Kenan, Amos, *Holocaust II,* 197n.12
Kibbutz, the, (and kibbutzniks), in Oz's fiction, 149-153, 155, 157, 161, 164, 168, 170, 172-174, 183-185; 197n.7
Kibbutz Hulda, 141, 183-185

Kibbutz novel, the, 149-150
Kierkegaard, Søren, 6, 119, 144
King Lear (Shakespeare), 101
Kiss of the Spider Woman (Puig), 188
Klausner, Abraham, 179
Klausner, Amos, 179. See Amos Oz
Klausner family, 162, 179
Klausner, Joseph, 179
Klieman, Aaron, xiv
Kosinski, Jerzy, 123
Kraus, Karl, 112
Kristallnacht, 28
Kufsa Shechora (Black Box) (Oz), 174
Kunitz, Stanley, "Father and Son," 19; reaction to father's suicide, 19; 36
Kurdestan, 137

Labor camps, 108, 120, 131
Labyrinths (Borges), 6
Lafayette Escadrille, 29
La Ferte-mace, 29-30
Laga'at Bamayim Laga'at Baruach (Touch the Water Touch the Wind). Oz, 156
Language, experimentation with, 37, 194; German, 131-132, 180; in Yehoshua's fiction, 55, 73; Yiddish, 132, 180. *See also* Hebrew language
"Last Commander, The" (Yehoshua), 46, 54, 57
Last Treatment (Yehoshua), 50
Late Divorce, A (Yehoshua), 37, 46, 59-63, 69, 78, 182
"Late Love" (Oz), 162, 164
Latin American writers, 178, 187-188, and individual authors
Lawrence, D. H., 6, 47; *Birds, Beasts And Flowers*, 82; "blood consciousness" in, 82; Carmi compared to, 82-83, 85-86; "Pomegranate," 82; "Snake," 82-83, 85-86; 140
Lebanon Campaign (Operation "Peace For Galilee"; the Litani Operation), 32, 92
Lehmann-Haupt, Christopher, 114
Levi, Primo, 108, 118, 133
Levitation, in Oz's fiction, 142, 156, 158-160, 167
Levitation: Five Fictions (Ozick), 6, 198n.14
Leyad Even Hato'im (At The Stone Of Losses) (Carmi), 81
Libya, 2
Light in August (Faulkner), 74
Likud Party, 178
Lind, Jakov, 127

Litani Operation, the. See Lebanon Campaign
Literary techniques: aesthetic distancing, 3, 59, 95, 108, 110, 114, 126; detachment, 109-110, 114, 120, 126
Little Red Riding Hood, 154, 169
Lo Me-Akhshav, Lo Mi-Kan (Not Of This Time, Not Of This Place) (Amichai), 9
"Long Hot Day, His Despair, His Wife And His Daughter, A" (Yehoshua), 47, 52-54, 56-57, 64
"Longing" (Oz), 166-167, 185-186
"Look: Thoughts and Dreams" (Amichai), 12-13
Love, Amichai's views on, 33-34, 95; in Carmi's poetry, 82, 88-89, 91-92, 95, 105; in Lawrence's poetry, 85-86; in Yehoshua's fiction, 51, 54, 68; 195
Lover, The (Yehoshua), 6, 46, 53-54, 56-58, 60, 63.
Lowry, Malcolm, *Under the Volcano*, 6, 172; 7, 31, 95, 160, 179
Lyricism, in Oz's prose, 141, 157, 176-177, 179; in Yehoshua's prose, 45, 59-60

Madame Bovary (Flaubert), 146-147, 167, 208n.8
Magic Mountain, The (Mann), 124
Magician of Lublin, The (Singer), 123
Maimonides, 137
Makom Acher (Elsewhere, Perhaps) (Oz), 142, 149
Malaise, in Oz's fiction, 144, 146; in Percy's fiction, 144; 194
Malamud, Bernard, xv, *God's Grace, 18; 39-40; The Assistant*, 139
Man Without Qualities, The (Musil), 187
Mandelbaum, Allen, 97
Mann, Thomas, 110, *The Magic Mountain*, 124, 187
Marital discord, in Appelfeld's fiction, 117, 129; in Oz's fiction, 144, 146, 148, 150, 165-166, 169-170, 176; in Yehoshua's fiction, 52-54, 62-63
Marx, Karl, "On Style," 90
Mathematics, 156-157, 160
Matter, in relativity theory, 7, 25, 158-159
Measure For Measure (Shakespeare), 101
Mediterranean Sea, area of, 8, 41, 71, 82, 179
Megged, Aharon, xvii, 4
Melville, Herman, 4, 142, *Moby Dick*, 143, 150, 182; 179, 183
Memory, in Oz's fiction, 145

Menschleitkeit, 20
Menucha Nechona (A Perfect Peace) (Oz), 168
Merkabah mysticism, 90, 99
Messiah of Stockholm, The (Ozick), 201n.3
Metafiction, 161
Metamorphoses (Ovid), 49
Metaphor and simile, 19, 21-26, 30-31, 82-83,
    94, 128-129, 156, 168, 177-178
Metaphysics, 159, 161, 188
Michael Sheli (My Michael) (Oz), 142
Middle East, the, 32, 71
Midsummer Night's Dream, A (Shakespeare),
    101
"Military Funeral at High Noon" (Carmi), 94
Mintz, Alan, 55
Mintz, Ruth F. ed., *Modern Hebrew Poetry A*
    Bilingual Anthology, 89-90
"Missile Base 612" (Yehoshua), 54
Mitchell, Stephen, 9; *T. Carmi and Dan Pagis,*
    Selected Poems, ed., 82
Moby Dick (Melville), 143, 150, 182
Modern Hebrew Poetry A Bilingual Anthology
    (Mintz, R. F.), 89-90
Montenegro, David, 19, 24
Mood evocation, in Appelfeld's fiction, 110,
    114, 120; in Conrad's fiction, 173
Moore, Marianne, 81, 97
Moraes, Dom, 81
Morahg, Gilead, "A Symbolic Psyche: The
    Structure of Meaning in A. B. Yehoshua's
    "Flood Tide," 201n.12
Morality play, the, 149, 155
Mosinzon, Yigal, 4
Mot ha-zaken (Yehoshua), 45, "The Death of
    an Old Man," 46; "The Evening Journey of
    Yatir," 47
Moviegoer, The (Percy), 144
Mozart, Wolfgang Amadeus, *Don Giovanni,*
    66; 189
"Mr. Levi" (Oz), 165-167
Mr. Sammler's Planet (Bellow), 74, 161, 183
Much Ado About Nothing (Shakespeare), 101
Mul ha-Ye'arot (Yehoshua) (Facing the
    Forests), 47
Mum Vahalom (Blemish and Dream)
    (Carmi), 81
Music, in Oz's fiction, 156-160, 166; in
    Yehoshua's fiction, 64-66
Musil, Herbert, *The Man Without Qualities,*
    187; *Three Women,* 187
"My Father" (Amichai), 36

"My Father in a White Space Suit" (Amichai), 36
"My Michael" (Oren), 208n.7
My Michael (Oz), 142-150, 156, 167,
    207-208n.2
Mysticism. See Jewish Mysticism; Kabbalah
Mythopoeism, 179, 188

Narrative constructs, in Oz, 141, 149, 152-155,
    162, 168, 184-186, 190
Nature, in Appelfeld's fiction, 110, 123; in
    Carmi's poetry, 82, 84; in Oz's fiction, 141,
    160; 195
Nazis, the (National Socialist Party), 108-109,
    113-114, 118, 121-122, 125-127, 161,
    164, 180
Nehash Hanehoshet (The Brass Serpent)
    (Carmi), 81
New Testament, 100
Newtonian absolutes (Sir Isaac Newton), 6,
    linearity, 7, 25, 39, 45, 55, 57-58, 63,
    110-111, 135, 162
New Wave Writers, 1-6, 141, 194, 198n.13
Nietzsche, Friedrich, 5, 119
Night in May, A (Yehoshua), 50
"No More Mozart" (Abse), 189
Norton-Harjes Ambulance Service, 29
Not Of This Time, Not Of This Place (Amichai),
    xvi, 6, 20, 25-29, 147; poetic imagery in, 29

Oates, Joyce Carol, 123, 126, 195
Olmert, Josef, xiv
"On Style" (Marx), 90
"Order of the Day." *See* "Author's Apology"
    (Carmi), 93-94, 99
Operation "Peace For Galilee." See Lebanon
    Campaign
Oren, Yosef, "My Michael," 208n.7
Orpheus and Eurydice (Gluck), 66
Ostjuden, 113, 115
Othello (Shakespeare), 101
Ovid (Publius Ovidius Naso), *Metamor-*
    phoses, 49
Owen, Wilfred, "Futility," 13; "Greater Love,"
    11; "The Parable Of The Old Men And The
    Young, 18, 55, 104; "The Show," 11;
    unpublished preface, 11; 32, 112
Oz, Amos, 3, animals in, 141 (jackals), 168,
    209n.18; background, 1, 141-142, 162, 179-
    181; causality, breakdown of, 142, 158-160;
    closures in, 155, 160, 171; creative process
    in, 143; Crusades, the, 162-163; desert in

141, 171-173, 179; desertion in, 150, 153, 166-167, 169, 186; dreams (and nightmares) in, 144-145, 147-149, 151, 156, 164, 166-167; earth-goddess in, 177; exotic realism in, 142, 145, 163, 165, 172, 174, 176-177, 179; fanaticism in, 164, 173-178; generational conflict in, 151, 170; Holocaust in, 142, 156, 158; imagination in, 142, 156, 165, 174, 177, 179, 185; infidelity in, 150-151, 166-167, 170, 175-176; irony in, 144, 146, 153, 159, 161-163; insanity (madness) in, 143, 146, 162-163, 170-174; the kibbutz (and kibbutzim) in, 149-153, 155, 157, 161, 164, 168, 170, 172-174, 183-185; levitation in, 142, 156, 158-160, 167; lyricism in, 141, 157, 176-177, 179; malaise in, 144, 146; marital discord in, 144, 146, 148, 150, 165-166, 169-170, 176; memory in, 145; music in, 156-160, 166; narrative constructs, 141, 149, 152-155, 162, 168, 184-186, 190; nature in, 141, 160; paternity, disputed in, 168, 175; politics (sociopolitical messages) in, 142, 149, 161, 165, 174, 178-179, 181, 188, 190, 193-195; psychology, use of, 142, 148, 165; relativity theory, use of 6, 158, 160-161; subjectivity in, 156, 158-159; symbolism in, 149; terrorism in, 145, 162; on translation, 188-190; visit to New Orleans, xvii; woman's psyche in, 142-143. Works: *Ad Mavet* (Unto Death), 162; *Artzot Hatan* (Where the Jackals Howl), 142; *Be'or hatkhelet ha'aza* (Under This Blazing Sun), 207n.1; *Black Box,* 174-178, 185; "Crusade," 162-163; *Elsewhere, Perhaps,* 147, 149-156, 168-169, 171, 186; *Har Ha'etza Ha'raah* (The Hill of Evil Counsel), 165; "The Hill of Evil Counsel," 165-167; *The Hill of Evil Counsel,* 93-94, 165-167; *In The Land Of Israel,* xvii, 167-168; *Kufsa Shechora* (Black Box), 174; *Laga'at Bamayim Laga'at Baruach* (Touch the Water Touch the Wind), 156; "Late Love," 162, 164; "Longing," 166-167, 185-186; *Makom Acher* (Elsewhere, Perhaps), 142, 149; *Menucha Nechona* (A Perfect Peace), 168; *Michael Sheli* (My Michael), 142; *My Michael,* 142-150, 156, 167, 207-208n.2; "Mr. Levi," 165-167; *A Perfect Peace,* 135, 168-174, 185-186, 190; "Reflections on an Anniversary," 163, 209n.30; *Soumchi,* 167; *Touch The Water Touch The Wind,* 6, 110,

155-162; *Unto Death,* 162-165; *Where the Jackals Howl,* 167-168, 183
Ozick, Cynthia, xv; 7, *Levitation: Five Fictions,* 6; 38, 40, 76, 95, 160, 183; *The Messiah of Stockholm,* 201n.3; "Shots," 198n.14

Pacifism, 33
Pagis, Dan, 82, 103
Painted Bird, The (Kosinski), 123
Palestine, 32, 64, 69, 78, 96-98, 101, 117, 162, 165, 180
Palmah, or Generation of 1948 Writers, 1, 4; as a political organization (Haganah), 32; 194, 197n.7
Pan-Germanism, in Appelfeld's fiction, 107, 110, 115, 123; 180
"Parable Of The Old Men And The Young, The" (Owen), 18, 55, 104
Parrinder, Patrick, 128
Past Continuous (Shabtai), 77
Past Perfect (Shabtai), 77
Paternity, disputed, in Oz's fiction, 168, 175
Peace Now movement, xvii
Penguin Book of Hebrew Verse, The (Carmi), 204n.16
Percy, Walker, The Moviegoer, *144*
Peretz, I. L., 180-181
Perfect Peace, A (Oz), 135, 168-174, 185-186, 190
Peri, Yoram, xiv
Perrault, Charles, "The Sleeping Beauty," 169-170
Personification, 24-26
Petah-Tikvah, 32
Pirandello, Luigi, 58-59
Pity, concept of, in Amichai, 11, in Owen, 11
"Platform No. 8" (Carmi), 95
PLO, 2
Poe, Edgar Allan, 4
"Poems for a Woman" (Amichai), 17
Poems Of A Jew (Shapiro), 10
Poetry, communicative function of, 24
Poetry, modern, 82
Poetry, Oz family, 180, 187, and Oz's poems, 187
"Poet's Continuing Silence, A" (Yehoshua), 46-48
Poland, 109, 111-113, 162, 164
Politics (sociopolitical messages), in Oz, 142, 149, 161, 165, 174, 178-179; 181, 188, 190, 194-195

"Pomegranate" (Lawrence), 82
Portnoy's Complaint (Roth, P.), 40, 76
Portrait of the Artist as a Young Man
    (Joyce), 61
Potok, Chaim, 76, 95
Pound, Ezra, 4, 35, 81, 97-98, 187
Preil, Gabriel, 97
Proust, Marcel, 4-5, 75, 110, 119; *The Remem-*
    brance of Things Past, 124; 140
Psychological differences, in Appelfeld's fic-
    tion, 134
Psychology, use of, in Oz's fiction, 142, 148,
    165; in Yehoshua's fiction, 47, 55, 63, 73.
    See also interiorized reality, the unconscious
Puig, Manuel, 178; *Kiss of the Spider*
    Woman, 188
Puritanism, in American literature, 40
Pynchon, Thomas, *Gravity's Rainbow,* 6, 161;
    7, 95

"Rabbi Ben Ezra" (Browning), 46
Ramras-Rauch, Gila, 158
Random movement, of particles, 7, 39; 26,
    31, 159
"Real Hero, The" (Amichai), 17-18, 55
Realism, 5, in Yehoshua, 45, 47; 156, 158
Reality, interiorization of, 5-6, 45; 21, 33-35;
    in Yehoshua's fiction, 45, 47, 55-56; 58,
    73, 77, 108-109, 111, 135, 139, 155-157,
    188, 194
"Reflections on an Anniversary" (Oz), 163,
    209n.30
"Relativity" (Amichai), 39
Relativity theory, in Amichai's fiction, 6, 25-27,
    29, 31, 39; in Appelfeld's fiction, 6, 110,
    127; in Durrell's fiction, 58; literary adapta-
    tions of, 6-7, 26, 193; in Oz's fiction, 6, 158,
    160-161; in Yehoshua's fiction, 6, 57
Religion, Amichai on, 34; Appelfeld on, 132;
    Shapiro on, 10
Remembrance of Things Past, The
    (Proust), 124
"René's Songs" (Carmi), 89-91
Retreat, The (Appelfeld), 123-127; 132
Right-wing orthodoxy, See Zealotry
Rilke, Rainer Maria, *Duino Elegies,* 34; 112
"Rime of the Ancient Mariner, The"
    (Coleridge), 85
Rise of David Levinsky, The (Cahan), 151
Robbins, Tom, 7
Romanticism, 142, 174

Rommel, Field-Marshal, 32
Rosen, Jacob, xiv
Rosenberg, Isaac, 32, 112
Rosenkrantz and Guildenstern Are Dead
    (Stoppard), 100
Rosenthal, M. L., 82
Rosovsky, Nitza, 154, 162
Rostand, Edmond, *Cyrano de Bergerac,*
    100-101, 105
Roth, Henry, 95; *all It Sleep,* 122-123, 183
Roth, Philip, xv, 7, *The Counterlife,* 27;
    Goodbye Columbus, 76, 139; *Portnoy's*
    Complaint, 40, 76; 139; "A Talk With Aharon
    Appelfeld," 207n.33
Rubens, Bernice, *The Brothers,* 70
Rugoff, Milton, 145
Russian literature: pioneering literature, 1,
    181; poetry, 102; and individual authors

Sabras, 1-2, 27
"Sailing to Byzantium" (Yeats), 46, 97
Salkinson, I. E., 100
Sartre, Jean-Paul, 6
Sassoon, Siegfried, 112
Satan, 14, 16, 83, 152
Satire, see Irony
Schacter, Yosef, 29
Schneller, Barracks, 166
Scholem, Gershom, 132
Schulman, Grace, 81, 93, 204n.16
Schwartz, Arnold, 50
Schwartz, Delmore, 36
Second World War, see World War II
"Secret Miracle, The" (Borges), 159
Sefer Yetsirah, 100, 204n.3
Selected Poetry of Yehuda Amichai, 9-10
Shabtai, Yacov, *Past Continuous,* 77; *Past*
    Perfect, 77
Shadows Within: Essays on Modern Jewish
    Writers, The (Shaked), 4, 110-111
Shaham, Nathan, 4
Shaked, Gershon, *The Shadows Within:*
    Essays on Modern Jewish Writers, 4,
    110-111, 198n.13, 205n.5
Shakespeare, William, 100-101, *Hamlet,* 101,
    155; *King Lear,* 101; *Measure For Measure,*
    101; *A Midsummer Night's Dream,* 101;
    Much Ado About Nothing, 101; *Othello,*
    101; 181
Shanim vesha'ot (Years and Hours) (Appel-
    feld), 111

Shapiro, Karl, attraction to Catholicism, 10, definition of a Jew, 10, *Poems Of A Jew,* 10; *V-Letter And Other Poems,* 33

Shelley, Percy Bysshe, 105

Shinhar, Aliza, xiv

Shlonsky, Abraham, 4. Translation: *King Lear* (William Shakespeare), 101; 102

Shosha (Singer), 121

"Shots" (Ozick), 198n.14

" 'Shots': A Case History of the Conflict Between Relativity Theory and the Newtonian Absolutes" (Cohen), 198n.14

"Show, The" (Owen), 11

Shrier, Pauline, 54

Siege (and siege mentality). See Trench mentality

Simeon ben Yohai, 91, 99

Simpson, Philip, 56

Simultaneity principle (simultaneous occurrence), 7, 26-28, 31, 58, 110, 160, 167

Sinai Campaign of 1956, 32, 136, 145

Singer, Isaac Bashevis, 95, 109-110, "Gimpel the Fool," 121; *The Magician of Lublin,* 123; *Shosha,* 121

Sivan, Emmanuel, xiv

Six Day War, the, 69, 136, 141, 157

"Sleeping Beauty, The" (Perrault), 169-170

"Snake" (Lawrence), 82-83, 85-86

Somnambulism, in Yehoshua's fiction, 58

Somnolence, in Yehoshua's fiction, 49

"Song of Thanks, The" (Carmi), 99

"Songs of Zion the Beautiful" (Amichai), 14-15, 17, 32-33

Sophie's Choice (Styron), 75

"Sort of Apocalypse, A" (Amichai), 103

Soumchi (Oz), 167

Sound and the Fury, The (Faulkner), 59-61, 75

Spinoza, Baruch, 170

Stern, David, 150

Stoppard, Tom, *Rosenkrantz and Guildenstern Are Dead,* 100

"Story" (Carmi), 98

Stream-of-consciousness, in Faulkner, 45, 59; in Oz, 145, in Yehoshua, 45

Styron, William, *Sophie's Choice,* 75

"Subject" writers, Yehoshua's view of, 68, 73-76

Subjectivity, in Appelfeld's fiction, 109-111; in Durrell's fiction, 58; in Oz's fiction, 156, 158-159; in Yehoshua's fiction, 45, 54-55, 58

Surrealism, 45, 47

Swift, Jonathan, *Gulliver's Travels,* 174

"Symbolic Psyche: The Structure of Meaning in A. B. Yehoshua's 'Flood Tide,' A" (Morahg), 201n.12

Symbolism and symbols, in Amichai, 21, 24; in Appelfeld, 110, 114-116; in Carmi, 86; in Oz, 149; in Yehoshua, 45-46; 49, 53-59, 63-66, 73, 188

Syria, 2, 137

"Talk With Aharon Appelfeld, A" (Roth, P.), 207n.33

Temporal and spatial configurations, 111, 193; experimentation, xv, 6, 26; displacement, 45, 114, 120, 128, 148-149; patterns, 63; 127, 135, 158. *See also* Relativity

Tennyson, Alfred, "Ulysses," 46

Terrorism, 3, in Oz's fiction, 145, 162

Theology, 181

There Are No Black Flowers (Carmi), 89

Thomas, D. H., *The White Hotel,* 75

Thomas, Dylan, "The Force That Through the Green Fuse Drives the Flower," 84

Thompson, John, 158

"Three Days And A Child" (Yehoshua), 47, 50-52

Three Days And A Child (Yehoshua), 47, 50, 52

Three Women (Musil), 187

"Times My Father Died, The" (Amichai), 36

"To A Pomegranate Tree" (Carmi), 82-83

To The Land Of The Cattails (Appelfeld), 6, 94, 127-128, 134-135

To the Land of the Reeds (Appelfeld), 128

To The Lighthouse (Woolf), 119

Tolstoy, Leo, 4-5, 72, 142, 168, 176, 182

Touch The Water Touch The Wind (Oz), 6, 110, 155-162

Trains, train stations and transports, in Appelfeld's fiction, 111, 116-118, 127-128

Translation, problems of, xv-xvi; Amichai's collaboration with Ted Hughes, 42; Carmi on, 100-101; Oz on, 188-190; Salkinson, 100; Yehoshua on, 78

"Travels of the Last Benjamin of Tudela" (Amichai), 13-17, 20

Trench (or siege) mentality, 2, 46, 54, 62-63, 155, 161, 164, 193-194

Tsedukah, 130

Tzili The Story of a Life (Appelfeld), 94, 120-123, 126, 128, 134-135

Ultraright orthodox community. *See* Zealotry
Ulysses (Joyce), 56, 78
"Ulysses" (Tennyson), 46
Unconscious, the role of, 6; in Conrad's fiction, 173; in Yehoshua's fiction, 45-46, 50-52, 63
Under the Volcano (Lowry), 6, 172
Unto Death (Oz), 162-165

"Vehi tehillatekha." See "And That Is Your Glory," 12
Vengeance, futility of, in Amichai, 28, 147; in Oz, 147, 162, 164
"Visit of the Queen of Sheba, The" (Amichai), 21-24, 28
V-Letter And Other Poems (Shapiro), 33
Vonnegut, Jr., Kurt, 7

Wachtel, Nili, 49, 55
Wandering Jew, the, 157, 160
War, dehumanization in, 30; Amichai's view of, 33-34; Carmi's view of, 92-94
War of Independence (Liberation), 1, 30, 37, 58, 78, 101-102, 136, 149, 165.
War poetry, 11; concept of pity in, 11; "Futility," 13; "Greater Love," 11; "God Has Pity on Kindergarten Children," 10-11; "The Show," 11; "Travels of the Last Benjamin of Tudela," 13-14; 33
Warren, Robert Penn, *The Cave,* 18
Wasteland, The (Eliot), 98
"Weeping" (Alterman), 174-175
Western literary tradition, 4-6, 45, 47, 81, 141-142, 193, 198n.13
Where the Jackals Howl (Oz), 167-168, 183
White Hotel, The (Thomas), 75
Wiesel, Elie, 29, 108, 118, 133-134
Wieseltier, Meir, xvii, 103
Williams, William Carlos, 102
Winesburg, Ohio (Anderson), 182-183
Wirth-Nesher, Hana, 148
Wolfe, Thomas, 134, 139
Woolf, Virginia, 6, 27, 47, 77; *To The Lighthouse,* 119; 140
Woman's psyche, in Oz's fiction, 142-143
World Is A Room And Other Stories, The (Amichai), 6, 29-31, 39
World War I Poets, 6, 122. *See also* Owen, Wilfred; Rosenberg, Isaac; and Sassoon, Siegfried
World War II, 32-33, 46, 75, 132, 147, 161
"World" writers, Yehoshua's view of, 68, 73-76

Wurzburg, in Amichai's fiction, 28; 32
Writer's games, contrivances, "magic," "tricks," 26, 158

Yad Vashem, 37
Yeats, William Butler, 4; "Sailing to Byzantium, 46, 97; 81, 87, 95, 177
Yehoshua, A. B., 3, 110, 138, 182, 194-195; animals in, 50-51; anti-hero in, 48; background, 69-71; the bizarre in, 46-47, 57, 62-63; causality, breakdown of, 58; child-women in, 52, 57, 63, 67; Crusades, the, 48-49; dreams in, 45, 51, 55-56, 58; existential despair in, 45, 47; eyesight, impaired or defective, in 48-49, 51, 53; family, 69; generational conflict in, 46, 48-49, 54, 62-63; Golah (Exile) in, 56, 62, 68; language, experimentation with, 55, 73: in Paris, 47; insomnia and insomniacs in, 52-53, 57-58; love in, 51, 54, 68; lyricism in, 45, 59-60; marital discord in, 52-54, 62-63; music in, 64-66; psychology, use of, 47, 55, 63, 73; realism in, 45, 47; reality, interiorization of, 45, 47, 55-56; relativity theory, use of, 6, 57; Sabra origin, 1; sense of alienation and futility in, 45; somnabulism in, 58; somnolence in, 49; stream-of-consciousness in, 45, 56; "subject writers in, 68, 73-76; subjectivity in, 45, 54-55, 58; survival of Israel in, 46, 50, 79-80; symbolism in, 45-46, 49, 53-59, 63-66, 73; on translation, 78; unconscious, use of the, 45-46, 50-52, 63; visit to New Orleans, xiv, xvi-xvii; "world" writers in, 68, 73-76; Zionism in, 46, 49, 57-59, 101-102. Works: *Between Right and Right,* 50, 79; "The Death of an Old Man," 46; *Early In The Summer Of 1970,* 54; "Early In The Summer Of 1970," 6, 46, 54-56; "The Evening Journey of Yatir," 47; "Facing the Forests," 46-51; *Five Seasons,* 46, 62-68; "Flood Tide," 47, 54; "The Last Commander," 46, 54, 57; *Last Treatment,* 50; *A Late Divorce,* 37, 46, 59-63, 69, 78, 182; "A Long Hot Day, His Despair, His Wife And His Daughter," 47, 52-54, 56-57, 64; *The Lover,* 6, 46, 53-54, 56-58, 60, 63; "Missile Base 612," 54; *Mot ha-zaken* (The Death of an Old Man, The Evening Journey of Yatir), 45-47; *Mul ha-Ye'arot* (Facing the Forests), 47; *A Night in May,* 50; "A Poet's Continuing Silence,"

46-48; "Three Days And A Child," 47, 50-52; *Three Days And A Child,* 47, 50, 52

Yeshurun, Avot, 97

Yiddish and Yiddishkeit, 110, 132, 180

Yizhar, Samech, (Yizhar Smilansky) xvii, *The Days of Tiklag,* 5, 78; "Hirbet Hiz'ah," 197n.12

Yom Kippur War, 3, 56, 58, 136, 141

Yordim (Israelis living in America), 29

Young, Vernon, 28; "It Makes You Wonder," 200n.24

Yudkin, Leon I., 173

Zach, Natan, xvii

Zealotry, right-wing extremist orthodox, Amichai's view of, 40; in Oz's fiction, 175, in Yehoshua's fiction, 57-58, 62-63, 67; 195

Zionism: idealism, 1, 58-59, 148, 164, 173, 194; relevance questioned, 2; Socialist aspects of, 4, 72, 101, 151, 168, 172; in Yehoshua's fiction, 46, 49, 57-59, 101-102; 79-80, 96, 101-102, 130, 173, 195

Zohar, The (de Leon), 84-86, 89, 91, 99, 203n.8 *See also* Jewish Mysticism and Kabbalah

Zoharic passages, Carmi's use of, 84-85, 87, 89, 91, 99; harmony in, 85; interconnectedness in, 85. *See also* Jewish Mysticism and Kabbalah